D0708329

THIS IS OUR FAITH

To fulfil a promise
and
with warmest regards

John Dow

3 St John's
Service Rd
Forfar

THIS IS OUR FAITH

An Exposition of the Statement of Faith of The United Church of Canada

JOHN DOW, M.A., D.D.
PROFESSOR OF NEW TESTAMENT, EMMANUEL COLLEGE
VICTORIA UNIVERSITY, TORONTO

ISSUED BY
THE BOARD OF EVANGELISM AND SOCIAL SERVICE
THE UNITED CHURCH OF CANADA

Published, September, 1943

PRINTED AND BOUND IN CANADA

TO

the little country church rising from the open prairie or the rocky shore-line, from the moorland or the brow of the hill, and to that friendly company of fellow-worshippers accustomed to gather there Sabbath by Sabbath, among whom I see through the mist of years the faces of my father and mother and many of the simple-hearted saints of earth.

PREFACE

This book offers a survey of the main doctrines of the Church. It was prepared to give fuller exposition to a short Statement of Faith presented to the Ninth General Council of The United Church of Canada in 1940. The line followed is Biblical throughout. I have endeavoured to reflect the views of the Commission which drew up the Statement; but, as I was left with complete freedom of interpretation, I must accept responsibility for what is here written. This is a task from which I shrank at first and finally accepted in the hope that in this way I might make some slight return for the generosity and friendliness of the ministers, laymen, and young people of the Church in which I serve. The work had to be overtaken in what little remains of summer vacation in these days of war, and has suffered from lack of leisure of mind.

I owe much to the discussion of the Commission. I would fain have drawn more heavily upon the learning and clarity of Dr. J. M. Shaw had distance allowed. Some of my colleagues on the Commission and on the staff of Emmanuel College did me the kindness of reading certain chapters, to my mingled encouragement and correction, notably Dr. W. Harold Young, Dr. John Line, Dr. A. S. Orton, and Principal Richard Davidson, the present chairman and the guiding mind of the Commission. Acknowledgment has been made in the footnotes of many whose published work has helped me; if any have been overlooked, I trust I may be forgiven. At every stage I have relied chiefly on the judgment and editorial skill of my wife.

JOHN DOW

Emmanuel College,
July 19, 1943.

CONTENTS

FOREWORD

Down through the ages men have been constrained to travel along lines of thought that lead them to One they call God. Standing back from this amazing universe, they have sought after the underlying Cause, the Real and Ultimate behind the visible frame. Peering into its intricacies, they have marked a magnificent purposiveness, a fitting of means to ends, a cunning contriving and designing that leads them on to One who must have planned it all. They have played with its parts like children with a jigsaw puzzle; and, finding it fall into an ordered picture, they have judged that, if it is intelligible to them, a Mind far, far greater than their own must have conceived it in the beginning. They have marvelled at their own hearts with their discerning between right and wrong, and they have confessed that this is no human invention, but surely, from its inescapability, it is an overriding authority from a moral Author above and beyond. They have been shaken by ecstasies and outreachings of the soul inexplicable in their universality and insatiableness unless Another has touched our nature and kindled within us the fires of the spirit. They have wondered how the idea of a God ever came over the threshold of the mind: could they have conceived Him had He not been there?

But it is not by paths like these that we arrive at the living, loving Lord of human life. We believe that God has actually been speaking across the years: He has a will to make Himself known, and in the Scripture of the Old and New Testaments we have the record of that self-uttering of the invisible God. He has confronted men of flesh and blood like ourselves. "It would seem," writes Professor John Macleod, "as if religious experience were a kind of collision, sometimes a violent collision. We know God, so to speak, only when God pleases to hit us! This is what the prophets stammer out at us in their great hours."[1] It is on these encounters we shall rely as persuasive evidence. And, confirming and sealing all these revelations, there is that incursion of

[1] In *A Faith for Today,* p. 17.

God into history in the Man of Nazareth: in Him we recognize the Yea and Amen to all the yearnings of the centuries. He is the Living Word who gives meaning to all the yesterdays, power to each passing day, and hope for the furthest tomorrow. And with a wise saint of God we would make confession: "We are more sure of the Person than of the doctrine about Him. We do not know it, as well as we know Him. You cannot represent theology with flaming Eyes and a healing Touch and a bleeding Heart. It is Personality that is writ that way, and it is in the revelation of Personality that we are to abide."[2]

[2] J. Rendel Harris, *As Pants the Hart,* p. 247f.

I. God.

We believe in God, the eternal personal Spirit, Creator and Upholder of all things.

We believe that God, as Sovereign Lord exalted above the world, orders and overrules all things in it to the accomplishment of His holy, wise, and good purposes.

We believe that God made man to love and serve Him; that He cares for him as a righteous and compassionate Father; and that nothing can either quench His love or finally defeat His gracious purpose for man.

So we acknowledge God as Creator, Upholder, and Sovereign Lord of all things, and the righteous and loving Father of men.

THIS IS OUR FAITH

CHAPTER I. GOD

A. The Doctrine of God

God is Spirit. Ps. 139: Acts 17: 22-31.

He runs a long, long way who runs from his conscience. The self-seeking son of Isaac found that out long ago (Gen. 28). He tried to cash in on his brother's rights, and had to make his heels his friends. Thoroughly weary and worn out with his own heart's torture, he flung himself down on alien soil well beyond the frontier of his own country. It was a cheerless bed, and the accusing stars looked down upon ridge beyond ridge of flinty rock; but he closed his eyes, and merciful sleep fell gently down. Then the mysterious universe opened its gates, ledges of stone fashioned themselves into a magic stairway, and angels began to flit to and fro. Where the truant had expected blissful forgetfulness there came the sense of a Presence that made even the rocks alive, and out of the darkness came an awesomeness eerie and challenging. What a place of dread and mystery! It was as if another world had touched the cold earth and transmuted its chilly garment into a vesture of glory. "Surely the Lord is in this place; and I knew it not." So Jacob discovered that God is One who confronts the fleeing spirit wherever he may lay his head. He outpaces our speediest feet, outdistances our swiftest thought. He is the great Spirit whose range is everywhere.

A young princeling turned his back on Egypt and his life's complications one fine morning before the dawn could catch him (Ex. 2: 15). He travelled on till he made friends and made new contacts. He let the years slip by and memories fade into dimness. He became a shepherd leading flocks. But his thoughts kept pursuing him closer than the sheep. Back yonder the slave gangs, the crack of the whip, the bricks drying in the hot sun, the whip cracking again, and the sound of weeping and the sharp cry of pain. He had the training for a leader, and yet he had run away from his suffering countrymen. But one day in the evening glory he stood a man transfixed. The desert bush burned with fire and yet it was not consumed. Only that which God has touched can pass through the furnace and live. Surely this was holy ground. He put off his shoes from his feet. A voice was sounding in his ears, a voice that would not let him go. There where he had turned his back on his people and his people's God, that same God had faced him and made His presence irresistible. So Moses went back to Egypt; for God is Spirit everywhere appearing and always besetting the kindred spirits He has made in His own image.

It was high noon, and a company of weary travellers had paused at a well head, and after a little parley they went into the unfriendly town to see if they could buy bread (John 4). The place seemed deserted; but one remained sitting alone craving the coolness of the spring water below. A woman drew near, empty pitcher upon her shoulder, a woman with a sad and wistful face. She came in the heat, when other women would not be there; she was minded to draw water, water that had a magic value for her because it was from the hallowed well of her great ancestor, the runaway who had found God crashing through his dreams into his waking life. She came then to avoid the taunts, the hints, the suggestive gestures, of those who had not made her grievous mistakes and who knew full well where to hurt. But today one confronted her when she least expected it, and He did not speak to hurt. He talked, and His words, strangely wise, went straight home to the better self she had so long hidden from the world. Seeking water with magic potency in it, she had found it—not in the well of her ancestor, but on the lips of One who convicted her, shamed her, roused a new yearning in her. The woman left her waterpot and hurried away to call others into a presence that had awakened her. "God is a Spirit," He had said, "and they that worship him must worship him in spirit and in truth." In the unlikely place He had flashed upon her path, and in the region of the past she had sought to veil, just there, He had discovered to her her real need and His will to forgive and make all things new.

God is spirit. The Hebrew word, like the Greek word, for "spirit" was used for air in motion, suggesting that man found this mysterious invisible reality all around, entering every corner and cranny of life, always penetrating, always alive, invigorating; sometimes jostling, imperious, compelling, like a tempest blast, sometimes gentle, wooing, caressing, like a summer breeze. God is always and everywhere near to those who seek. He is not far from any one of us. "In Him we live and move and have our being" (Acts 17: 27f.). He had prompted the Athenians to build an altar to the Unknown God. They felt an urge they could not define. Israel needed a wise guide who would hear the heavenly voice in tempestuous times; so He mysteriously nourished a mother's hope and Samuel came. The nation was growing rich and drawing to herself corroding influences, foreign gods; so the Spirit came on Elijah, man of one-ideaed devotion to the one true God. The forces of corruption and injustice were crushing the poor; so Amos, a herdsman and a fig-dresser, found his mind filled with a blazing passion for righteousness and alive with words that burned like tongues of flame. The times had been hard, and the nation seemed to have paid double for all her sins; so God touched the soul of Isaiah, making him a great-hearted comforter. From every phase of life, in every kind of circumstance, there was a movement from behind a veil, and people knew that it was a Living One who had broken into their national or into individual concerns, warning, arousing, comforting, as the mood of the moment required.

We humans know the severe limitations of time and space. We are confined by the brevity of our days and the scant reach and resources of our earthly frame. But God is not so restrained. Experience tells us that He is everywhere and always available to His people. Whenever we come to the end of our strength or our folly, He is there. Wherever sin or defeat or death reveals our helplessness, there He appears with healing for our soul's distress. In the beauty and grandeur of the world, even in the terror and the darkness, we are stirred to seek and search beyond ourselves for the Mind that fashioned the loveliness of the rose, for the creative Power that set the stars in the bowl of night and forges the lightning bolt. And in the soul within there is an awareness of right and wrong, a moral demand that arises—how and why we wonder. On every side of our world and in every phase of our nature there is this invading mystery that we come to know as the Spirit of the Living God.

Whither shall I go from thy spirit?
or whither shall I flee from thy presence?
If I ascend up into heaven, thou art there:
if I make my bed in hell, behold, thou art there (Ps. 139: 7-8).

God is Personal. Ps. 63; Is. 1; Jer. 12: 1-6; 20: 7-18; Acts 9: 4-6; 2 Cor. 12: 7-10.

These encounters of a Jacob or a Moses were all personal. "Son of man, stand upon thy feet" (Ezek. 2: 1): the prophet felt himself addressed directly. "Save me, O God: for the waters are come in unto my soul" (Ps. 69: 1): the Psalmist could make appeal to a sure and tried friend. "Come now, and let us reason together . . . though your sins be as scarlet, they shall be as white as snow; though they be red like crimson, they shall be as wool" (Is. 1: 18): as if God and people could come together in a heart-to-heart talk. And sometimes it would be an argument: "Let me talk with thee of thy judgments: Wherefore doth the way of the wicked prosper? . . . How long shall the land mourn?" And the counter thrust would come: "If thou hast run with the footmen, and they have wearied thee, then how canst thou contend with horses?" (Jer. 12: 1ff.).

We cannot fathom or define the nature of God, how far His being is like or unlike personality as we know it. But He is personal in that He addresses us, comforts us, and is addressed and confronted by us in the direct way of person to person. He is One with whom we can enter into an intimate and reciprocal fellowship. We feel we are not dealing with some vague principle, some blind urge or force unresponsive to our call, some hard and intangible law or necessity in things. Many think of God in that impersonal way; but that is not the testimony of the saints, of Scripture, or of the Christian Church.

"My heart and my flesh crieth out for the *living* God" (Ps. 84: 2). That is the passionate hunger of the Old Testament saint, and that yearning was satisfied. The veneration of Israel was fixed on Jehovah because He had delivered the nation from bondage, and by mighty acts He was ever affirming that *aliveness* and *sensitiveness* to the needs of His people. The Psalms unfold the record of the most intimate communion with that Living One: they are studded with the first and second *personal* pronouns.

The law of the Lord is imperative and precious because it was His *personal* will, the expression of a righteous nature. To the prophets He communicated in words and thoughts, thoughts that were so new and outreaching that they had not arisen from any human brain, but from a mind that was vaster. "For my thoughts are not your thoughts, neither are your ways my ways, saith the Lord" (Is. 55: 8). The Messianic yearnings after One who would be the shadow of a great rock in a weary land were seen as the sacred promises of a Love that had made tryst with suffering human kind and surely in the end would bring a gladdening consummation. The beauty of the earth was His fashioning; because it was the Eternal who set His glory in the heavens, man, made in His image, could behold and commune with Him. The Sovereign Soul conversed with His creature souls in the language of colour and light.

How does modern man reason? I value above all else truth, honour, righteousness, and how can I conceive these except as first divine creations, expressions of the Eternal Mind? How could the splendours of cloud and sunshine, the starry heavens, the glories of field and flower, speak to me in the accents of beauty if the Divine Artist had not first uttered His soul therein? Surely it is not an accidental concatenation of atoms and colours that thus happens upon loveliness? I see only what the One who made me first saw and gave me the power of seeing after Him.

The Christian does not need to argue: he knows. As he follows the moving story from Nazareth to Olivet, he is constrained to acknowledge that in the man of history it is a mind far-sighted beyond the human who is speaking forth His loftier thoughts. To read the Beatitudes is to experience an elevation of the human soul. It is like passing out of the mists into a clear view of the everlasting hills that seem literally to lift you up to the grandeur of their snowclad tops. "An eye for an eye, and a tooth for a tooth"—so did mean man stiffly hold the balance for his pound of flesh. "Love your enemies, bless them that curse you"—at once man owns that Truth in person utters His voice there, transcending all human values. The Christian lives by faith, prayer, love. His faith is not the acceptance of a mass of dogma, but trust in a *Person* who has come seeking him, drawing him with bands of love in Christ Jesus. He prays not to persuade himself, as if he could pull himself up by his bootstraps. He prays to One whose heart is open to his cry, and he continues praying because he has assuring answers. Above all, what he experiences as the Love of God is the outflow of a *living* Heart whose compassionate tenderness is proven by the mighty acts of Christ's life, death, and resurrection. Because God is personal the Incarnation was possible. "In Jesus we are in contact with a Divine Moral Self, with a God who takes sides, who stands for right and against wrong, in whom the deepest and constitutive reality is not pure thought or absolute knowledge but Personality constituted by infinite Holy Love."[1] Our supreme need is deliverance from the awful thraldom of sin, and that need can be satisfied by no formal remission or mechanical cancellation. No vague principle within us or without can cleanse our heart. We know the peace of pardon because God comes *personally* to us in Jesus Christ. We know it is real because the cost was paid in a real Person's tears and agony. Christians throughout the ages have gone on affirming that they are in constant touch with that same dynamic, renewing love that was in Jesus. Dr. L. P. Jacks has expressed the reality of the living God in his inimitable way: "There is that in the world, call it what you will, which responds to the confidence of those who trust it, declaring itself, to them, as a fellow-worker in the pursuit of the Eternal Values, meeting their loyalty to it with reciprocal loyalty to them, and coming in at critical moments when the need of its sympathy is greatest; the conclusion being, that wherever there is a soul in darkness, obstruction or misery, there also is a Power which can help, deliver, illuminate and gladden that soul. This is the Helper of men, sharing their business as Creators of Value, nearest at hand when the worst has to be encountered; the companion of the brave, the upholder of the loyal, the friend of the lover, the healer of the broken, the joy of the victorious—the God who is spirit, the God who is love."[2]

God is Eternal. Ps. 90; 2 Pet. 3: 8-18.

"The eternal God is thy refuge, and underneath are the everlasting arms" (Deut. 33: 27). Man is ever seeking something more dependable than himself. He knows that he is unstable in

[1] H. R. Mackintosh, *The Christian Apprehension of God*, p. 130.
[2] L. P. Jacks, *Religious Perplexities*, p. 60f.

character, and he yearns for One who can be counted on always. He sees his purposes falter and fade away: a hope like world peace that has fascinated him and called up all his energies slips out of his grasp in the present age, and from the depths of his being springs the longing that there may be One who can bind together the broken purposes of the passing generations. The tides of history sweep on and bear away frail man and all his treasured structures; yet in his heart he knows that with him and his works there pass away ideas and hopes and dreams that all humanity would fain bring to birth, to enrich the life of those who are yet to be. If only there were One who was master of all time, and able and willing to outlast the passing defeats and bring to harvest all the sowings of the years! There are moral and spiritual values continually emerging in the lives of the saints and the poets and the musicians and the scientists. Are these to be wrecked by the hand of death, or stand rebukingly like the ruined doorways and shattered arches of a once great and beautiful cathedral, tragic memorials of a grace and a piety that have been and are no more? Is there no Supreme Genius who bestrides the centuries, who goes on building with invisible stone the sacred fanes where men have toiled and worshipped and prayed their last prayer? Is history an endless series of trials and errors and recurring cycles of failure? Is there not One living above change and decay who sees all things from the beginning, holds His hand on all passing events, and transmutes all frustrations into final victory? Is there not a consistency behind all seeming accidents, a purposiveness that threads its pattern through all mutation to climax in the end?

We are creatures compacted of emotion and desire. We have had our Bethel and our Peniel in life's journeyings, and we look at our children and bethink ourselves of the evil world where they must pass their days. Our prayer goes out that the goodness and the mercy that have followed us may meet and protect our children likewise. Our God must needs be the unfailing friend of every age and time. As He has set love in our heart, we crave eternity in His faithfulness. Such is the divinely implanted thought behind man's cry to the high and lofty One that inhabiteth eternity. "For the mountains shall depart, and the hills be removed; but my kindness shall not depart from thee, neither shall the covenant of my peace be removed, saith the Lord that hath mercy on thee" (Is. 54: 10). Thus the hunger for the

Eternal points towards a Kingdom where God's purposes have their consummation. Ultimately reason cries out to God's love to bind together the flying terms with bands of gold.

Sovereign Lord Exalted . . . holy. Is. 6: 1-8; 37: 15; Ps. 89: 1-18; Ps. 93; Rev. 4.

> Holy, holy, holy, is the Lord of hosts:
> the whole earth is full of his glory.

Such was the revelation that came to Isaiah when the burden of an earthly disillusionment bore heavily upon his soul. What patriot had not been proud of King Uzziah's reign, long, glorious, and prosperous? Then suddenly fell the blow inexplicable. "The Lord smote the king, so that he was a leper unto the day of his death, and dwelt in a several house" (2 Kings 15: 5; cf. 2 Chron. 26: 16ff.). Wealth and luxury had mounted during a long reign, so that the blessing of God seemed to rest with king and people. Then came the tragedy that tore the king from his people and made him, for all his greatness, an outcast, unclean, shut off from the house of God and the society of man. How terrifying a judgment! By one stroke court and people stood forth as rebuked and smitten by the unseen Hand. The Majesty on high had been offended, and so the proud nation was rudely awakened to a Power beyond princes, a Will sensitive as it was inscrutable. Here was One who lay beyond the limits of the human intellect. The Jew was deeply conscious of this dark side to the greatness of God that would brook no irreverence or transgression. Abraham had a human pity for the doomed people of Sodom, yet hardly dared to plead for them: "Behold now, I have taken upon me to speak unto the Lord, which am but dust and ashes" (Gen. 18: 27). Moses turned aside with a very natural curiosity to see the burning bush: "Draw not nigh hither: put off thy shoes from off thy feet" (Ex. 3: 5). Job was proud in his conviction of innocence, bold in the face of men, and clamorous to appear before his Vindicator; but when confronted by the Presence he confessed: "Wherefore I abhor myself, and repent in dust and ashes" (42: 6). "He is the living God . . . at his wrath the earth shall tremble, and the nations shall not be able to abide his indignation." Thus the most tender and spiritual of all the prophets (Jer. 10: 10). The New Testament continues to sound that note. "It is a fearful thing to fall into the hands of the living God" (Heb. 10: 31). "Our God is a consuming fire" (12: 29). Paul sees in history a very real wrath of God, and he interprets the hateful lusts and the vile passions of paganism as the purposeful sufferance of an outraged God who lets sin mount to a crisis point at once to enlighten and to punish men: He "gave them over to a reprobate mind" (Rom. 1: 28). The author of the Apocalypse pictures the vials of the divine anger overflowing, and in the very chapter where the Evangelist proclaims a God who so loved the world that He gave His only-begotten Son there is the awful penalty suspended above the man who rejects the offer: "the wrath of God abideth on him" (John 3: 16, 36).

It is hardly adequate to explain away this dread element in Scripture as simply gross human misunderstanding of the Divine. Familiar with the capricious Eastern potentate of unchecked power, the writers of the Old Testament may sometimes ascribe unworthy passions to the Almighty and so reduce God to our human likeness. It is true that gradually they became more clearly aware of the *moral* grandeur of their God. But there is an overplus here that cannot be so explained, a profound sense of One overwhelmingly magnificent and transcending all imagination, endowed with a will and nature that cannot but be terrible and implacable in a world of unrighteousness, One of purer eyes than to behold iniquity, One who is of another sort than we humans can know, One who in the radiance and splendour of His being outdazzles us men and all our seeing. He is the Creator: we are but creatures. Language clumsily calls Him "the wholly other." "Holy" does not initially describe His moral perfection, but rather His Separateness and Aloneness.

Have we overlooked this elevated awesomeness in the Gracious God of the New Testament? Did not Jesus set that majesty in the forefront of our thought when we pray "Our Father who art in heaven, *hallowed* be Thy name"? Proof of the reality of this "otherness" appeared in the Jesus who revealed Him. Yet we have so read the Gospels after our own liking that we have missed the majesty that glows alongside of the gentleness. But turn to the opening chapter of the first and freshest picture of Jesus (Mark 1). Note how, when He appears in Galilee, He, their familiar friend, the carpenter they knew, unveils a *commandingness* among His fellows that is superlatively amazing. At His word they forsook their vocation (1: 18), the livelihood we men naturally cling to; they forsook their parents (1: 20), and how strong was the family bond among the Jews; they forsook their religious leaders (1: 22); they prepared even to forsake the devil's chains (1: 24), and how strong is that hold. "The Holy One of God," He is acclaimed. A cityful gathers at His door; but before dawn He is up and away even while men seek for Him: He is possessed by other standards and values than men can understand. He has a Kingdom to preach (1: 38); He belongs to another universe that is breaking into our earth. There must have been something manifestly otherworldly or numinous in the man about whom they could testify that even the winds and waves obeyed Him, and death itself gave back its captives. Obedient to a heavenly commission, He goes on and ever on to Jerusalem, while fascinated men walk after Him *afraid* (10: 32). He clears the Temple courts at a word, and holds men spellbound (11: 18). His very silence before His judges makes the accusers the accused, and even on the criminal's cross from the midst of its pain and horror He stands out to a gruff soldier's frank surprise the One who is truly the Son of God (15: 39).

Yet when Jesus has done His work there is a new appraisal of this God of power and mystery. The author of Hebrews who terms God a consuming fire yet assures his readers that they come no longer to a mount of dread (12: 18ff.), but to a God who is judge of all *and* to Jesus the Mediator of a New Covenant. One who has learned to pray in the name of Jesus has not the hesitation of Abraham when he would plead for sinful men. When we feel ourselves in the Divine Presence, we are not like Job, silenced by the mysteries of the natural world, the eagle, the ostrich, the wild ass, but we are constrained to bow before a grander mystery, the love that seeks and finds us in the Cross of Jesus. God is still the unsearchable, baffling human reason. But the focal point of Revelation is no longer His undefined sublimity and power; it is to His moral grandeur that men turn their eyes in wondering awe. He has declared Himself above all as mighty to save.

It is because of this "otherness" of God that we have failed to understand His ways. In one of his sermons Professor H. R. Mackintosh pictured our unlikeness to God as "an obscuring screen impeding our view" so that we see such a mystery as the Atonement "through the frosted glass of our own lovelessness."

"It is because we are such strangers to sacrifice that God's sacrifice leaves us bewildered. It is because we love so little that His love is mysterious. We have never forgiven anybody at such a cost as His."

Righteous and Loving: His Wise and Good Purposes. Ps. 145: Is. 45: 18-25; Amos 4; Hosea 11; Mark 10: 17-27; Rev. 5.

God stands at the beginning of all history; He continues with us to the end of the story. "The prophet's faith is that the whole ongoing process of nature and human life is in God's control. His hand is on it all every moment, all His creatures are in His care. Confusion and terror abroad may be too much for us; it is not too much for Him."[3] This prophetic conviction was verified and sealed by the advent of our Lord Jesus Christ to crown the destiny of His world. Throughout all the hurrying centuries God has been for ever initiating, overturning to build better, a Doer who worketh up to this hour. And all that creative energy is but the outflow of a character that grows ever more clear in successive flashes of revelation. Because He is the Living One at the heart of things, nature and history are full of meaning and mystery. He is "a just God and therefore a Saviour."

To the mind of man came ever broken lights: the fullness of the Everlasting Light was there, but only gradually could it be received. In the struggle for land and liberty a Moses or a Joshua or a Saul found Him as the mighty Doer; an Elijah in a day of debasing contacts recognized Him as a jealous God with a will to break the servitude of His people to all that was false and corrupt. His love and His righteousness, *never contradictory, but two sides of one nature,* glowed ever more clear before the eyes of His servants. Amos, the shepherd and dresser of sycomore trees, would not have known Him as One who "let judgment run down as waters, and righteousness as a mighty stream" (5: 24) had he not also confessed Him as concerned in love that the needy were sold for a pair of shoes. Hosea could not have plumbed the depths of His love had he not experienced in his own soul the divine abhorrence for the wickedness of unfaithfulness in a wife: he could measure the exhaustless patience of love only by knowing how much he hated the evil of the disloyalty he struggled to forgive. Isaiah was

[3] Richard Davidson, *A Faith to Live by,* p. 3.

fondly proud of his king and his compatriots before he came to be appalled by the tragedy of unrighteousness, of dwelling among a people of unclean lips: the all-holy majestic God who was high and lifted up had a tenderness towards His thoughtless people who did not consider. "To do justly, and to love mercy, and to walk humbly with thy God": so Micah (6: 8) saw mercy and righteousness commingled in the God who spoke to him. Jonah pictures a God who was at once inflexible, inescapable, and yet ready to spare alien Nineveh with her thousands of helpless innocents. Joel knew what dread visitation it meant when the Day of the Lord was at hand, but he knew likewise the gracious promise: "I will restore to you the years that the locust hath eaten" (2: 25). What other nation so set before all eyes the demands of the God of Sinai and yet knew equally the exultant cry: "Who is a God like unto thee who pardoneth iniquity?" So were the lines laid for that supreme unveiling of the divine nature in Jesus of Nazareth, the Word incarnate of His righteous judgment *and* His unsearchable love. And the master purpose running like a golden thread throughout the centuries of conflict and suffering came at last to completion in the grand design whereby the Cross, the Resurrection, and the gift of the Spirit finally spread the glory of His Kingdom before mankind. That Kingdom was a rainbow of hope overarching human history. There His love *and* righteousness were to reach their perfect expression. Paul as he hastened from city to city, adding group after group to the bright believing band, was God's instrument in creating the holy fellowship of the Church, the heirs of that Kingdom. That ever-expanding community afire with love and righteousness was to leaven the whole lump of human kind and so create that perfect society wherein His Holy Spirit uttered forth the ultimate meaning of the universe. There at last in the larger incarnation of the Church of Christ was bodied forth the God of the Infinite Righteousness and Graciousness, manifest as the Redeemer and Lord of all mankind.

Creator and Upholder. Gen. 1-2: 3; Ps. 8, Ps. 19; Is. 40: 25-31; Col. 1: 16-17; John 1: 1-18.

"Lift up your eyes on high, and behold who hath created these things, that bringeth out their host by number: he calleth them all by names by the greatness of his might, for that he is strong in power; not one faileth" (Is. 40: 26). The prophet is very sure of the limitless grandeur of the divine power; and for him that means that there is available for frail man a God of gracious purpose who has not made the wonder of heaven for no end; He who has created is ever willing and able to recreate: "he giveth power to the faint . . . they that wait upon the Lord shall renew their strength" (29 ff.). The interest of Scripture in the fashioning of earth and all the starry firmament lies not in the "how" of creation, but in the "why." Whether the process was long and gradual, whether it came by one dramatic whirl of natural forces or by a series of sudden leaps, whether it happened by divine fiat or evolutionary development—these are marginal questions. What matters is the fact that *God willed it all* and that everything came into being for His high and gracious purposes. Thus the narrative of creation in Genesis reaches up to the climax in v. 26: "And God said, Let us make man. . . ." The fair world has arisen out of the void; but why? That man might step forth, made in His own likeness, with power to think and feel and will, and so be able to enter into fellowship with the Creator of all. The story goes on to recount the first Sabbath day—the day set apart for intercourse between the creatures of earth and the Maker of the heavens. The amphitheatre of things—the fair green earth and the star-strewn skies, the clouds above and the waters stretching to the far horizon—these are but the scenery, the stage for the actors; the play begins when God addresses man, when Spirit communes with spirit.

The narrative in Genesis needs a supplement. It is like a palimpsest, an ancient manuscript which thrusts before the eye an obvious text, but which carries underneath the faint lines of a deeper and richer story. That further illumination is given in the Prologue of the Fourth Gospel (John 1: 1-18). There the real culmination of the creation story comes to light: on the scene of earth the Word became flesh and dwelt among us, full of grace and truth. The Son of Man reveals at last the true image in which Adam was made. And His coming to redeem fallen, undeserving man sheds glory upon the name of the Creator, showing Him as the *Father* whose will it is to call many sons of earth into glory. Thus we learn that "there is a world because the will and wisdom of God called it into being."[4] Love reached out to find those whom it could love, and so there came into being the world

[4] John Macleod, in *Expository Times,* Jan., 1940.

and man. The world was made for spiritual ends by the Word of God. When the early fathers spoke of creation out of nothing, a phrase not used in Scripture, they were claiming that God did not merely re-shape material that already existed, as the Gnostic heretics believed. What lies behind their contention is something richer—that there is nothing beyond the range of God's initiative. He made all things, and therefore, as everything is His framing, it must fulfil His purpose and depend on His activity alone, and that activity is for spiritual ends. A God of love and purpose surely did not fashion us and our world to be a plaything for an hour and then fling us back into the void. He has continued His spiritual work all through the ages. "My Father has been working up to this very hour, and I too continually am at work" (John 5: 17). There can be no cessation of the divine interest in the objects of His creation. As we came "from His hand," we remain "in His hand." The potter is for ever at work fashioning and refashioning for use or beauty, for service or delight. He "upholds" what He has created.

And what does Paul mean when he declares that "the whole creation groaneth and travaileth in pain together until now"? "The earnest expectation of the creature waiteth for the manifestation of the sons of God" (Rom. 8: 22). Divine sonship is to be realized in humanity at last, and that consummation is one towards which nature strains forward with "absorbed, persistent expectation—waiting, as it were, with uplifted head." For that great spiritual end "the whole frame of creation, all its parts together, *unite* in sighing and in pain."[5] Jesus came among men preaching the coming of the Kingdom of God and He died for the cause of that Kingdom. Upon the blood- and tear-stained earth where had risen and fallen so many empires of man's shaping, in the place where hopes had so often been dimmed, and the utmost striving of humanity had raised but perishing structures of frustrated zeal, there God has laid out the lines of a new foundation, a spiritual Kingdom, a temple not made with hands. The Rejected One was the chosen cornerstone, the Apostles were the pillars, men and women were the living stones being built daily into the sensitive frame. Men had looked for God's Presence in houses of stone and lime; now they would find that Presence in the living society of the Church. That is the "poem" of God, as the author of

[5] James Denney, *Expositor's Greek Testament.*

Ephesians sees it: He completes the work of earth with its far-flung beauty and its over-arching glory of the heavens by crowning it with a cathedral of living flaming souls aglow with His grace and His love. So creation is revealed finally as the theatre of the glory of God, the scene of the spiritual order He had designed and brought to consummation. The artist is gladdened when after travail and toil he has set upon the canvas the lines and colours of a thing of beauty. But God had to satisfy a deeper nature, a profounder purpose. He fashions that which will satisfy not merely the eye or a single sense, but the whole nature of man. Here is something so rich and rare that "eye hath not seen, nor ear heard, nor hath it entered into the heart of man."

John Keats called this world a vale of soul-making. He voiced a truth. Here through the testing and refining, the tempting and the scourging, the toiling and moiling, character is formed, and the glory and grandeur of man's nature appear. But the soul has a greater glory to reflect: *the face of God* has to shine from the faces of men. The end of life is not to discover ourselves: that is but the first step that leads the prodigal back to discover the Father. The end of creation's story is not that the Word became flesh, nor that to those who believed He gave the power to become the sons of God, but that from that living flesh the grace and truth of the Father at last appeared (John 1: 18). The spiritual temple is not an end in itself: it radiates forth the saving Presence of the Living God. "Fatherhood is at the world's great core."

Yet this very recreating of His in the womb of time pushes to finer issues still. Do we fulfil our destiny within time and space, or may we reach further into the enlarging universe of our spiritual desires? What lies beyond this bank and shoal of time? For what end has God touched us with His glory? If creation leads to a new creation, to what does redemption open out? Do watchers see the outlines of a new Jerusalem coming down from God out of heaven?

B. The Doctrine of Providence

God Overrules.

How far, and in what way, is God in touch with the world in which we live? Is He just a struggling God, striving to unwind the tangled ball of things? Is He a prisoner in His own world, a spirit diffused through nature and permeating our being, but never above us or beyond us? Or is He the master clock-maker who has conceived and set agoing the whirling, interlocking mass of cyclic motion, leaving it to run slowly down in the end of time?

There are times when the encompassing universe seems uncaring, unfeeling, and man is strangely deserted and alone. Frustrated and defeated, the sensitive soul has often looked around in vain for understanding and sympathy.

> Ye banks and braes o' bonnie Doon,
> How can ye bloom sae fresh and fair?
> How can ye chant, ye little birds,
> And I sae weary, fu' o' care?

Not only is nature callous, but the whole course of human life seems to tumble precipitately down past rocks and shallows, over narrows and through dark defiles, with disaster and capsizal always threatening and no arm ready to save. The realist novelist tortures and benumbs us as he describes the immortals pursuing relentlessly, and finally finishing their sport with Tess. Over the gaiety and glamour of modern civilization hangs a pall of despair. The march of history is seen as no triumphal progress, but rather like the pitiful recession to the sensuous and bestial laws of the dark jungle.

But Scripture knows nothing of such defeatism. The saints of the Old Testament passed on to mankind the assurance that our God is a transcendent God neither external to and aloof from His world nor chained and limited within it. He is the great sovereign overlord who has called the world out of the void and can always call it back again, an Almighty One constricted by no sinister arbitrary chain of fate, but who holds in His sure hands all events, One moreover who is a hearer and an answerer of prayer, able and always willing to respond to the call of man. The Hebrews knew that the Shekinah, the eternal Presence, was ever in the midst, where God's folk could freely resort: His people were never under the mercy of some malign star. God might be often invisible, holding off for long, leaving the world, it would seem, to the free play of evil powers; but in the end He would assert His overlordship and out of the seeming struggle and defeat snatch victory and vindication for His own. But that faith did not come to its splendour all at once. Let us hear the Psalmists and the saints thinking their thoughts aloud about the ways of God.

Pss. 37, 49, 73, 91, 147; Amos 1-2: 3; Hab. 1, 2; Ezek. 18; Jer. 18; Job 38, 39.

1. There is no evading of the hard facts of life. "Truly God is good to Israel. . . . But as for me, my feet were almost gone; my steps had well nigh slipped" (Ps. 73: 1-2). In words like these we see that beneath the piety there is a questioning. The facts of life are against faith. It was the wicked who prospered: they were not in trouble as other men. "Verily I have cleansed my heart in vain, and washed my hands in innocency" (Ps. 73: 13). "Is it for the dead thou wilt do wonders?" asks another Psalmist, turning cynic (Ps. 88: 10). There were times when the mind turned to bitterness: "My sore ran in the night, and ceased not: my soul refused to be comforted" (Ps. 77: 2). The people of God were not sheltered or spared. They lived on a land that knew continual invasion; the shock and the cruelty of war and death were commonplace (Is. 5: 26-29; Hab. 1: 6ff.). They knew the horrors of plague and pestilence. A land flowing with milk and honey was the shining place of promise; but where can we find a picture of locust-invasion more realistic and dramatic than in Joel (ch. 2)? Life, they were told, had opened in the idyllic Garden of Eden; but what were the drab consequences throughout the centuries? Toil and sweat for man, and for the woman travail and pain, and for all time, barring both from the life that might have been, a flaming sword which turned every way (Gen. 3). Yet amid the hardship God was ever leading them out in revealing thought and vision.

2. There was the lesson to be drawn from the long view of history, solemnizing in the range and depth of the national experience, fascinating in the turning of individual fortunes into the grand pattern of His Providence. "I have considered the days of old, the years of ancient times. . . . I will remember the years of the right hand of the most High" (Ps. 77: 5, 10). Memory loved to linger on the dreamer Joseph, set upon by his own brethren and callously sold—thus to be a link in the saving of his people; on Moses, so marvellously preserved and trained for the historic hour; on Saul, called from seeking his father's asses; on David

summoned from the sheepcotes. Moreover, by terrible acts in righteousness God had redeemed His people. Egypt knew it, and Babylon and Syria: the hosts of Sennacherib had melted mysteriously away from the very gates of the holy city. The conquering tyrants had come sweeping their helpless victims like fish into their net; but a Habakkuk could always mount his watch-tower and from a vantage point of revelation see the meaning of all the tumult and the wreckage: the vision might tarry, but the heirs of such a history could surely wait for it with confidence.

3. There was the confirming evidence of a Divine Purpose in the course of revelation within Israel. "The Lord took me as I followed the flock," said Amos. "In the year that King Uzziah died I saw the Lord," proclaimed Isaiah. "Before I formed thee in the belly I knew thee": so came the word to Jeremiah. And expressly it came to Ezekiel and to many others, each chosen in his season to utter forth truth, and the whole constituting an insight and penetration into the mysteries of the divine counsel such as had been given to no other people. Contrasted with the surrounding nations who had the same or even higher levels of culture, and disciplined by war and death and desolation not dissimilar, Israel experienced a movement of soul, a deepening understanding of the character of God, that was altogether unique. By what uncharted movement of the Spirit was it achieved that under the revealing words of this succession of prophets and seers God stood forth in His Holiness, Justice, and Mercy as the covenant God of this one peculiar people? Whence came that sense of separateness and high destiny that out of her should go forth the divine law for all the earth? "Thou didst lead thy people like a flock" (Ps. 77: 20). There was a mystery about this guiding. God's way was in the sea, His path in the great waters, and His footsteps were not known.

4. There was the personal reconciliation with God that came to the individual mystic. Envious at the prosperity of the wicked, plagued and chastened with each new day, the rebel of Psalm 73 went into the sanctuary of God, and there came to appreciate the issue of things, the desolation in front of the wicked, and for himself the joy of the eternal Presence. "Nevertheless I am continually with thee. God is . . . my portion for ever." It is a sort of anticipation of that word spoken later to the grumbling elder

brother: "Son, thou art ever with me, and all that I have is thine" (Luke 15: 31).

The book of Job offers the classical example of this personal triumph. Sorrow is piled upon sorrow, disease upon affliction, and by the accepted standards he stands before his fellows a man under punishment for his sins. He cuts through the web of arguments that his friends address to him and holds on to his innocency and his hope of a vindicator. That he can suffer so much without cause and *still* trust in God is a proof that God had not created the human species in vain. But even to Job is not vouchsafed a clarification of the ways of Providence. He gains a deeper realization of God's wisdom and power as seen in nature: "Thou doest all things. I have heard of thee by the hearing of the ear: but now mine eye seeth thee" (42: 2-6). He is like a man looking through a telescope for the first time. He sees a larger and grander universe, a more intricate and stupendously ordered world. The mind reels before the wonder and majesty of it. In the presence of One so far transcending all human thought one may well say: "He who is wise enough to fashion this mystery can surely be trusted to have set a meaning in my little circle of experience. It is for me simply to accept and have faith." Yet how much has he come to know of God? His Creator still remains in the dim shadow of impenetrable mystery. There is a splendour in God's ways that human eyes cannot penetrate. Here is something to carry on with: God has not left His creature unanswered. He has spoken, lifted the veil of His majesty enough to let the glory through. It is only a glimpse from Mount Nebo, but it gives sweet content to know the God of all the promises has acknowledged His servant. It is as if in the story of the blind man in John 9 we heard the utterance: "Neither hath this man sinned, nor his parents: but that the works of God should be made manifest in him"—and the narrative stopped there, with no account of what the Christ did to sightless eyes.

5. There was a glimmering of light to come in the prophetic portrayal of the Suffering Servant of God (Is. 53). That suffering might not be due to one's own misdeeds, but might be heaped upon the innocent one to awaken the unthinking guilty ones to see "it is for *our* sin he suffers, the chastisement of *our* peace is upon him"—that was a new and strange light to cast on the mysterious ways of God. When a dissolute son comes home and sees how his

follies have set upon the face of a mother the indelible marks of suffering, he awakens to a fact of life, to a way that Providence has used to break a hard and callous heart. When Czechoslovakia began to suffer dismemberment and the unplumbed sorrows that followed, there came upon the mind of many the sense of shame and guilt that it was by policies they had supported that this agony had come upon the defenceless. To detect this thin red line of unmerited suffering running through the pattern of history is to have foretaste of the truth and tragedy of the Cross of Christ.

6. There are hints of a Beyond that will compensate for the ills of life and adjust the balance. "Wherefore should I fear in the days of evil?" asks the Psalmist (49: 5). "The fool and the brutish man perish . . . their beauty shall consume in the grave. . . . But the Lord will redeem my soul from the clutch of Sheol" (10-14, 15). Belief in an after life is slow to come distinctly into view; but there is the feeling that the Living God can quicken a valley of dry bones. Judgment is looming up on the far horizon: the Day of the Lord rises afar off in grim colours, but after the upheaval there will be a new day for the righteous. The assurance deepens that as the Lord is just so also is He merciful. "Many of them that sleep in the dust of the earth shall awake, some to everlasting life, and some to shame and everlasting contempt. And they that be wise shall shine as the brightness of the firmament; and they that turn many to righteousness as the stars for ever and ever" (Dan. 12: 2-3).

Matt. 6: 24-34; Luke 13: 1-5; John 9: 1-5; John 11: 6-10; Luke 12: 54-56; Matt. 4: 14-16; Matt. 11: 3-6; Matt. 23: 34-35; Rom. 8: 18-39; 1 Pet. 4: 12-14; James 1: 2-17; Eph. 1: 3-14; Rev. 21: 1-8.

To pass to the New Testament is to find that "all the trumpets of the spring are sounding."[6] God has come down among men and taken upon Himself the weight of that sin and suffering that make the burden of this unintelligible world. Jesus steps out upon the human scene with a power that gives Him mastery. He puts our human heritage to the test and carries it back undimmed and unashamed. He accepts the limitations and the frustrations of the earthly portion, and yet leaves life aglow with the glory of

[6] D. S. Cairns, *The Riddle of the World.*

God. He vindicates Providence by accepting the darkest road and holding the unseen Hand to the end. What can we learn from Him?

1. Jesus sees the world as fashioned and preserved by a Father's hand. "Are not two sparrows sold for a farthing? and one of them shall not fall on the ground without your Father. But the very hairs of your head are all numbered" (Matt. 10: 29-30). Thus pointedly and picturesquely Jesus declares His faith in an overruling Providence. The meanest of His creatures are followed by His care: how much more does grace precede the noblest of His creatures in all his undertakings! The lilies of the field, the common grass we cast upon the fire, have received their glory from Him, passing though it may be. Faith is the air that Jesus breathes. Are there not twelve hours in the day? All that is appointed to us to do can be done with the assurance that there will be time enough even though death has laid hold upon Lazarus and great distances divide us from his side (John 11). This is the Father's world. As the Lord's Prayer teaches us, we can simply turn to Him with the affectionate trust of a child, whether it is but daily bread we need or the grander gift of forgiveness.

Do we realize how much it means that Jesus accepted the conditions of common life? He had to grow as a child grows and toil as a man toils. The effort, the struggle, the weariness, the hope deferred—He knew them all. He would not make stones into bread: He accepted the law laid down for all. What Genesis regarded as the human *curse,* to toil with the sweat of the brow, He deliberately prefers as better than the easy way. When He calls men to share in the wonder of the Kingdom, it is fishermen and tax-gatherers and common folk that He names. Evidently He rejoiced in the rugged character of a Peter, the fierce intensity of the sons of Zebedee, and He had patience with a doubting Thomas, and even a Judas was worth pleading for to the end. A world that calls for the exercise of faith, hope, courage, patience, is essentially a good world. How if, with all its pathos and tragedy, it is the only kind of world that can produce heroic human souls, the faith that can remove mountains, the love that never faileth, the hope that maketh not ashamed?[7] A rigorous existence with toil and travail and tears in it is a world in which

[7] D. S. Cairns, *The Riddle of the World,* p. 265.

man *must* reach out for a Father's hand and so live as to glorify God and enjoy Him for ever.

2. Jesus makes it clear that fatherliness does not mean favouritism. He would demand no special providences for Himself. Again and again asked for a sign, a demonstration of a power to disrupt the natural order, He refused. The temptation to cast Himself from the pinnacle of the Temple was an invitation to defy the appointed laws of God's world, and He would not. Galileans even in the holy act of sacrificing must not count on special protection from the sword of Pilate's soldiers. When a tower in Siloam collapses, the ordinary laws will hold for good and bad alike (Luke 13: 1-5). God sends His rain upon the just and the unjust (Matt. 5: 45).

There is no thought here like the modern scientist's with his jealous eye for the unerring laws of the natural world. Trained in that school, we moderns must seek what light we can by viewing nature in the large and seeing catastrophes as balanced by the good. Earthquakes, flood, hurricane, and volcanic disturbance, shocking in their mass destruction of life, must be seen as the occasional explosions of essentially benign forces working within the universe to make possible animal and vegetable life, forces without which human existence would not be possible at all.[8] The pitiless desert must not be classed as a flaw in the divine craftsman's handiwork, as we know how much may be due to man's improvident use of the soil—*e.g.,* in the dustbowl of the United States and Canada. What we regard as pests have their uses in nature. The sandfly that makes life unendurable for the white men on the hot desert plains is the agent that fertilizes the date palm, and so ministers to the production of one of earth's delicacies. The wasp, unwanted visitor to our fruit trees, is nine-tenths beneficent when we reckon how many enemies of growth he has devoured. Famine and pestilence, once passively accepted as divine visitations, are challenges to be overcome by sharing, planning, and increased medical knowledge.

But Jesus here confronts us with a new view of God in relation to His world. God's sun rising on the wicked and His rain falling on their fields is, Rabbi Klausner claims,[9] an act of unfairness: it is not absolute righteousness. This is a disruption of the

[8] Weatherhead, *Why Men Suffer.*
[9] Klausner, *Jesus of Nazareth,* pp. 379-380.

moral order and thus also of the natural order. This world with its fixed laws of sun, moon, and tide ought to perish as it did in the Flood. To Jesus, however, there is a largeness in the divine purposes. He views us, not as driven slaves, but as persons with mind and imagination and a moral grandeur above a nicely calculated exact-to-the-inch justice. He cheerfully accepts a universe where there are heavy odds, and teaches a spirit that is victor over these odds. How smug we would be if we had but to pull the lever of goodness and, lo! in our hands the elixir of immunity! Workers in God's vineyard may bear the heat and burden of the day and yet have no priority rights over late-comers (Matt. 20: 1-16). Prodigals are honoured at banquet tables: that gives their brothers no ground for complaint—His whole universe is still ours (Luke 15: 11-32). Jesus assumes a lack of equality in talents and circumstances; the one to be condemned is the small-minded man who refuses the rough seas of commerce (Matt. 25: 14-30; Luke 19: 12-27). Jesus saw a depth of design in God's disposition of things: the human field is not for the self-regarding, the seekers after a guaranteed safety. "Foxes have holes and the birds of the air have nests," but the Son of Man enjoys no cloistered security.

3. Jesus saw in freedom the only way of life for man. In the Third Temptation He refused to have the kingdoms of the world by one dramatic gift: He would be king only by the free choice of men. It was His own way: it was of His own will that He had taken up life and by His own will He was to lay it down (John 10). "He that hath ears to hear, let him hear": so He left His appeal open to man's free choice. His sadness over Jerusalem and His tears were because His own people had the chance and would not. The strongest of all His condemnations fell on the Pharisees because they neither went into the Kingdom themselves nor would give freedom to others to enter. The favourite picture of God in the parables is as Father: that best expresses the free relationship in which He stood to His children: He lets even the foolish son have his way (Luke 15) and accepts the rebuff of the churlish one (Matt. 21: 29). And when God is pictured as a king, He goes away to a far country and leaves the servants as free agents. Here is a God who deliberately delegates His powers, limits His authority. Constraint is so foreign to the divine mind that even Judas is suffered to make his choice and

Caiaphas to lay his schemes unchecked. That means foolish choices, sin, tragedy, death. But evidently that is the only atmosphere in which spiritual beings can come to know themselves, their weakness and their Father's exhaustless love. Then we come back to be *voluntary* bond slaves.

That very freedom throws upon us an enormous responsibility. God is always opening our eyes and giving us glimpses that should lead us on. And God is justified by the fact that it is in the free countries of the world that there have come the greatest social advances. It is to free countries that we can look for finer social services, wiser industrial legislation, extension of medical and scientific research, and above all it is to a free association of the peoples of the earth that we must look for an order of world peace. But that freedom can find its dynamic only in a religious sense, a knowledge of the debt we owe to a Father's generosity, a Father who has spared nothing that we might have life and have it more abundantly.

4. Yet Jesus sees our freedom fit into a divine over-ruling: all human history is but a grand pledge of the coming of the Kingdom of God. Jesus believed, as did the prophets, that the footsteps of God could be detected in national history: it was possible to read the signs of the times, and guilt lay heavily on those who refused to see (Luke 12: 56). He does not elaborate a philosophy of history as Paul does (Rom. 9, 10); but His woe over Jerusalem (Luke 19: 41-44: cf. Matt. 23: 37-39) and His sense of urgency show His awareness of a God whose purposes brooked no delay. He saw His own coming as an intervention of the divine into history: His Messiahship was a culminating point of human destiny. His message to His people, especially in the later days when rejection seemed imminent, was weighted with a sense of His nation's doom (Matt. 23).

Yet He did not see that doom as inexorable. In the parable of the Fig Tree He makes it plain that He has prayed to a God who could stay judgment, and He encouraged His hearers to lean heavily on the effect of importunity (Luke 13: 6; 18: 1). To Him penitence and limitless faith have power beyond all calculation. As Paul later prayed that the thorn in the flesh might be taken away, so Jesus in Gethsemane sought that the cup might pass from Him. He does not upbraid the heavens when the answer is in the negative: He continues to look to the unanswering sky and say "Father" (Mark 14: 36).

5. Jesus looked on suffering as a call to action or to faith. He had more than eyes of compassion: He had hands that were stretched forth readily to heal and to help. He had no complacency towards the ills of the body, but rather showed a will to break the bondage of the unfortunate. In His eyes it was Satan who had bound in physical pain many of the children of Israel, and that was a reign to be broken. He had nothing of pious Eastern passivity towards affliction, but rather approached it as an evil to be crusaded against.

Our scientific age regards pain as a sign of life, a mark of that sensitivity without which we could not have the feeling of our delicate organisms: our pain is often a danger signal and a salutary warning. That constitutes no problem. But where a man has been thirty-and-eight years in his infirmity, or where a child is at death's door to the anguish of a father's heart—that is the kind of situation where faith is tried, and there it is that Jesus is moved. There is a suffering that seems excessive and undeserved. His quick sense of reality diagnoses sin as at the root of a case like the paralytic, and he deals with that unerringly. But there are cases that do not fall under the catalogue of human responsibility: "Master, who did sin, this man, or his parents, that he was born blind?" (John 9: 2). The answer must have been startling: "Neither hath this man sinned, nor his parents: but that the works of God should be made manifest in him." There is often a deep mystery about suffering. It is the cruel portion that can drive man nigh to madness, but it is equally the crucible that transmutes man into sainthood.

> My vision Thou hast dimmed that I may see
> Thyself, Thyself alone.

So said Milton; and many another can add his testimony. "A world without a contingency or an agony could have no hero and no saint and enable no son of man to discover that he is a son of God."[10] If men had not walked in darkness, they had never discovered the stars. The maimed and crippled life, meaningless to the human eye, may be caught up into the inscrutable purposes of God. The one inexplicable thing is really our own blind-

[10] Martineau, in a sermon on "The Uncertainties of Life."

ness. Jesus saw in His own bitter experience not the hand of Satan, but the hand of God. "Jesus," writes Otto, "did not believe that he was Messiah although he had to suffer, but because he had to suffer." To the very human mind of Peter—and here Peter reflects the average thought of the commonplace man—suffering was an impossible intrusion into the lot of God's chosen ones: but that showed how far off Peter was from the thought of God. Suffering is an instrument of redemption. By that very fact it is removed from the denials of God's Providence and is set among the proofs of His livingness among men and His purposiveness. The singer of the Suffering Servant songs had seen vicarious suffering as an instrument in God's hands for the spiritual awakening of cruel and callous men. "The whole creation groaneth and travaileth until now," says Paul; but the travail is just the sign that God is there, achieving the redemption of His sons. If suffering is that without which Christ could not have done for men His work of salvation, then we can expect that it is the threshing floor on which the flail of His judgment will separate the finest of the wheat. By the alchemy of suffering He prepares many sons for glory.

Jesus saw farther than our seeing. It would be a dull and adventureless world where all things were plain to the human understanding. Prematurely proud of a little knowledge, we lose the child's eye of wonder; driving our concrete roads through forest glades, we lose the songs of the birds and the Never Never Land. Who has shared the intimate home life of a crippled invalid without awakening to another world of values? Bereft of our power of commonplace speech or facile mental life, the children of sorrow create their own world of fancy, croon their own songs, and let thoughts go roving into altitudes that are beyond us. They have their own intercourse with the unseen, and reap a harvest of happiness that we cannot estimate. With their own gifts and genius they teach us our limitations. And if their condition is often pathetic and helpless, do they not work a miracle in the souls of their rough brothers and gay sisters, evoking in them a gentleness and considerateness and a sensitivity of heart that will contribute richly to the society where they later mingle as men and women? Where do men learn the beauty of uncomplaining patience, the radiance of undefeated courage, the power of mind over body, if not from those who have made the bed of pain the place of victory? The interlacing of our destinies to unreckoned good is past all calculation.

> The sexton tolling his bell at noon
> Deems not that great Napoleon
> Stops his horse and lists with delight
> Whilst his files sweep round yon Alpine height:
> Nor knowest thou what argument
> Thy life to thy neighbour's creed has lent.[11]

6. Jesus recognized in sin the deepest evil in life, the source of our most tragic woe and hopelessness. He takes His first public stand among penitents who have come to John seeking baptism, and He dies by sin's intrigue and for sinners. In the prayer He taught His disciples forgiveness stands out beside bread as the need of all, and His dying prayer is for those who had sinned against Him. The prayer that, in a matchless parable, He held up for approval was the simple cry: "God be merciful to me a sinner." The other evils that beset men—disease, hurricane, idiocy, war—have their reign and terror in this life and cease to be. But sin is that which the soul carries before the judgment-seat of God. Other afflictions cut us off from health, happiness, human friendship; but sin administers the supreme deprivation: it shuts out the face of God. Made in the image of God, we can know life at its highest only in fellowship with Him. Sin robs us of our present joy and our hope of the life to come. So it is for the lifting of this burden from mankind that Jesus set His face towards Jerusalem, took the bitter cup in Gethsemane, and gave Himself up on Calvary.

But Calvary had its consummation in the Resurrection morn. Through the darkness of the Cross the Son of Man was ushered into light. So to those who have faced life's hard and cruel blows there is given not a mere human hope of immortality, but the certainty that the Resurrection provides that evil is finally overcome by good. This is our sign and surety that "nothing can either quench His love or finally defeat His gracious purpose for man." Meantime we can experience foretaste of victory. God has let down a ladder to us where we are in the place of testing, the ladder upon which His angels ascend and descend. There is the ever open gateway of prayer through which the soul can pass

[11] R. W. Emerson, "Each and All."

immediately into the presence of the Eternal. It was before the staggering weight of the Cross was finally thrust on His shoulders that Jesus had resort to the Mount of Transfiguration and the Garden of Gethsemane. Under the hallowing contact of prayer His face was transfigured before His disciples, and in the strength of that experience He was able to set His face to Jerusalem. In the Garden the prayer was not granted; but there He found that the lips did not falter as they closed on the familiar name: "Father." And later, when the blackness of darkness enveloped His destiny on the Cross, when the world's coldest cruelties were heaped upon His head and there appeared no light at all breaking through the cloud, He had still a hold of the intimate name: *"My* God, *my* God."

II. Jesus Christ.

We believe in Jesus Christ, the Son of the Father, Who for us men and our salvation became man and dwelt among us.

We believe that He lived a perfect human life, wholly devoted to the will of God and the service of man.

We believe that in Him God comes face to face with men; so that they learn that God loves them, seeks their good, bears their sorrows and their sin, and claims their exclusive faith and perfect obedience.

We believe that in Jesus Christ God acted to save man, taking, at measureless cost, man's sin upon Himself; that the Cross reveals at once God's abhorrence of sin and His saving love in its height and depth and power; and that the Cross is for all time the effectual means of reconciling the world unto God.

We believe that Jesus was raised victorious over death and declared to be the Son of God with power; and that He is alive for evermore, our Saviour and our Lord.

So we acknowledge Jesus Christ as the Son of God Incarnate, the Saviour of the world.

CHAPTER II. JESUS CHRIST

A. Jesus the Christ

Who Became Man and Dwelt among Us.

The New Testament opens with four Gospels. Of these admittedly Mark is the earliest. It gives the impression of a breathless story. Incident follows incident in a style marked by the vivid present, "and" chasing "and" in the manner of the eager hurrying narrator who has barely finished one thrilling scene before he is off on the trail of another and plunging after that with undiminished ardour. From the voice of John crying in the wilderness "Prepare" and "Repent," forward through clash after clash between the hero and the religious dogmatist, we are borne swiftly on from Galilee to Cæsarea Philippi, from Gethsemane to the Judgment Hall and along the sorrowful way to Calvary. We pause only when we come to the amazing story of the open tomb and the women standing by awestruck. It is a record of startling happenings, of a human figure who appears in a real world, speaking in such vivid accents and performing such deeds of power that dazzled onlookers are both thrilled and alarmed. It is an unmistakable incursion into history of one who was a phenomenon, an enigma.

When we read through St. Matthew's Gospel, we find the story set in a fuller context. The life of Jesus is seen as an emergence in the history of the Jewish people, the fulfilment at last of many prophecies, the proclamation of a new law of revolutionary demand; and as the narrative gains momentum towards its later scenes, the clouds of foreboding and imminent judgment gather overhead, and the central figure appears as the Man of Destiny in His national history, the culmination of the long process of the ages, and the judge of mankind. The challenge throughout is that of a King to whom the wisest must come to offer homage, a royal proclamation of a new law that revolutionizes all values and sets men over against the standard of the Kingdom of Heaven, and woe be unto those who have not ears to hear. The Son of Man has come in judgment.

The Gospel of Luke has this same story to set within the

framework of world history. But it is the coming of a Graciousness, an act of Redemption for which angels in heaven and shepherds on earth and sainted seers at the Temple door are waiting. It is a proclamation of deliverance for the poor, the opening of eyes for the blind, and release for all mankind, sinner and Samaritan sharing with Pharisee and Jew. It is the message of a God who goes out after the lost, who has forgiveness even for His enemies, paradise even for the penitent thief. And yet it echoes a sad woe over a Jerusalem that knows not the time of its visitation; a warning that, except we repent, we shall all likewise perish; an urgent appeal for importunity in prayer. Thus it is Graciousness that must not be rejected, a sword of division that cannot be evaded. And that life of Jesus is not a finished story, but a prelude: it issues into a waiting Church that is to be filled with power from on high. Jesus has come into the history of men, and He is to remain in history, in His Church and in the life of His people, their hearts burning within them when He meets them on the way.

Thus the Gospels portray a figure of history, rooted in one generation, yet fulfilling the hopes of past ages, and reaching forth with power to bless all mankind.

But within the historical framework there is obviously another and a dominant interest. Always this Jesus is constraining men to decision for or against Him. As soon as He issues into a public ministry there is conflict around His name, conflict in His own country of Galilee, conflict in His own city of Nazareth, conflict of the deepest in the central city of Jerusalem. This man provokes strongest emotions; ignorant Gadarenes would drive Him out of their coasts because He has uncanny powers; natural enemies—like the court party of Herod and the conservatively pious—combine their forces to thwart Him. His own mother felt a sword pierce through her heart as she watched His perilous career, and sought to draw Him from His course. The sick of every sort come flocking to Him, and even the outcast publicans betray a strange interest in His passing by. But those Galileans who have been closest to Him in His ministry come to hail Him as the Anointed One of God; even a Syro-Phœnician woman comes worshipping; a Roman judge can find no fault in Him; and an honest Roman soldier, confronting Him under the torture of a criminal's cross, pronounces Him truly a Son of God. Evidently this is a man who cannot be ignored: He utters a doctrine at which people are astonished, and exercises powers that startle the cleverest observers. He passes on amid blessing and cursing; He is set for the falling and rising of many in and beyond Israel.

Thus this man of human story has constrained men to set Him on a place apart. The historical figure has become a Saviour of men. Here is a power that transcends the earthly scene: He must be seen in the heavenlies. To the records of His life story must be added an estimate of another kind. His Church has ever treasured a Fourth Gospel, the spiritual Gospel in which from the opening page to the close it is the living Word of God which confronts men. This is frankly written "that ye might believe that Jesus is the Christ, the Son of God; and that believing ye might find life through his name."

A Perfect Human Life, Wholly Devoted. Luke 4: 16-22; Matt. 11: 25-30; Luke 12: 49-50.

By what power did Jesus thus impress His name indelibly upon the history and conscience of mankind? Simply by living the life of a human being, growing up to man's estate in the simple home of a carpenter, sharing the intimacies of the family life with sisters and brothers, and then at the call of God passing out into a ministry among His fellows of teaching and healing and witnessing. He did not attempt to cater to men's greed and to dazzle them by miracle or mass hysteria. He relied immeasurably on simple personal contacts: by voice, hand, and eye He made appeal; the quiet word, the healing touch, the searching look won Him victories. With utter frankness and sincerity He set men face to face with God and with their true selves, leaving the men they were gazing ashamedly across the chasm at the men they might be. He never sought to arrest attention by adopting the garb of a desert ascetic. His authority from the beginning rested on His own penetrating mind and blameless character with an ever-haunting sense of a Something beyond and with Him; truth on His lips flashed clean and clear in accents which there was no mistaking; and there was a flawless harmony between His own life and His commanding precepts. The daily sights and scenes of everyday life supplied all He needed to point His lessons: He made humanity learn ever from its own nobler heights, from the widow's indefatigable persistence for her share of justice, from the father's heart that could not but receive back with joy the undeserving prodigal.

Living thus completely on the open levels of village society without concealment or privacy, thrust up against prying eyes and listening ears, He lived out a life on which even His enemies failed to fix any clinging slander. Nor was this a mere negative flawlessness, a blank white sheet of an existence: it was a vivid swift-moving career of positive action, of unceasing self-giving for His fellow-men, especially for the ailing and the discouraged, with bold and challenging words and contacts for the sinner and the outcast. Throughout the months of the ministry there was an unresting interest in the needs and hopes of each individual soul who made approach to Him, an eager willingness to expend virtue without counting the cost. There was in all His activity a big-mindedness and tender-heartedness that made His days a triumphal progress of the delivering Spirit of the Lord that the prophet had dreamed of—the opening of sightless eyes, the releasing of imprisoned souls, and the gladdening of weary hearts. Plainly this Son of Man came not to be ministered unto, but to minister.

The compelling urge, moreover, came from no fevered eagerness for popularity or personal glory. Always His coming and going were under constraint from on high. At the moment of His baptism He heard the direct call, and in every crisis He found His way to the Father's presence, on the mountain top or in the garden, on the dusty highway and even on the cruel Cross. Necessity was laid upon Him, and how was He straitened till it be accomplished. He had a baptism to be baptized with, a cup He must needs drink, a greater will before which He bowed in obedience and agony. We can observe between the lines of the story how other forces beat upon Him in vain. A whole cityful of people would gather at His door eager to encourage Him towards popularity, to persuade Him to accept the grateful homage of the masses as the wonderful physician. After the Feeding of the Five Thousand the awestruck crowds would fain have carried Him away to be their king and leader of a long-delayed *revolution* for a people's freedom (John 6: 15); and behind the enslaved Jews were other nations aplenty ready to follow a bold lead for the overthrow of Rome and the setting up of a new empire of larger liberty. His closest friends sought to divert Him from any premature encounter with the hate and death in Jerusalem. He became so detached from them in His out-soaring thoughts that He walked before them as one apart, while they followed behind a prey to fears and alarms (Mark 10: 32). He saw there was treachery among His followers; but He would not save Himself by any drastic purge of traitors. He found a Roman judge so impressed by His innocence as almost to hold the door open for His escape, and He would not. No voice would He hear but the voice of God; no road would He follow but the will of His Father. Surely this was a perfect life wholly devoted to the will of God and the service of man.

The Son of the Father. Matt. 16: 13-28; Matt. 12: 6; Luke 11: 31-32.

Who then was this phenomenon of history, Jesus of Nazareth? We all know from the thousand fallibilities and limitations of each passing day that we are but men, poor creatures of need and shame who live only by the great God's pity and tenderness. But this Jesus wheeled round upon His intimates one day and startled them with the question: "Whom do men say that I am?" Here then was one man who was a problem to Himself: as Denney puts it: "The question, it might almost be said, is more significant than the answers. Jesus is not only conscious that He is a problem to men, He assumes that He ought to be. It is not right that people should be indifferent to Him. . . ."[1]

They had left the Galilean crowds and excitement behind them, and for days they had travelled northwards towards the lofty ranges of Lebanon and the majestic snow-clad peaks of Hermon. It was a region for pause and reflection, for there was much in that landscape to stir thought and imagination. Yonder lay the sources of the mighty and historic Jordan: "The place is a very sanctuary of waters, and from time immemorial men have drawn near it to worship."[2] From the boulders and debris of a high cliff, dank and red, wells forth, as if from hidden sources, the thirty-feet-broad tumultuous stream. In the cliff is a dark grotto above which are carved Greek shrines recalling that fittingly here was worshipped the great nature-god *Pan* whose name still lingers in the modern Banias. Here too by command of Herod the

[1] James Denney, *Jesus and the Gospel*, p. 323.
[2] G. A. Smith, *Historical Geography of the Holy Land*, p. 474.

Great another and more ambitious shrine had been raised, a temple in white marble with the bust of great *Cæsar* Augustus. Thus, where beside the mysterious grotto deep called unto deep, across the heights of Hermon, men had been constrained for long ages to offer homage. Was this the highest height to which the soul could rise—the worship of the seductive and mysterious power manifest in the productivity of nature as represented by *Pan,* or the pomp of power based on the sword as centred in a mortal man, great *Cæsar?* Nature-worship and Führer-worship still claim allegiance. But Jesus had come upon the scene, bringing with Him a majesty of another sort, the glory of the God of love. Already men had begun to link Him with the Spirit of the Most High; for He recalled to the people who saw Him in action those men in whom the divine Word had burned and glowed, Elijah of the passionate zeal and consuming one-ideaed devotion, and Jeremiah, the prophet of exquisite tenderness combined with the strange aloofness of the Suffering Servant of God.

"Whom say ye that I am?", asked Jesus of His Galilean friends, those men who had been so close to Him that nothing of His human action could be hid from their searching gaze. Yet these men, near enough to read each and every flaw, were still prepared to put upon Him the highest title in their vocabulary: "Thou art the Christ." It was an amazing acknowledgment of one who walked before them as a common man; for it meant they reckoned Him worthy to be given the supreme commission God had to offer—to be the one chosen to bring in the dream of the long ages, the resplendent new order for mankind. There was that in Jesus evidently which compelled His intimates to set Him closer to the mind and counsel of Almighty God than any other man, saint or prophet or king.

Jesus must have confessed to Himself that this estimate from without only corroborated the conviction that had sprung up within His own soul. As a growing boy in the Temple He had spoken of the High and Lofty One intimately as "My Father." At the baptism, threshold of His life's work, He had heard the voice claiming Him as son: "This day have I begotten thee." In His parables as He expounded the ways of God with mankind He pictured Him as a Father among His sons. When He lifted up His petitions, He addressed Him naturally and unaffectedly as Father. The one title He constantly bestowed upon Himself was Son of Man. That, according to the vision of Daniel 7, meant that, when it pleased God to end the reign of worldly powers with their bestial and savage policies, it was to this Son of Man that He would commit the new everlasting Kingdom to be established by His own divine power, a Kingdom humane and spiritual as the earthly powers had been brutal and despotic. That Kingdom, Jesus declared, had come, and He Himself must be the one chosen to introduce it. He had hinted at the glory of that new epoch as something grander than the wise Solomon had embodied (Luke 11: 31). And, still more significantly, He had asserted that something greater than the *Temple* was there (Matt. 12: 6) : which meant that with Him, Jesus, and the new society He brought, the Presence of the Living God was confronting men with a life-giving power that even the storied Holy House on Mount Zion had never known. Because He knew He brought the Presence with Him He had startled the paralytic into health by telling him his sins were forgiven; and the radiance of that Presence convinced even the woman of the city that she too could win free from her gilded chains into a larger liberty—a delirious surprise to which only falling tears could testify (Luke 7: 38). This surely was a remarkable consciousness that Jesus possessed that in Him, and through the new society He inaugurated, all the glories that the wisest seers had glimpsed, all the health and spiritual healing that had centred in the ancestral fane, now were immediately and directly available for mankind. In a unique and absolute way He was the Son of the Father.

At the heart of this disclosure was a blameless beauty of soul. Men saw an outer glory; God knew the inner secret, the unstained loveliness of the holy heart. "Behold the Lamb of God, which taketh away the sin of the world." He wore a white radiance, a winsome serenity, the living symbol of the flawless sacrifice.[3] When the Baptist saw among the penitents this man coming to a rite of cleansing, instinctively he drew back: this was highest, holiest manhood by whom, not to whom, the sacred water should be ministered. The eager, blustering, self-confident Peter was suddenly aware that his beloved and familiar friend stood on another level of being: "Depart from me, for I am a sinful man, O Lord." This man embodied the moral standard He preached.

[3] On the sinlessness of Jesus consult A. Martin, *The Finality of Jesus for Faith,* ch. iv.

"Lord, how oft shall my brother sin against me, and I forgive him? till seven times?" (Matt. 18: 21). Peter was normally never at a loss for an answer, but he was speechless when he heard the reply, "Until seventy times seven!" He might have put that saying away as an impractical word for a real world. But he revised that opinion when he heard these whispered words reported from the shadow of the Cross: "Father, forgive them; for they know not what they do" (Luke 23: 34). To be in this man's company was to know that there could be no half-hearted allegiance. He carried an atmosphere of values with Him to which one had to *surrender* the heart. A man had to turn his back on the alluring world *absolutely* before he could answer the straight query, "Lovest thou *me?*" (John 21: 15ff.). It was hard for one who knew his own evil heart to answer boldly "Yes." There must have been a haunting sense of glory on His face before the rich and the clever came running and kneeling to one who was the village carpenter. The rich young ruler, with that sensitive fineness of soul that drew the Master's love, felt the heavenward pull so strong that he went away exceeding sorrowful; it was a hard choice: this man or an unsatisfied heart all life long.

> For ah! the Master is so fair,
> His smile so sweet on banished men
> That those who meet it unaware
> Can never rest on earth again.

Nathanael was an Israelite indeed in whom was no guile. Something lies unexplained in John's story (1: 45ff.), but evidently there was in Jesus an appeal to this rare spirit that threw him into complete homage. Under the fig-tree he had given himself to the study of the law, seeking to find God there. Probably he had been deeply stirred by the Baptist. But now he had found a King of Israel, a spiritual Saul among the people. Nay more, One in whose presence the dividing screen fell away and heaven became open for continual intercourse with the sons of earth. Mary of Bethany had rare vision. She knew the better part which was not to be taken away from her. She could not declare in words of sober prose how this friend sanctified the supper table. She could only make a broken alabaster box declare her will to yield her all. This man was not a mere echo of the divine voice: He was the authentic Word, uttering the Divine Holiness.

In Him God Comes Face to Face With Man. John 1: 1-18; Phil. 2: 1-11; Col. 1: 14-17; Heb. 1: 2-3.

That claim and consciousness of Jesus made a landmark in religious history. Scripture and all Christian experience corroborate His estimate of Himself. More and more men have become convinced that it is impossible to disengage the ministry of Jesus from the activity of God: it was God who was in Christ reconciling the world unto Himself. What was the uniqueness in His presence that made the unclean spirit give voice: "Let us alone; what have we to do with thee, thou Jesus of Nazareth? . . . I know thee who thou art, the Holy One of God" (Mk. 1: 24)? "Follow me," Jesus had but to say; and, though He had just stepped from the carpenter's shop, authority rang in His voice and His word was accepted as a command to be obeyed. "Ye have heard that it hath been said by them of old . . . but I say unto you . . .," and before the astonished ears of tradition-revering and devout Israelites the law of Moses was cast into the shadow, and the utterance of this contemporary human shone out as transcending the ten words spoken amid the thunders of Sinai. Only a voice acclaimed as *God's* could set aside the law of God. Pharisee and Scribe, honoured for piety and knowledge of the sacred lore of the Rabbis, were overawed into gaping silence before His penetrating pronouncements. "Never man spake like this man." "He spake with authority and not as the Scribes." To a Hebrew the one authority to be obeyed was the voice from heaven: that voice reached men's souls in the accents of the Man of Nazareth. The remote God about whom the Scribes debated and the prophets used to speak had come near and faced men.

That truth found classic expression in the Fourth Gospel. The Word became flesh: that self-disclosure that God had granted in passing manifestations had now blazed forth in a life that awakened men to a new consciousness of the Graciousness and Reality of the Creator and Redeemer of men. If from the void had issued in times past notes and intimations that broke and died away leaving a haunting sense of an unfinished harmony beyond, now at last there had poured forth upon human ears a voice that set all men's hearts a-singing. "God, who at sundry times and in divers manners spake in time past unto the fathers by the prophets, hath in these last days spoken unto us by his

Son" (Heb. 1: 1). Men looked upon a human face, but recognized in the light of it that they were gazing at last upon the unveiled glory of God. As there was a time, reflected the Apostle Paul, when upon the darkness and chaos of the unfinished universe the voice said, "Let there be light," and there was light, giving colour and outline and character to the shape of things, so upon the confusion and sorrow of earth, in the dark night of sin and death, there had flashed forth a radiance from the Son of Man: it was the *likeness of God* that thus appeared above the maze and the tangle of humanity, the enlightening vision of the Eternal One Himself, majestic and gracious (2 Cor. 4: 6). It was *God* who came right into the homes and hearts of men in the preacher of Nazareth. It was not just that truth was spoken from a prophet's mouth: it was a creative Personality touching individuals to a new splendour of living. The prejudiced human of the first century with a Jewish tradition of exclusive self-righteousness would not have done the things this man did. He stepped right out of all the conventions, walked right in among the social outcasts, and sat down to eat with publicans and sinners. He went unasked across forbidden thresholds; and, confronting a quisling publican at his own hearth, He awakened his sleeping soul and discovered a son of Abraham: with the power of His presence salvation came to this house. Sensing at once His pity and His purity, the sinner who under a life of shame had long concealed a heartache broke through her reserve, and in a swift and startling act of love and penitence began a new course of life. The Baptist had by his words reached men's souls and sought to confirm his message in a rite; but here was One whose touch was immediate and direct: He brought gospel and regeneration at one and the same time.

He Seeks Their Good. Matt. 5: 45; Mark 2: 14-17; Luke 7: 36-50; Luke 19: 1-9.

Conventional religion drew back in horror before this upsetting of ancient values. The divine had been set down as holy and unapproachable; but here was a blameless Son of God who sought out and made friends with sinners. This was a signal departure from the precedents in the religions of mankind whereby sinful man must stand afar off from the All-Holy One and approach only after he had purified himself by rites and penitence or by priestly intervention.[4] *Here was God in a new guise seeking out and standing beside the sinner in his sin.* Instinctively the publican in the parable stood afar off, beating his breast and crying, "God be merciful to me a sinner." "This man," said the typical Pharisee in a famous scene (Luke 7: 39), "if he were a prophet, would have known who and what manner of woman this is that toucheth him: for she is a sinner": proximity between a true Son of God and the sinner was unthinkable. "Lord, who shall abide in thy tabernacle? who shall dwell in thy holy hill? He that walketh uprightly, and worketh righteousness . . ." (Ps. 15: 1f.). The practices of primitive religion might be summed up as ways of attaining purification, in order to come near to God. Higher religions that have freed themselves from ritual ideas of uncleanness still are concerned deeply with the need for spiritual cleansing as the only way to have community with the deity. To the Muslim when a man tells a lie the foulness of its odour drives his guardian angels a mile away; none shall touch the *Qur'an* except the purified. The Greek was much concerned with *katharsis* (purification): for communion with the god or participation in the mysteries purity was essential. The Orphic sects imposed a stringent code of abstinence on all who sought happiness in the next world. Thus *universally* the sinner must not dare to seek the divine *till he has performed the stated ritual.* But Jesus began His public life standing among the penitents under John's baptism, and with His last breath He opened the gates of Paradise to a penitent thief. In the hour of her public shame He stood with the woman taken in adultery over against her accusers. This concern for the seeking out of the sinner was so complete a revolution in religious thought that it can only be described as God breaking through to make a new revelation of His nature.

Naturally here Judaism took sharp issue with Jesus. This, the Rabbis held, was dethroning the righteousness of God. That God should send rain upon the just and the unjust alike was unrighteous: it was to put sinners upon the same level as saints in the sight of God, and that surely was impiety offensive to a Holy God. But this was God as Jesus knew Him. Love was His own nature, as was righteousness. What the sinner has to expect

[4] Cf. Karl Holl, *The Distinctive Elements of Christianity,* translated by E. P. Dickie.

is not offended dignity that averts its face till the sinner does penance, but a heart grieved, so grieved as to initiate a means to awaken and recall and redeem the erring one. This is the Christian Gospel that is a religious revolution. God is revealed in Jesus as concerned less with the punishment than with the cure of sin. Right at the opening of His ministry forgiveness is the word He must speak. The divine nature does not wait for penitence, but goes out to meet the sinner in his sin with a love so warm that the frozen heart melts in tears. The sinners and the outcasts in consequence were storming the Kingdom, while the righteous Pharisees strove in vain to attain the goal of a perfectly kept Sabbath in Israel. He who waits for perfect conditions before he puts his hand to the plough never reaps a harvest in the natural world, and God does not insist on our perfection before He calls us into His company in the spiritual sphere. The greater our need, the readier He is to come to our aid.

Will anyone suggest that in thus making approach to the sinner God in Jesus undermined morality? Was Peter less troubled about sin because Jesus made him His friend? Did not Zaccheus surrender his ill-gotten gains when Jesus stepped into his life? Did not Matthew leave the lucrative trade altogether when the word of Jesus gripped him? When the Magdalene was received with a gracious pardon instead of a stinging rebuke, did she go back to her old trade light-heartedly? Did the woman taken in adultery fail to feel the sting of her wrongdoing when He challenged her accusers? Did the rich young ruler live comfortably with his great possessions when Jesus left a command in his soul? Can anyone read the record of the life of Jesus and not feel the constraint of His blameless purity? Has any mind ever met a sterner challenge than the Sermon on the Mount? No, the strange power of this gentle Son of Man was to set man before the judgment seat of absolute love. Beside the austerity of His demand there is the pressing obligation His love casts upon us. Beside the purity that condemns our sinfulness there is the constraint of His generosity upon us. We are twice-judged.

In the attitude of Jesus toward the capital city of Jerusalem we see as in a mirror the mind of God toward us men and our contentment in our settled ways. Almost any other place would have offered Him a kindlier reception, but it was there at the last that He would go. "He set his face to go to Jerusalem." "How often would I have gathered thy children together, even as a hen gathereth her chickens under her wings, and ye would not!" (Matt. 23: 37). But because the clouds of doom were gathering over the obdurate city as the revolutionary party whetted their knives for a foolish clash with all-powerful Rome, it was all the more incumbent upon love that it must declare itself. As He looked down upon the city He burst into tears, so intimately did He take to Himself the burden of the city's sins and her sorrows past and yet to come. He rode in defencelessly that He might make clear His will to her peace and welfare. Right within the ancient sanctuary He proclaimed the nearness of the grander spiritual temple of His person and society, but their only answer was to demand His authority. Yet authority He had, and He claimed it. With all His patience and His love He insisted that they must give Him alone their trust and loyalty or perish. "If thou hadst known in this thy day the things which belong unto thy peace!" (Luke 19: 42). In the Divine name He brought this last offer, but they discerned not the time when God Himself was visiting them. Truth was hid from their eyes, and the doom of desolation must come. God was long-suffering, but He must have exclusive faith and obedience.

B. The Necessity of the Cross

At Measureless Cost. Matt. 16: 21-23; John 12: 1-9; 20-23.

When Peter reached the grand climax of belief and hailed Jesus as Messiah, He straightway began to lift a corner of the veil for them: "He began to teach them, that the Son of man must suffer many things, and be rejected of the elders, and of the chief priests, and scribes, and be killed, and after three days rise again" (Mark 8: 31). Again and again He returned to the theme (9: 31; 10: 33ff.). Indeed it became His one concern and preoccupation.

Nothing can be more clear than this, that Jesus saw before Him in the capital city a commission from God from which there was no escape. Every Gospel portrays Jesus reaching forward toward this crisis. Once He had been hailed as Messiah, there was only one direction He could take—toward that place where the national life surged and the people's hopes centred. No more does He confront great crowds or linger much in casual encounter: He stays by the Twelve and seeks to make more secure the links of loyalty and hope that bind them to Him. And the kernel of His conversation was this theme of suffering to come. At first the rebound of the most loyal like Peter was sharp: such a fate could not befall such a chosen one. But Jesus rebuked the dream of a grander road, and persisted. When they talked of places of honour, He pushed them up against the stern demand of endurance and sacrifice: there is a cup to be drunk and a baptism to be baptized with. What a chasm of spirit divided him from the Twelve! What was first in His thought was last in theirs. This is reflected in the unvarnished but vivid picture: "They were in the way going up to Jerusalem; and Jesus was going before them: and they were amazed; and as they followed, they were afraid" (Mark 10: 32). This is a glimpse of a leader resolved and absorbed, pushing ahead as He had never pushed before, and followed with a reluctance and an apprehension and misgiving such as had never before emerged. It is here that Luke reveals the face set resolutely, and here, too, the stern words to a would-be disciple: "No man, having put his hand to the plough, and looking back, is fit for the kingdom of God" (9: 51-62). To this period also belong the words: "I have a baptism to be baptized with; and how am I straitened till it be accomplished!" (12: 50).

The words in which Jesus justifies His line of action are introduced by a Greek word (*dei*) that implies that this dread journey was *divinely* appointed. God's will was behind this decision (Mark 8: 31). He had begun to pay the bitter cost when He broke away from His home and took a course that seemed the mark of madness to His nearest and dearest. What more bitter anguish could be thrust on a loving son than to know that a sword was even now piercing His mother's heart, and what would it be when she saw Him on a criminal cross? To one who held John Baptist to be one of the greatest born of woman it was cruel to take a line that made John feel deserted by his likeliest disciple, adding thus disappointment and distress to the hard lot of the prophet in prison (Matt. 11). When close friends like John and James appeared before Him brimful of eager expectation of coming glory, it was hard to dash in their faces the chill reality of a gruelling baptism and a bitter cup (Mark 10: 35). How difficult it must have been to struggle daily with the uncomprehending roseate hopes of these simple souls who followed Him, and to know that in the end He must leave them victims to a grim awakening and the clutch of pitiless forces! He betrayed a mind often preoccupied with the costliness of sacrifice. What fascinated His interest in Mary's extravagant gift of precious ointment was that she parted thus with what she dearly loved—as so must He; for He enjoyed human life and all its myriad contacts and interests (Mark 14: 3). So too the widow's mites that she willingly flung into the treasury were hard to come by and were her *all:* it was throwing away her bread (12: 41). He spoke the parable about the king who must needs count the cost before he went on an expedition (Luke 14: 31), and He did not conceal from Himself that some could enter into life only at the cost of being halt and maimed (Mark 9: 43).

When the Greeks were waiting for an audience and His mind was thrilled by the prospect of the harvest to be gathered, He knew full well that first the corn of wheat must fall into the earth and die (John 12: 24). Gethsemane was a costly ordeal, but He had been paying in drops of blood all the way—in the cruel disappointment of men's unresponsiveness, in the stinging taunts that ungenerous folk cast at Him, in the malignant opposition with which the officials and the religious countered Him, in the hypocrisy that remained impenetrable to pleading or exposure, in the awful responsibility that saw a nation blindly heading for disaster and failed to stab it awake, in the crushing weight of heedless sin and indifference in the people who alone had the vision of the true God. Upon that uniquely sensitive heart the fearful burden daily rested, and there was no human friend who even dimly understood or dumbly tried to help. Thus we see as in a mirror how the divine bears the sin of man—at measureless cost. Foxes had holes, birds of the air had nests, but the Son of Man had not where to lay His head.

God's Abhorrence of Sin and His Saving Love. Hosea 11; Is. 53; Matt. 26: 20-24; Luke 22: 37.

In these days of ruthless totalitarian war the heinousness of sin has come home to us. The pitilessness and the blatant savagery of it have struck deep into even our insensitive souls. When men are seized by stealth in the privacy of their homes, dragged forth and lined up in barrack squares to be shot in dozens, without trial or even accusation, simply because they dared to think differently from others; when engines of death are hurled down upon crowded tenements, and mothers and children are thrown from sleep into the awful agonies of pain and death; when in the darkness without warning helpless souls are capsized in mid ocean and left to the pitiless waters while the perpetrators look on and laugh; then indeed we awake to the ugliness of sin. And when these horrors come to those we ourselves love and cherish, to the innocent we have ourselves fondled, our wrath becomes a terrible thing. Ordinarily we avert our eyes from sin or seek to chase it from our minds because our own hearts accuse us of like transgressions. But how must sin appear to the All-Seeing God and the all-sensitive heart of love? Set down the story of a year's life in a crowded city block in peace time where poverty and drink and lust hold sway, unroof in imagination one single row of houses for one single night and look in upon the crime and hopelessness and misery, and the heart is too full for words, the eyes too hard for tears. The imagination refuses to picture the ills we could daily know. Enough that we face those we must share, and hide our thought about the rest.

But the Creator of all human souls cannot be indifferent to the world He has made; He cannot single out the loveliness and pass unheeded the fevers and the woes. Sin that we comprehend only in the mass He knows in the single tragedies of each tenement of clay. It was characteristic of Jesus that He dealt lovingly and patiently with individual after individual. The personal concern of the Father was mirrored in the personal ministries of the Son. He lived in Galilee, remote to all appearances from the great world's throbbing life; but the heaving seas of worldwide humanity laid at His feet evidence aplenty of the sorrows of the untraversed oceans.

His first ministry was that of forgiveness. But forgiveness, glorious and life-giving as it is to the redeemed soul, is but a drop that falls on a single blade of grass. Behind the Magdalene's sin was a whole context of transgression, a history of wilfulness and lust and careless parenthood, it may be, a story of disappointment and momentary abandon that cruel and gross minds had turned to gain without pity. Behind the ill-gotten gains of a Zaccheus lay his disloyalty to national ideals, and behind that again the crushing yoke of Rome that brought the doubtful gifts of bread and games to the imperial city as it brought penury and frustration to the subject peoples, a system that drowned many in the debauchery of excessive wealth and power in and around the palace as it defrauded multitudes of a just price for the crops they grew and of that greater harvest of the soul and spirit that belongs to free men and women. Behind the betrayal of a Judas, a disappointed Zealot, lay the malignity of a Caiaphas and his fellow-lovers of office and power, and beyond them lay centuries of privilege by which the service of God had been corrupted and debased. The redeeming acts of Jesus to individual souls were but candle lights that revealed the limitless darkness beyond.

How then could the Almighty contrive to send to earth's remotest bounds and into its depths some awareness of His abhorrence of the ravages of sin? A beacon must be lit in the land that would throw its light far and wide, and that beacon must have a strange singularity about its fires that men would look up and take thought. What stark and challenging deed could be lifted up before men's eyes that would at once declare the exceeding sinfulness of sin and at the same time reveal the power that alone could bring health and healing to its victims and martyrs? If sin was to confront mankind in all its hideous reality, then love likewise in all its heroic winsomeness must flaunt its glory in the skies. So there came to be that incredible tragedy of the ages, the Crucifixion on Calvary.

Premonitions of that grand act of history had come to a lone singer in Israel when he burst into poetry in the songs of the Suffering Servant (Is. 42: 1-4; 49: 1-6; 50: 4-9; 52: 13 to 53: 12). There he had pictured an Israel pure and innocent, suffering incalculably under the murderous cruelty of stronger surrounding powers, yet bearing herself with such lofty allegiance to a higher will that gradually it began to smite with shame the minds of her oppressors. Surely there fell upon them as they watched a wonder that one should suffer so inexplicably and unprotestingly. And as they marvelled, the flash of insight lit up their dull understanding and they knew that it was a divine mystery they beheld—the innocent was suffering for their sins, the chastisement of their peace fell upon the tortured one. Such a premonition must reach the stage of reality.

The Son of Man must needs suffer, Jesus had striven to teach. It needs blood, sweat, and tears to lay upon the conscience of men the terrible toll of heedlessness. Men excused Rome her despotism because she was just; then let her representative in Jerusalem face the angry and scheming priests with all their power to stir bloodshed and rebellion, and show if justice could dwell in the heart of a despot, if power would forego its alliance with policy and cunning and let the innocent go free. If she with all power at her command laid hands on innocence, then her subservience to sin was proven and exposed. Let the corrupt and worldly priests be faced with the choice of losing their prestige or doing to death the Man of Nazareth, and the crisis would show how they hugged their sin—lust of power and greed. Let the people even, with all their professed admiration for the Galilean and their willingness to follow Him, be faced with the choice of a Barabbas and bloody vengeance or the pale Galilean who talked of meekness and peace, and see if sin did not win the mastery. And that choice of sin by rulers, priests, and people would be exposed for all time as upon the cruel cross was hoisted the innocent victim, the purity that no slander could tarnish, the blamelessness that no cruelty could provoke to strike back. Strange that it should need the bitterness of death to release the truth. Some flowers must be crushed to give out their fragrance; the great divide must be crossed before the view on the other side can be unveiled. The Son of Man could not stop short of death if the dark hideousness of the world's sin was to stand out clear.

With the exposure of sin must be revealed the grace that redeems, else the spectacle of his own misdoing would have been too terrible even for sinful man. It was one thing just to *talk* about meekness on the Mount in Galilee, but it was quite another to see it *lived out* in the agony of a courtroom and the long stretch of travel under a heavy cross along the sorrowful way while soldiers scoffed and enemies grunted satisfaction. Such meekness impressed even a proud Roman. It might be airy rhetoric to talk of surrendering an offending eye or a limb; but there was a saving salt in the sacrifice when one calmly gave up life itself rather than betray a principle. It was just a startling paradox to be exhorted to love your enemies and to pray for them that despitefully use you, but it gave men furiously to think of love as no mere sentiment when it enabled a man in the agony of death and torture to pray for those who had actually raised the cruel cross and driven the nails into His hands. It was no surprising thing that Pilate after a superficial examination and without calling many witnesses should say that he found no fault in this man; but it was matter for pondering when a blunt soldier who had looked on many executions gazed with a strange awe at this quivering figure on the Cross, marked His words and demeanour, and exclaimed, "Truly this was a righteous man." Thus the sordid tragedy of a criminal's death could be viewed as no mere exhibition of the evil heart in man, but as the exaltation of that spiritual quality whereby the evil could be met and overcome. If there are depths unplumbed in the wickedness of man, there are also heights unscaled in the spirit that God gives to those who look in faith to Him.

But this demonstration of the eternal love, to be on the grand scale, must be made by a divine protagonist. There must be no unreal shadow figures on the screen. God Himself must enter the human stage and prove beyond contradiction that it was His will to wrestle with sin and it was His power that would overthrow the evil. No common ties must bind the Son of Man to the Father in heaven. God must be in Christ reconciling the world unto Himself. And yet man must feel that this warfare was not a remote conflict in the heavens, but a combat where the conditions and the weapons were human. The Son of God must be a son of man, bone of our bone and flesh of our flesh, so that when in the shock of battle He met the dread enemy, it would be by no supernatural wizardry that the mortal blow was given and victory won, but by means that were spiritual, by qualities that had their parallel and counterpart in the life of a common man. So Calvary became the ordeal of the Son of Man and at the same time the victory of God.

The Effectual Means, Heb. 2: 17-18; Heb. 4: 15-16.

The method chosen for the grand hope of reconciliation for the whole world was a strange one: a simple carpenter turned preacher in remote Palestine and among a subject people, an inconspicuous beginning and the prelude to a drab ending—a criminal's cross of shame on a bare eminence outside a city wall. But has it proved an effectual means? Principal Alexander Martin has affirmed: "It is matter of experience that morally distracted souls do thus find the readjustment with Reality which they crave. They do, in plain spiritual fact, pass into 'the Holiest of all'—to the very heart of Existence where alone a spiritual nature can rest—through the rent veil of this Man's flesh. . . . Nothing is surer to Christian faith than that we are 'made nigh by the blood of Christ.' "[5]

C. The Resurrection

Victorious Over Death. Mark 15; Matt. 28; Luke 24; John 20-21; 1 Cor. 15.

When the sun went down on the bleak tragedy of Calvary, hope might very well have died in Israel. The purest life ever lived in its long history had ended on a criminal's cross, and it seemed as if it but remained to cast the earthly frame to rest ingloriously in a common felon's grave. Loving hands might intervene and place the body reverently in a new tomb, but that was only a seemly act of farewell. Pious women hurrying with spices to pay the last dues were but adding the touch of beauty and love to relieve the grimness of the inevitable end. The birds on the bough might fittingly have tuned their notes into a sad requiem.

From the human side nothing more was expected from Jesus of Nazareth. His story had passed into history, and even His closest associates had no eyes for marvel to spring forth. A resuscitation in any shape or form was entirely unexpected. All the records testify to the Resurrection as a complete surprise: it was not a mere hallucination that grew out of notions earlier cherished in circles from which the disciples came. The disciples out on the lake were surprised (John 21: 7); on the way to Emmaus it was of a lost leader they spoke when lo! He was in their company an unsuspected fellow-traveller (Luke 24: 21); it was an obstinately unbelieving Thomas whom his Lord confronted (John 20: 25); it was to women who had gone to pay the last

[5] *The Finality of Faith,* p. 174f.

offices to the dead that there opened up the vision of the empty tomb (Mark 16: 1); and it was to Paul an enemy and an unbeliever that the Risen Lord spake startlingly on the Damascus Road (Acts 9: 4). The event indeed was so far out of their expectation that the women at the tomb were left afraid (Mark 16: 8), the disciples were changed from disheartened and fleeing men to bold preachers of a living Lord (Acts 4: 13), and Paul always spoke of having been "apprehended," laid hold on, arrested and turned round in his thoughts and life purposes by a Power and Presence that confronted him suddenly (Phil. 3: 12). It was as if an unseen world of reality had invaded this common earth, and men of flesh and blood, earth bound and earth centred, had their mind opened to a Divine Presence that recognized no barriers.

It was the faith of the singer of the Suffering Servant songs that the only end to long travail was glorious triumph:

> Behold, my servant shall achieve,
> He shall be exalted, lifted up and very high . . .
> Many the nations that shall wonder,
> Kings shall shut their mouths in awe:
> What they were never told shall they see,
> What they had never heard shall they ponder. . . .
> From the travail of his soul he shall see light
> And rest satisfied with the knowledge of his vindication
> (Is. 52: 13ff.).

So had Job reached the conviction: "I know that my Vindicator liveth" (19: 25).

So it had fallen out in the actuality of living history: Jesus Christ was risen from the dead. The God of love had declared His righteousness; the God of righteousness had certified His love by raising from the dead the sinless Son of Man.

It is a vain study to turn to the written records and place under a microscope divergences in the Gospel testimonies. This is a field of experience where redemption counts and not mere records. As James Denney has put it, "It ought to be apparent that, so far as the fact of the resurrection of Jesus is concerned, the narratives of the evangelists are quite the least important part of the evidence . . . It is not this or that in the New Testament . . . which is the primary evidence for the resurrection; it is the New Testament itself. The life that throbs in it from beginning to end, the life that always fills us again with wonder as it beats upon us from its pages, is the life which the Risen Saviour has quickened in Christian souls. The evidence for the resurrection of Jesus is the existence of the Church in that extraordinary spiritual vitality which confronts us in the New Testament."[6]

With a strange premonition the Psalmist, from his close grasp on the God of his faith, had exclaimed: "Thou wilt not suffer thine Holy One to see corruption" (16: 10). That was a verse on which early Christian thought seized (Acts 2: 25ff.). What was involved in this life was not just a span of ordinary existence. Here was a life proved blameless in the sight of men, a life in which the moral qualities were gathered in all their purity and power: it was a thrusting through and a flourishing on the common earth of that peace and joy, that love and pity, that faith and tenderness, which man's eyes looked for as sign and symbol of the heavenly reality. If that the noblest Son of Man could know no happier issue than to be rudely haled from a Gethsemane, shuffled through a travesty of justice along the Via Dolorosa to a criminal's cross and a transgressor's grave, then the divine honour was for ever besmirched and His righteousness denied. If the heavens remained brass over Calvary, faith and hope in the mercy of God was stifled in every sensitive soul. So even Jesus was deluded, and for all His living grasp on a Father's hand He too was cast into ignominy and devouring death! Surely it was proven that the divine arm was shortened that it could not save.

Jesus through His ministry had been the incarnation of human yearnings as of the divine mind. He had confidently declared the forgiveness of sins—unveiling, and by His deeds and attitudes making vivid and real, the outreaching love of the Father. He had brought to the common earth the qualities of mind and soul and spirit that awakened the sensitive to the inrush of a new order: the Kingdom of God had arrived among men. *Could that be all a vain dream?* He had persuaded His listeners that God set human values above rigid laws, willing rather that His healing should make a Sabbath in the soul than to hold to a harsh formalism without (Mark 2: 27-28). He had opened invitingly the gates of prayer, assuring the most defenceless of humans that their importunity won vindication from the pitiful and righteous

[6] *Jesus and the Gospel*, pp. 111-112.

God (Luke 18: 1-8). He had penetrated behind the forms and falsities of legalistic rules, and set men face to face with the deadliness of evil desire and murderous thought (Matt. 5: 21). *What if the Almighty One refused to honour that revelation of His name and nature?* All that discerning minds had come to see in the words Love, Righteousness, Holiness, Peace, Meekness, Joy, Forgiveness—all that was inextricably associated with Jesus of Nazareth. For these realities He had lived and died. If the Almighty honoured and vindicated that sacrifice, then these realities were approved of God and shone as stars in man's heaven. If the tragedy of Calvary aroused no action in the God of all Justice, then He did not care.

But God did care, and the power of the Resurrected One descended upon living men with a transforming touch past all denial. It was not just that Peter saw a vision or Paul heard a voice on the Damascus Road. These men were quickened by a new spiritual dynamic: the stumbling, fumbling, denying Peter became a leader radiating confidence and conviction, and Paul outstripped all his contemporaries in zeal and insight and moral grandeur. A company of disillusioned, disheartened followers gathered out of nowhere to testify after Pentecost to a transfiguring faith and a consuming love that set a Church in motion, a Church that has gone on spreading its roots throughout the lands of earth and still defies the death that falls on earthly societies. Whence has come that driving force, that persistent energy of renewal, that inherent quality that sustains the saint and heals the sinner of every class and kind?

The Church knows only one explanation: Jesus Christ is risen —not that He was raised up merely in the long past to walk the earth for a season, a phantom spirit coming through closed doors, haunting the shore line of the old familiar fishing-ground, disappearing from the grasp of would-be worshippers in the garden where He had been laid. The Church does not rest on the bare memories of a re-animated body that came and after forty days passed from human vision. The Church knows her Lord as one who was exalted to another order of being, one who was declared to be the Son of God with power. The gift of the Holy Spirit, the renewing vitality that still animates the saints of today as it has glorified the faithful of all the generations—that is the evidence that He lives at the right hand of God.

III. The Holy Spirit.

We believe in the Holy Spirit by whom God is ever at work in the minds and hearts of men, inspiring every right desire and every effort after truth and beauty.

We believe that the Spirit of God moves men to acknowledge their sins and accept the divine forgiveness and grace.

We believe that the Spirit was present with power at the beginning of the Church, enabling the disciples to bear witness to what they had seen and heard, filling them with love of the brethren, and hope of the coming Kingdom, and sustaining them in the sense of Christ's continuing presence in their midst.

We believe that by the same Spirit the Church is continually guided and empowered, and her members fortified against temptation, fear and doubt, and built up in faith and holiness unto salvation.

So we acknowledge the Holy Spirit as the Lord and Giver of life, through whom the creative, redeeming love of God is ever at work among men.

CHAPTER III. THE HOLY SPIRIT

As the Wind. Gen. 2: 7; Ps. 104: 29-30; Ezek. 37: 5-10.

Far back in the time story it must have happened many a time in the days when men dwelt in tents, trekked much under the stars, and paused to bivouac for the night. The mother laid down her ailing child and watched her through the livelong night with anxious eyes. The laboured breathing of the little one grew softer and died away. Was it death? Was life still flickering there? How could one tell? Did the mother hold her hand across the lips? Or was her hand too rough with toil, and insensitive? Did she hold her cheek over the motionless mouth? She was testing life by breathing, by air in motion. Satisfied and grateful, she passed out into the night. It was sultry and heavy. Then came the soft something upon her cheek like the breathing of her child. It was air in motion; the wind was rising. It came so mysteriously out of the nowhere, and into the nowhere it would pass as silently. She used the same word to describe the breath of her child and the current of air that blew in from the sea. It was *ruah,* the Hebrew word which means breath, air in agitation, and so came also to mean the spirit, the living viewless reality that declares its presence in the body by the act of breathing.

St. John takes us across the years to a housetop in Jerusalem (John 3). The learned Rabbi talks by night with the Master of all life about the deepest of all human concerns, the coming of God's reign to the soul. How shall a man be born again when he is old? The answer comes from the viewless breath of the night, the wind that, suddenly arising as if from nowhere, begins to fan his cheeks. The same Greek word *pneuma* is used for wind and for spirit. The mysterious zephyr comes and goes, incalculable and unpredictable. So with the visitations of the Spirit of God. You recognize the movement; but to the human eye the wherefore of it is unexplained, yet real. It can come soft as the breath of even: as a friend of Théodore Monod described his conversion: "I just felt happy in the love of God. God did to me as a mother will sometimes do to her child who has overslept himself: He woke me with a kiss." But that same power can descend with all the fury of a tempest casting souls like ships from ocean troughs to dizzy heights, from the "O wretched man that I am!" of St. Paul to his glorying in the Cross of Christ.[1]

Ever at Work. Ps. 51: 11; Ps. 139: 7; Ezek. 11: 5, 19; Is. 11: 2-4; Is. 42: 1; Is. 61: 1; Joel 2: 28-31; Nu. 11: 29.

Among the Hebrews abnormal powers or sudden frenzies experienced by men were ascribed to the action of a spirit, good or evil. It was a spirit that gave Bezaleel the craftsman's skill to devise cunning works in gold, in silver, and in brass (Exod. 31: 3); it was a spirit that came to Samson so that he rent a lion as if it were a kid (Judg. 14: 6); it was an evil spirit that filled Saul with a mad jealousy so that he threw the javelin at David (1 Sam. 19: 9). The inexplicable and potent quality of spirit is often expressed in the language used about it. It may "leap upon," "rush upon," "fall mightily upon," "carry away" men. It can be "poured out" with fertilizing power on nature (Is. 32: 15, 44: 3). To the prophets in particular the gift of the Spirit was ascribed. In earlier days the schools of prophets were prone to induce enthusiasm and high ecstasy by dancing and wild music (1 Sam. 10: 5-11), but in the later days of the writing prophet it was rather with thought and grave utterance and stirrings of moral passion and religious truth that the Spirit marked its tarrying (Amos 7-9; Is. 6; Hos. 1-3; Jer. 1). The mood varied from the tempestuous Elijah to the gentle Hosea, from the rugged moral strength of Amos to the tender sensitiveness of Jeremiah. And, grand though the Spirit was, it was in the Old Testament ever fitful: it comes and goes unaccountably, and no man claims it as an abiding possession. As Jehovah unveils His nature throughout the centuries the Spirit comes to be known as pre-eminently holy (Ps. 51: 11).

As we turn over the pages of the Old Testament we note with what dignified simplicity and moral purity the story unfolds from the first beginnings down to the hectic days of the Maccabees as reflected in Daniel; and as we compare the literature of other nations—*e.g.*, in their delineations of creation or in the records of their boastful kings—we are very conscious of a lofty ethical

[1] Cf. *ERE* vol. iv. art. 'Conversion.'

strain in the deposit of the Hebrew genius. Where can we find utterances of such deep and moving quality as are provided by the Psalms? We become aware of a gracious Spirit at work there in these singers of Israel as in the prophets. What is the meaning of this distinctiveness in a whole literature? And in the facts of their history as well as in their interpretation of that history there is the sense of a leading and guiding power, of a redeeming and purifying fire, that constrains one to exclaim: Surely a Presence was there through all the years, not always seen and known, but ever moving in the shadow! The Old Testament itself is a proof of the reality of the Spirit of God; as is also the whole story of the uniqueness of Hebrew development, not towards power or culture like other nations, but simply and frankly towards the knowledge of the Living God and the clearer vision of His coming Kingdom.

With Power at the Beginning. Luke 1: 35; Matt. 3: 13-17; Matt. 12: 28; Mark 3: 28-29; John 14: 16ff.; John 15: 26ff.; John 16: 7ff.

Jesus in the Synoptic Gospels has remarkably little to say directly on the Holy Spirit. He recognizes the truth that we have just noticed, that the Spirit of God is behind the rich legacy of the Psalter: "David himself said in the Spirit" (Mark 12: 36; Matt. 22: 43). The part that the Spirit played in emergencies when His presence was removed from the disciples, as in the early history of the Church, is forecast in Mark 13: 11; Matt. 10: 20; Luke 12: 12. One late version, in Luke, of the Lord's Prayer instead of "Hallowed be thy name" reads "Send thy Holy Spirit upon us," and there is the Lucan version of the saying about prayer: "How much more shall your heavenly Father give the Holy Spirit to them that ask him?" (11: 13). But there is one pre-eminently clear and unmistakable pronouncement—that the unforgivable sin is sin against the Holy Ghost. What is this unforgivable sin? It is to see His good deeds and call them the work of Satan—the sin of deliberate resistance to the truth as we know it in our souls, a stubborn obstinacy that calls good evil and falsehood truth rather than acknowledge our defeat (Mark 3: 28-30; Matt. 12: 31-32; Luke 12: 10). That saying is the key to understanding the fewness of His words about the Spirit. There was no call to speak much of it, because its presence was obvious in all He said and did. "If I by the Spirit (or finger) of God cast out demons, then is the Kingdom of God come upon you" (Matt. 12: *27*; Luke 11: 20). At the baptism under John the Spirit came to rest upon Him, and from that moment onward the beauty, strength, tenderness, and intensity of His daily life found their explanation in the continuing presence of the Spirit of God. In the experience of other men the heavenly visitant came and went; with Him it remained and shone so conspicuously from His words and deeds that not to acknowledge its presence was to turn one's back upon the Living God.

But perhaps even the disciples had not fully understood the source of His strength. They were to recognize the divine reality only when bitter need came upon themselves. As a young man often fails to mature while his parents are at his side but, when death takes away his father, rises suddenly to responsibilities and capacities his timid nature had never suspected, so with the disciples: "It is expedient for you that I go away: for if I go not away, the Comforter will not come unto you; but if I depart, I will send him unto you" (John 16: 7). These apostles were to be like men on trial before an accusing world, and they would need an advocate at their side, a power that would clarify the truth of life for them.

Enabling the Disciples. John 20: 19-23; Acts 2; Acts 4: 31-37; Acts 5: 3, 32.

The Fourth Gospel does not own a time when the bereaved disciples did not know the sustaining of the Spirit. It is the first act of Jesus when He returns to them gathered behind closed doors for fear of the Jews: "Peace be unto you . . . Receive ye the Holy Ghost" (John 20: 19-22). And who can doubt that there was a Presence with them in the hours of bewilderment, grief, and prostration, as they groped their way out of darkness into light, out of the dull stupor of astonishment and desolation into the gladdening knowledge that made even gloom-set Thomas exclaim, "My Lord and my God!"?

But it is on the dazzling day of Pentecost that the remembrance of the Church has ever been focussed (Acts 2). That stands out in Christian history as the real birthday of the Christian Church, the advent of the Holy Ghost with power. It is not to be dismissed as merely a case of mass hysteria, a flare up of emotional exuberance in a company of startled men and women. That day must be known by its fruits, and its fruit was the realization that God is God not of the dead but of the living; the Holy Ghost is a power that turns the world upside down. "As in the earth's core, so in the core of every vital religion lives a fire; on occasion it will break the crust of decent routine and will excite the terror or the laughter of the 'rational.' Yet without this fire there would be no spiritual life, and without its volcanic outbursts there would be none of life's cleansing and renewal."[2]

The crucifixion of Jesus took place at Passover time, and we can imagine with what sadness of heart His disciples and other followers had sought to gather up once again the broken strings of life. Most had scattered to their homes, and the precious fellowship was broken into fragments. Yet there must have been meetings of friends with friends and communings like that of Cleopas and his companion on the way to Emmaus in the melancholy strain: "We trusted that it had been he which should have redeemed Israel." It was now the month of May, the unlucky month when no marriages took place to gladden the family and village life. It was the busy season of the ingathering of the grain harvest. But surely in the fields parables as Jesus told them were recalled and experiences exchanged. News must have travelled of the visions to the disciples, and a breath of hope and the thrill of surprise quickened even in shadowed souls a wondering and expectation. Thus seven long weeks passed away and then came Pentecost, so called because it was the fiftieth day from the offering of the first sheaf of firstfruits at Passover time (Lev. 23: 15-16). It was one of the great festivals that brought Jews from all lands to keep tryst in the Temple, and for the first time since the tragedy of Calvary Christian sympathizers from all parts had opportunity of coming together again. Kindlier seas and spring weather made it possible for many of the faithful to come from the greater distances of the Dispersion, and thus it was a more cosmopolitan company than gathered at Passover time. It was really a joyous harvest thanksgiving, and on this occasion Providence had marked it out to celebrate the beginning of a new and richer harvest.

[2] Andrew Lang, in his biography of Lockhart, quoted in J. Moffatt, *Jesus Christ the Same,* p. 63.

By what planning or mysterious prompting the adherents of the Christian hope came together in one place we do not know. Soon after dawn, as good Jews, they would find themselves in the Temple for the morning sacrifices, and thereafter by a common impulse they sought each other's company in a generous home such as that of John Mark's mother, perhaps in the upper room of sacred memory; and there they would give themselves to prayer and worship, not breaking their fast until noon. Testimonies would be given by those who had seen the Lord, and new insight and hope would spring in the bewildered and wondering questioners as disciples recalled the Master's great utterances and showed how prophecy shed light on the strangely moving sequence of events. Then came the unexpected, the invasion by the Spirit of God, sweeping away all doubts and fears and rousing the whole assembly to heights of vision and expectation.

The psychological preparation, the tension of these long weeks of suppressed hopes and of wonders afoot, and then the eruption of gladness and thanksgiving in one cataclysmic experience—all that we can dimly discern. But there is an overplus that we cannot explain. There was the return of boldness and conviction to those who in panic had forsaken the cause and fled; there was the illumination of soul that changed a forlorn hope into a Gospel; there was the sense of power that swept unlettered men into confident and ardent testimony; there was an impetus that transformed a broken remnant into a fellowship able to consolidate and establish its life in the very heart of hostile Judaism. Leadership does not come to a man like Peter out of nothing, nor does the will to follow fall easily upon men who were so lately rivals for place and position. Most remarkable was the voluntary selling of property and the coming together in a communal family life of those who had not been lacking in either the acquisitive or the class spirit (Acts 2: 42ff.). Disciples who had been stubborn enough learners under Jesus became teachers, and a spontaneous flow of prayer and devotion inevitably centred in the breaking of bread. We might accuse Luke of painting too idyllic a picture; but we have to admit he does not suppress or extenuate: do we not read of Ananias and Sapphira caught in their fraudulent designs and of bickering between the Hellenists and the Palestinians? What emerges here is life on a new level, life that carried forward through misunderstanding and persecution, life that illuminated the minds of a Philip and a Stephen just as it opened the heart of a Barnabas, life so conspicuous that authority had to take steps to stamp it out, life so challenging that an ardent young Rabbi like Saul of Tarsus thought it must become the consuming concern of his days to hunt out and destroy its representatives already raising their heads as far away as Damascus. Yes, so swift was this current that Saul himself was speedily drawn into it. Onlookers must have marvelled at the momentum of this movement. It flowed relentlessly on across the frontiers of Palestine and Syria into Asia, Macedonia, Greece, and Rome. And still it moves irresistibly: the Christian Church has never stood still through all the centuries.

This was obviously a superhuman force. Starting out from a group of Jews, the proudest and most aloof of peoples, to whom the common contacts of daily life with other nations had been reckoned defiling in the sight of God, this movement yet opened its heart to all the races of earth. Age-long enmities and ancestral feuds were buried in this fellowship. Class division was broken down, slave and master met on the same platform, women were received on the same terms as men. "There is neither Jew nor Greek, there is neither bond nor free, there is neither male nor female: for ye are all one in Christ Jesus" (Gal. 3: 28; Eph. 2: 12ff.). Springing from a nation that centred its religion in the *holiness* of God that none might draw near save by the stated ritual of Judaism, and cherishing the belief that all the nations would yet come to her to learn her law, this movement changed the emphasis to the *love* of God, proclaimed His will to seek after and bring into the fold all sorts and conditions of men, and sent out from Jerusalem apostles of this gospel of the open door to all the ends of the earth. Such conversions only come from a divine impact, and that impact made itself felt first at the festival of Pentecost.

The Spirit . . . of God. Acts 6: 3-5; 7: 55; 8: 15-24; 8: 29, 39; 9: 17, 31; 10: 19, 44; 13: 2.

How then are we to designate this power that was the enabling and creating factor that sent the early Church on its way and sustained its developing life? It is plainly insufficient to call it vaguely a force or influence. It is a propelling energy, no doubt, but it is more: it enters the mind and widens the sympathies and broadens the horizons; it invades the whole manhood, appropriating and heightening the gifts and graces of the soul. It has all the varied qualities of personality, and to the New Testament writers it is *personal,* affecting as it does the thought, the will, and the emotions. It is none other than *God Himself* reaching into the souls He has made and firing their world with His purposes. Nay more, it is God Himself, somehow brought into closer relationship than before, now speaking in more intimate terms, expressing His mind and master concerns in compelling ways and drawing men with bonds of love. It is indeed the God who had drawn near and made Himself known in the graciousness of Jesus Christ and was now available in a new way to His people. It was like having *Jesus Christ back again* among men. And indeed that was the truth of the matter: through this outflowing the dynamic work and worth of Jesus were being multiplied and made contemporary and effective to men in the changing circumstances of individual lives. God was in Christ, or was it Christ in God, reconciling the world unto Himself?

Is the Spirit then a supplement to the work of Jesus Christ? Does this cast the shadow of insufficiency on His life and death? No, it is rather that the once-for-all-ness of His unique service to mankind must continually be made present and potent in the here and now. The Jesus of history must be revealed as also contemporary, "the eternal contemporary of every human soul," as Dr. Cairns has expressed it[3]. It would be an unconvinced and dissatisfied world that merely heard that God was *once* alive and available to a needy world in the life and ministry of Jesus of Nazareth in the first century of our era. It would be an unpersuaded humanity that learned of the efficacy of a mighty deed once done by the love of God on Calvary *long ago.* There must needs be that movement of God to and within the soul in this very hour that makes real and credible that storied entrance into history in the witness and death of the Man of Nazareth. Souls that fell in love long years ago are for ever flowering forth in gifts and tokens that declare how love renews its ardour. So the Spirit must ever be taking of the things of Christ and be shewing them unto us (John 16: 14). The revelation made in

[3] *The Riddle of the World,* p. 359.

the beginning of our Christian era is made real and effective *now* through the work of the Holy Spirit.

Does someone object that this constraining Spirit of God must violate the unity of the human personality? If it comes cajoling or coercing, are we any longer free, with sovereign rights in our own souls? But our experience of God's Spirit is not that He is an imperious dictator staking upon us totalitarian claims. "Behold, I stand at the door and knock" sums up the facts of the case. It is a constraint like the moral constraint of person upon person. The nearest parallel that we know is the persuasive power of that ever new affection that we call love. Love is insistent, sometimes to our thinking unreasonable, but never a blind force. Personality is not disrupted by such constraint, but rather developed and enriched. In fact we go farther and claim that this gracious pressure of spirit upon spirit is creative, a continuation and renewal of that first act of God in touching us and making us men. Organisms of sensitive and delicate structure once planted in mother earth and furnished with the means of appropriating the virtues of the soil yet need the continual ministry of the dew and the rain, the sun and the cloud. So we who are set in the complex of human life and environment and draw virtue daily from the culture and activity of our civilization still need an elixir of life from above, a power that will open our sordid nature to the inflow from that higher realm made real to men once in Jesus Christ and renewed to us daily by the ministry of the Holy Spirit. Happy is he who has his soul open to a universe of larger dimensions.

By whom God.

What then is the function of the Holy Spirit today?

1. It assures us that we are in the hands of a Creator who keeps faith with His creatures. God has made us in His own image and set us down with bodies of strong passions in a world of conflicting forces. We have ideals and aspirations, a dream universe in the soul of us, a will to climb and strive and set the marks of our achievement ever on higher heights; and yet we are continually baffled and beaten back from without or dragged down by the dead weight within. With failures behind us and formidable foes to right and left of us we lose heart and would

give up the battle. That is how the first disciples felt with the tragedy of Calvary behind them, their own fears within, and enemies without to discourage any further cherishing of hope in a dead cause. But God did not leave these disconsolate men without a witness. A Presence came upon their bewildered sight, and now they knew that they were not alone. They had been encouraged by the presence of Jesus in their midst to believe that God had set about the consolation of Israel. They had left their nets, the counting-house, the claims of home, and had fared forth in faith like voyagers braving the ocean in search of a new world. And then came Calvary, and God seemed to have failed them, leaving them gazing at the wreckage of their hopes and of the nation's cause. But with the return of Jesus they became aware of a breeze that was filling their sails and bearing them out of the torpid seas where they had been becalmed. God had kept tryst with them and would keep faith to the end. So to us today the Spirit is the guarantee that God is alive. Now we know that the God who burst into history in Jesus Christ has still the will to keep a world astir. Our God is one whose name is Yea and Amen, the one who is ever coming (Rev. 1: 8).

Inspiring. Acts 6: 3-5; 1 Cor. 2: 4ff.; Rom. 8: 26-27; Eph. 4: 3-15; Rev. 1: 4, 8, 10; Rev. 2: 7, etc.

2. The Spirit moreover spells inspiration and illumination, invigoration of will and enlarging of mind. What made Peter arise after all his blundering and his betrayal? What gave the others, equally discouraged, the strength to rise and follow him? The poet knows the divine afflatus. There are seasons of dullness when no idea will take shape in music and no words will flow in rhythmic order. Then in a trice comes the flash of illumination and the poem is born. Christian men have given us their testimony to like effect. The blind preacher Dr. Matheson was passing through the most severe mental suffering. Suddenly in his brooding sorrow he was moved to take the pen and write, and in so few moments there flowed forth the moving hymn, "O Love that wilt not let me go." "I had the impression of having it dictated to me by some inward voice."[4]

Some of us lived through the period of the Great War 1914-

[4] Alexander Macmillan, *Hymns of the Church,* p. 270.

1918, and recall the promises and hopes of "a world fit for heroes to live in," "a world safe for democracy," "a peace that would put the war-mongers out of business for a thousand years"! And we know the disillusionment that has mocked our days. Yet in the midst of a conflict far deeper and more bitter the same voices rise in confident hope: this time it will be a better order, a stable and enduring peace, a lasting victory for the democratic ideal. What makes the Christian statesman lift up his soul in fervent hope? Is it not the Holy Spirit of God that all through history has awakened men from the despondency and despair which their human plight would justify? There is an urge in the midst of Christian civilization that will not let us acquiesce in a fatalistic "Wars will always be as they always have been." There is an impetus that ever sends another flight of birds into the summer sky.

The recognized sphere of operation for the Spirit is the Church of God (Eph. 4: 3ff.). The Christian society is the temple of the Spirit. Yet we must acknowledge that God is at work beyond ecclesiastical frontiers. The Old Testament conception owned the Spirit at work in the artist who adorned the Temple, and in Samson, a man of extraordinary power. What of the amazing gifts poured out on the masters of Greek drama and sculpture? What of the pioneer spirits of Socrates and Plato? In the experience of a scientist like Henri Poincaré, a modern French mathematician, there have been time and again startling upsurgings of ideas and problem solutions when his active interest was for the moment elsewhere. Dr. Richard Roberts[5] quotes examples of these and makes the comment: "That there is at work in the world an influence which may be described as creative wherever it operates, which is capable of reinforcing life and enhancing natural faculty and of producing characteristic effects in the intellectual, aesthetic and ethical fields—for this there is impressive evidence." Without entering that field of enquiry we may reflect that a poet like John Milton, born in pre-Christian times, would have been a master craftsman, but his poetry would not have had that depth and grandeur and enlargement of soul that only one inspired by the specifically Christ Spirit can know. He would be a brave person who would

[5] *The Spirit of God and the Faith of Today,* p. 52ff.

say that *always* down the centuries the Church has been led by the Spirit into truth. There were churchmen who upheld the institution of slavery, and non-churchmen who had more of the divine leading in that matter. There have been times when Christians have been less than hospitable to insights of the mind that should have been recognized as the Spirit's pleading. The way of revelation by the Spirit is not that of the mechanical dictaphone, but the way of the human mind with its proneness to error and confusion and self-deception.

It is impossible to distinguish mental illumination from inspiration. They are so often interlaced. The classic example is the vision and truth flashed forth by the inspired Hebrew prophets. The sharpened insight of Stephen blended with the heightened will that sent him boldly to proclaim that new truth. The inspiration of the Spirit that guided Paul throughout his volcanic career firmed his resolution amid difficulties, but it also forged the Rabbinically trained and cramped mind into a statesman's massive judgment and far-sightedness. Delivered from the thraldom of law and tradition, he thought with a new clarity and set the issues before men with a penetrating power. It is not mere accident that Renaissance and Reformation overlap in history, and it is unescapable that there is a direct connection between the coming of the Protestant faith to England and the flowering forth of the manifold brilliance of the Elizabethan age. The revival of religion of which John Wesley was the instrument saved England because it gave the common man a new appreciation of those things that make for a nation's greatness. So also we cannot study Italian art without recognizing the fresh beauty and delicate sensitiveness that religious inspiration gave to the artist and the craftsman.

Convicting. Acts 5: 3.

3. The Spirit must often intervene to cross our human wills. Our foolishness, stubbornness, impetuousness, unpreparedness are checked by a power gentle as it is strong. We see how Paul was turned aside in his missionary campaigns (Acts 16: 6, 7). He was all eagerness to set up the standard of Christ in Ephesus, the religious and intellectual centre of Asia. But the Spirit diverted his path. He had first to cross the Dardanelles to

Europe, found his bestloved church at Philippi, discover in cold, critical Athens that the Gospel is not preached easily by logic to the intellectuals, but that Christ crucified appeals to the needy sinners of corrupt Corinth. Even then he had still much waiting and journeying before he could set up the standard of the Cross under the shadow of the great temple of Diana of the Ephesians. Paul had to learn likewise that for a good end in the spiritual life a thorn in the flesh is not removed at the first asking (2 Cor. 12: 7ff.). Many of God's servants have reached their vocation only after the Spirit closed this door and that before them. We need discipline and the frustrations that teach patience before we are ready and able for our destined tasks.

But in particular the Spirit convicts the world of sin and righteousness and of judgment (John 16: 8), confronts man when he wills to take the downward path. How often did the Spirit strive with a Judas before he succumbed to the tempter, and how often did He return after the tempter had won and peace of mind had gone! The Spirit is the Holy God warning, pleading, claiming. He must stab the soul broad awake before the angels of faith and penitence can do their work and open the way for grace and forgiveness. The ice-bound Niagara can yield no power. So with sinbound men and women. There must be a thawing of our cold hard natures. The obstructions must be removed, the dead mass melted away, before there can be the free flow of the Spirit of God. Jesus starts with that fact in His intercourse with men. "Thy sins are forgiven thee": that word alone can release the pent-up energies in the paralytic and let health tides surge again through the body. Peter was the leader in the first gladness of the early community because he came fresh from contrition and forgiveness and restoration (John 21: 15ff.; Acts 2: 38). The dynamic power that made Paul so nervous and daring and challenging a preacher can be charged to the enormous sense of indebtedness he had for sin piled up in persecution and bitter hate being taken marvellously away in the grace of a great love. The source of his consecrated energy was that indebtedness he felt towards Him "who loved me and gave himself for me" (Gal. 2: 20). He had opened his heart in faith to the stupendous news of pardon, and into that open heart the Spirit could be poured without stint. So with the other members of that first community. They had all been faithless, unbelieving, despairing, and yet to them the undeserving the gracious God had come in the Risen Christ; so, touched to the heart, they swung back and were roused by the Spirit to the eager and ardent passion that made the first Christian history. And so in the years since, the saints have testified again and again in their experience to this activity of the Spirit. It comes dramatically often in the mission-field with the burning of books of magic (Acts 19: 19), the abandonment of slavery and immorality, and in the home field there is the eternal warfare against the practices that destroy life. Evangelism is ever the nerve of social service and redemptive effort.

Filling Them with Love of the Brethren and Hope of the Coming Kingdom. Acts 2: 44-47; Acts 4: 32-37; 1 Cor. 13; 2 Cor. 1: 22; 2 Cor. 5: 5; Eph. 1: 13, 14; Eph. 4: 3-15.

The Spirit opened the Christian era by drawing together in one place the scattered adherents of the Master. It was the first considerable congregation of the faithful that was startled by the sound of a mighty rushing wind and the appearance of tongues of flame. So the creation of the Christian society claims the opening pages of the Acts of the Apostles. This was no act of men: they were possessed and propelled by power from on high. The Spirit of the God of love inevitably confronts men with the obligation to come together and to love one another (Eph. 4: 3ff.).

Yet religion has been defined as what a man does with his solitariness. And there is much to support that view. Scripture shows the founder of the people of God as a lonely spirit Abraham setting forth from Ur of the Chaldees. Moses faces the burning bush alone. Elijah sought the desert alone. Jeremiah was a solitary. Ezekiel was a man apart from his fellows. Each prophet comes forth to make his pronouncements from a brooding silence before God. Jesus was driven into the desert alone, and Paul went unaccompanied into the peace of Arabia.

But the retreat with God is only a preparation for bringing God to the people, setting Him in the midst of society to judge or heal. An Amos could not speak except after living close to his folk, observing what was destroying society, and his aim was to bring about a better society. The Incarnation was a birth into a real home among brothers and sisters, and the Preacher of the

Kingdom drew about Him the nucleus of the kingly society. To preach God as love is to lay low for ever the notion that the hermit is a religious man. To link the Second Commandment of Jesus close to the First means that neighbourliness becomes a supreme concern. The Good Samaritan is closer to God than self-centred priest or Levite. Holiness under the old law depended on a kind of decontamination from the dust of one's fellows. But holiness to Jesus consisted in sharing the dust of the sinner and the outcast. The altar was no place to find God, even with splendid gifts, unless you were first reconciled to your brother. The prayer our Lord taught begins and ends on the first person plural—*Our* Father.

Paul's greatness was that he compassed Europe and Asia founding the finest clubs the world has ever known. But these "clubs" were not based on co-opted membership. They were societies of the redeemed, each member chosen by the Spirit of God, forgiven and called to be a "saint." And there were but few membership rules—to practise the mind of the Master, to seek much and often the Divine Presence in prayer, and to bear one another's burdens in the spirit of patience, faith, and charity. The little companies had one end—to seek and await with eager hope the coming to the world at large of that of which they had already a foretaste, the Kingdom of God.

Empowering Rom. 8: 1-15; Gal. 5: 18; 2 Cor. 3: 17.

The spirit is the life-blood of freedom for the Christian man. The Jew in old days had the law as his guide, and the oral teaching of the Rabbis sought to provide a rule for every occasion in life, in the home, the field, or the highway. But these elaborate rules—so intricate that it takes a book of many pages to set out the rules for keeping the Sabbath—were like a heavy pack strapped on the back. The Spirit by contrast put a spring in the step. The burden was dropped from the shoulders and believers were exuberant, joyous people in a new-found freedom.

The teaching of Jesus must not be used as a new law to be automatically applied. Ours is a modern complicated social life with situations never contemplated in the time of Jesus. We cannot therefore expect to turn to the line and page of His teaching as to a lightning calculator to solve our problems. We have our God-given moral senses, and these senses must be exercised like our muscles, or they will atrophy. We have the general principles like the stars in the sailor's heaven, and we must navigate by the stars. There is a margin always of human responsibility like the sailor's sea sense in the face of mists and storms, rocks and shallows. And human responsibility falters sometimes and knows its inadequacy. But there is always the guiding Spirit of God. As God has given us freedom in the Christian life, so He has left Himself freedom to intervene and aid us in our perplexities. The Spirit can always take of the things of Christ and shew them unto us.

"Where the Spirit of the Lord is, there is liberty," said the Apostle (2 Cor. 3: 17). But he had to warn his emancipated converts that they must never use that liberty as license. We have to keep the strait and narrow way. His liberty is freedom to serve—to serve God and our fellow-men. As Christ's men we voluntarily enlist to uphold the principles of goodness, truth, and beauty. There are temptations without, enemies of fear and doubt within, and always we must fight to conquer. But we can fight with confidence in the knowledge that the Spirit of God is free to aid us. That is what the Spirit of God means. He is not limited by time or space. His Spirit is with us at each critical juncture to fortify our faith and keep us true to our responsibilities.

Upbuilding. 1 Cor. 12-13; Gal. 5: 16-26; 1 Thess. 5: 19-20.

The Spirit that came dramatically like a mighty rushing wind and roused a whole company to an exhilaration and boldness and speaking in strange bursts of language might well have been identified only with the abnormal and the enthusiastic. But God gave the Church the gift of wisdom and understanding, and by the time that Paul was writing some twenty years on from Pentecost he was able to set a truer estimate on the manifestations of the Spirit. He recognized the variety of gifts and owns his own ability to speak with tongues; but the chief place is not to be assigned to such spasmodic utterances, but to the quiet, restrained, and enduring gifts—faith, hope, and love (1 Cor. 12-14). And when he enumerates the fruits of the Spirit for the volatile Galatians (5: 22), he lists love, joy, peace, longsuffering, gentleness, goodness, faith, meekness, temperance. Of the wilder outgrowths of the Spirit he has not there even a mention. The fruits enumerated, be it noted, are in part the marks of the individual Christian life; but for the most part they are social qualities, those graces that make for the upbuilding and enriching of community life. Paul valued the more spectacular gifts of visions and revelations; but he knew how broken, embittered, and chaotic the common life could become where the ecstatic ran riot and cultivated individualism at the expense of the solidarity of the whole. Hence he stressed the gifts that are not ostentatious, but quietly transfiguring, those steady spiritual graces that grow with discipline and restraint and scatter their fragrance over the whole common life. The testimony of the centuries approves his wisdom. God has blessed the self-abnegating humble disciples who without parade or vainglory have never wearied in welldoing. But that does not mean that there is no place or time for the visionary and the exuberant. On the contrary the Church has often been awakened as from sleep by the trumpet notes of a clamant evangelism, and in the strength of that arousal she has kept her witness through long years of dullness. God tempers His visitations to our varying needs. "Quench not the Spirit" (1 Thess. 5: 19).

There is a river I see in imagination now. Far up in the hills I have climbed, tracing its beginnings in spreading bogland and mountain tarn, but never quite reaching its hidden sources. That is like the Spirit issuing from the high and mistbound places and drawing from its unfathomed springs. The river is glorious in its upper reaches with cascades of waterfall and turbulent torrent foaming between rugged overhanging crags, sites for the power house and the dynamo to create light and heat. But on either side are only narrow strips of pasture land, just enough to carry a few crofters and their hardy sheep. Such was the course of the Church in the days of Pentecost with the fresh exuberance of the first believers who had seen the living Lord—a glorious time, romantic, exhilarating and uplifting, shared by few. But in the lower reaches the rivulet has become a river of peace, slipping through fertile fields with mills and factories and farms, villages and towns, upon its banks, alive with the manifold activities of douce folk—a sober stream, broad and dignified, with a wealth of water that "moving seems asleep" amid the quiet beauty of fields and wild flowers and on either side a plenitude for bird and beast on its wide acres. Such is the life of the Spirit in the more developed stage of the Church, its earlier ecstasies dissolved into warm helpful fellowship of love, joy, meekness, and temperance. Life on the upland continuously is for the few or for the occasional visitor who seeks reinvigoration. But existence on the plain is for the many who with restrained emotion practise the graces and virtues of simple folk weaving Christlike patterns daily on the loom of their living.

To sum it all up we may say that it was the Spirit that sustained the life of Jesus in its beauty, strength, and elevation; it was the Spirit that created and illumined the Christian Church, transforming the cosmopolitan company into the unity of a new race; and it is the Spirit that daily works the miracle of fashioning the new man. Finest of all terms used to describe this gift is that of Paul—"the *earnest* of the Spirit." It is the pledge or promise (in modern Greek the engagement ring) of God, the foretaste of that new life that shall be ours in the consummated Kingdom of His love (2 Cor. 1: 22; 5: 5; Eph. 1: 13-14).

IV. The Holy Trinity.

Knowing God thus, as Creator and Father, as Redeemer in Christ, and as Holy Spirit working in us, we confess our faith in the Holy Trinity.

So we acknowledge and worship one God, Father, Son, and Holy Spirit.

CHAPTER IV. THE HOLY TRINITY

2 Cor. 13: 14; Jude 1: 20-21; Rev. 1: 4-6; Matt. 28: 19-20.

> The grace of the Lord Jesus Christ,
> and the love of God,
> and the communion of the Holy Spirit,
> be with you all (2 Cor. 13: 14).

How often a moving act of worship has reached its crown and culmination in the beauty of that threefold benediction! It brings home to the mind the movement of the Divine towards us in prayer and in the hearing of the Word in the sanctuary. The soul has come face to face with a gracious reality, a story old but ever new, the living and dying of the Lord Jesus for us sinful men: that is the first, the most immediate, the freshest contact that a modern Peter or Mary or Philip can know. But that close contact would be meaningless if it were but a human touching a human, a friend greeting a friend, as moving as a glimpse of his mother's portrait was to Cowper, but just one other encounter among the episodes of history. But that grace that found us was something more: it was nothing less than the Eternal Love that reached out and "kissed me in a glad surprise," the Love that fashioned me, followed me down the years into the places of my sin and my despair and lifted me into the circle of the redeemed: it was the Great High God who made the stars who set His thought upon me and redeemed me. But how was it possible for me in the Word preached to see Jesus and in Him to recognize God Himself appropriating me? Why did my soul tremble in that joy and not another's? Because there is a third participant in that vitalizing contact. A power took hold of me and gently but irresistibly made me confront Jesus: I enjoyed a sharing of, or partnership in, the Spirit of God. Any worshipper knows that time and again in the same holy place with the same Scripture being opened before us with eloquence and imagination the contact is not made: we are *not* in the Spirit on the Lord's day. Thus the grace of the Lord Jesus Christ and the love of God are ours just inasmuch as we are in touch with the Spirit, not otherwise.[1]

[1] Cf. Moffatt, *Grace in the New Testament,* p. 153.

So Christian experience acknowledges a threefoldness in the encounter with God. And that acknowledgment of the Apostle comes early, just some twenty-five years after Pentecost. "The wonderful kindness of Christ is historically the first thing in the Gospel, the porch through which the believer enters the building, and comes to know what God is to him and what the Holy Spirit is. . . . After Christ's grace or kindness has brought him into the building the Christian finds the love of God around him, which he would not have known without that introduction."[2] And what opens his eyes to the beauty of the porch and the glory of the building is the Holy Spirit. Paul affirms that truth elsewhere in speaking under the figure of adoption (Rom. 8: 15-16). We sinners, he implies, know a strange stirring in our souls when we awaken to the fact that it is for people like us that Christ died; then we realize that for a forgiving love like that there can be only one name: that must be the love of a Father; we hail Him as such (Abba). When we say that, he asserts (v. 16), it is the Spirit witnessing with our spirit that we are children of God. Again we notice the same threefoldness in Rom. 5: 5-8. Christian hope, he affirms, can hold its head high; for *God's love* has been poured out into, and keeps flooding, our hearts through *the Holy Spirit* which was given to us . . . God makes good His own love towards us in that while we were still sinners *Christ* died for us. There we note the author of our salvation, God in His love; the Christ who died for us; the power that opens our hearts and floods them with that love, the Holy Spirit.

Father, Son, and Spirit. Matt. 16: 17; Mark 12: 36-37; Luke 10: 21-22; John 14: 16-26; John 15: 26; John 16: 23; 1 John 4: 2-3; 1 Cor. 12: 3; 1 Cor. 6: 19; Phil. 2: 1; Rom. 8: 9-11; Acts 5: 29-32; Acts 11: 15-18.

The threefoldness in the Christian experience does not mean that we have to deal with three separate divine figures with distinct functions. Suppose we set side by side two confessions, that of Peter and that of Paul. Peter was the first to set Jesus on the higher plane. He broke forth in the words: "Thou art the Christ, the Son of the living God." It was an amazing insight that the young Galilean fisherman had that day, so amazing that it was

[2] Menzies, *The Second Epistle to the Corinthians, ad loc.*

recognized at once that "flesh and blood hath not revealed it unto thee, but my Father which is in heaven" (Matt. 16: 17). Then Paul exclaims: "I give you to understand, that no man can say that Jesus is the Lord, but by the Holy Ghost" (1 Cor. 12: 3). In the old days as an embittered young Rabbi, offended by the idea that a crucified criminal could be proclaimed as the Messiah of Israel, he must have burst out: "Accursed be this Jesus!" Now he knows, having once stood on that very human viewpoint, how great a force was needed to lift him to a new vision: only a power from on high could so open a man's eyes to see in the rejected and humble carpenter the glory and dignity of the Son of Man, enabling him to give the title: Jesus is Lord. It is the Holy Ghost that enables a man to give Jesus the right predicate. But in Peter's case it was the Father who revealed it. Are these sources of revelation really different entities? Is it not rather that in the one case we think of the primal originator of all insight, the Father, and in the other case we think rather of the means by which that revelation comes, His Spirit?

Again, read Rom. 8: 9, 10: "But ye are not in the flesh, but in the Spirit, if so be that the *Spirit of God* dwell in you. Now if any man have not the *Spirit of Christ,* he is none of his. And if *Christ* be *in you* . . . " In quick succession Spirit of God, Spirit of Christ, Christ in you, tumble from the same pen, different terms apparently for the same reality (cf. 2 Cor. 3: 16-18). So also in the Fourth Gospel: "I will not leave you comfortless: I will come to you" (14: 18). Further on it is the Comforter, the Spirit of truth, who comes (15: 26; 16: 7). Again we have the assurance: "If ye shall ask any thing in my name, I will do it" (14: 14). Compare 16: 23: "Whatsoever ye shall ask the Father in my name, he will give it you." It is as if a man enjoying the glow of re-invigoration in the garden will say, "It is the spring" or "It is the lovely air" or "It is the fragrance of the flowers," whereas it was no single one of these but all together happily commingled on a May morning.

How shall we explain this reference at will to the Living Christ, the Holy Spirit, the Eternal Father? Is it not that we enjoy a rich redemptive experience and in that mystical operation we seem to discern a face now on this side now on that? As Professor Donald Baillie has finely summed it up: "They all stand for the vital truth that we have more than the story of the historical Jesus, we are united by faith to a Living Spirit who becomes supremely real to us through that story. If Christians speak of that Spirit as the Living Christ, they should be careful not to allow this to eclipse the idea of the Living God, or (worse still) to suggest that in the distant background there is a God who is less friendly and intimate than Christ, or (in another direction) to obscure the features of the historical Jesus and the importance of reading the old, old story of Him."[3]

Knowing God Thus. Ps. 33: 4-9; Prov. 8: 22-36.

What came upon those early Christians was a recreating of personality that could not be analyzed. Jesus the man of history had set new life glowing in them. But that Jesus always drew men's thoughts beyond Himself to the Father. And the Father since the life and death of Jesus had become accessible through His Spirit as He had never been before. It was a Trinity of experience that they were in process of formulating. The God who had long disclosed Himself as the Creator and the Righteous Author of the moral law had now drawn closer to men in the Son, the Redeemer, and He continued in that deeper intimacy opened up by the Son through His abiding Spirit, the upbuilder and sanctifier of the new life.

This development was not really untrue to the Hebrew heritage. Jehovah had never been a remote and aloof God, but one who was ever intervening in the history of His people. The Spirit of God was a reality in the life of Israel, especially in the experience of the prophets. Often that Spirit had been spoken of as the Word, and in later thought it had been almost personalized. "By the word of the Lord were the heavens made," said the Psalmist; "he spake and it was done; he commanded, and it stood fast" (Ps. 33: 6-9). "He uttered his voice, the earth melted" (Ps. 46: 6). There was dynamic in the divine Word, as had been from the beginning: "God said, Let there be light: and there was light" (Gen. 1: 3). His Word went forth with power: "it shall not return unto me void, but it shall accomplish that which I please" (Is. 55: 11). As they came to feel that God was too pure to put His hand upon evil matter, they thought of God as having an agent or agents. The Wisdom of God in Proverbs 8 is pictured

[3] *Faith in God,* p. 263.

dramatically as if it were a separate reality alongside of the Almighty: "When he prepared the heavens, I was there . . . . I was daily his delight, rejoicing always before him" (vs. 22-30). So while God remained the One and Only in Hebrew thought, the way had opened up for speaking as if there were other divine realities beside Him.

Then came Jesus, so manifestly uplifted above His fellows in the strength and beauty of His living and able to make men aware of a divine radiance in His words and actions. To come under His influence was to know that this could be nothing less than God expressing Himself in a new freedom. And even when He disappeared from the human scene, that new accessibility of God continued, His Spirit came upon men with an explosive energy as at Pentecost, or with a power of inner renewal as in a Peter. Where could men place this reality except by linking it with God and with the Risen Christ?

Creator and Father, Redeemer, Spirit.

The doctrine of the Trinity certainly gathers up and affirms the *manifoldness* of the self-disclosure of God to many an individual soul. Consider Paul's experience. (1) There were the long years a-growing within the privileges of a Jewish home and the mercy-laden inheritance of the family of Israel. Under the inspiration of the Scriptures of the Old Testament there came to him the sense of awe before the God of Power and Judgment and Holiness, an awe that showed up the cleverness of the university youths of Tarsus as empty and superficial, an awe that constrained him to go to Jerusalem and give himself to an intenser study of the law. That same disclosure, he found, had come to his fellows in Gamaliel's classroom. (2) Then there came the vision on the Damascus Road: an outreaching love, ignoring all his persecutions and his bitter hate, apprehended him and startled him with the magnanimity of its mercifulness; the love spurned in the crucified Messiah came back to plead with him. It had pleased God to make a disclosure within his soul of the meaning of the Son of Man (Gal. 1: 15f.). That new revelation of the love of God in Christ was for ever after the essential element in his thought of God. That was a depth in the divine nature that never met the gaze of the scholars in Gamaliel's classroom. (3) Then there was the active ministry of the Apostle of Christ with its adventures and wrestlings, its conflicts mental and spiritual, its visions and revelations in hours of crisis and upheaval—a career which daily depended on the quickening and illumining of the Spirit, that glory of God that he had first seen in the face of Jesus Christ. That too was an enablement that the pupils of Gamaliel never knew. His contemporaries still in the synagogue no doubt had the Spirit of the God of Israel to guide their path. But they lacked that immediacy of contact that came not from law and prophecy, but from Jesus only. Thus Paul could not adequately confess his faith in the One God in the fashion of his fathers and Jewish contemporaries. He had to affirm a God who had entered into history in Jesus with a fresh declaration of His Word, and had continued to enlarge that disclosure in the movements of the Spirit. The Christian thus asserts in the doctrine of the Trinity that he has an enlarged and deepened understanding of God.

Working in Us.

Again, the conception of the Trinity has supreme value in reminding us that God is *personal in a most ardent and active sense,* One who thinks, wills, and acts in movements that penetrate our human world. The philosopher might be content to think of God as high and lifted up in lonely contemplation, unmoved by the trivial and the transitory that make up so much of earthly existence. But the sinner has need of a God of another sort—a God who has entered the human scene and is ever willing to enter it again with the will and purpose to redeem and restore. The Christian God does not live to Himself: He has ever sought to express Himself, to communicate with the creatures He has made, to impart to the world the spiritual life that is within Himself. If we cannot penetrate the mystery of His *being,* we at least must proclaim that we have experienced the wonder of His *doing.* We cannot think of Him without recalling the mighty act in which He came near to men in the life and death of Jesus Christ. We dare not attempt to sustain the redeemed life except by drawing freely from the inspiration and illumination of the living Spirit. And we are concerned to assert that that unique episode of revelation that men experienced in Jesus Christ and that grace upon grace that we draw upon in life's crises are not just casual and accidental touchings of His pity: these define for us what is His essential nature and abiding character as the God who is Love.

The doctrine of the Trinity affirms that it was from the depths of His own rich nature that God called us, His creatures, into being, reclaimed us, and continually renews us. It confesses that there was a purpose behind our coming into being, our life here, and our final destiny. It asserts that we are ever confronting a God who has put meaning into all the works of His hands, a God who never loses personal hold of His own, a God who crowns us with glory and honour by the very fact that He cares for us everlastingly. We stake our all on the belief that His essential being must be like unto His doing.

Three in One. John 1: 1-18; Phil. 2: 6-11; Col. 1: 15-16; Heb. 1: 3-5.

While the New Testament does not formulate the doctrine of the Trinity, it opens up the truth that later thinkers were to expand. The Fourth Gospel starts off from three assertions that were probably already enshrined in a hymn of the Church. (1) *In the beginning was the Word; i.e.* the Word is not a mere part of the created order, made within time: He was there when time awoke. (2) *And the Word was with God; i.e.* He was not a mere phase of the divine being, but a reality with independent existence, a person confronting God. (3) *And the Word was God; i.e.* the Word was not just of divine quality or rank (*theios*), but actual God (*theos*). Then the Evangelist goes on to claim that this pre-existent Word entered human history in Jesus. There we have already a belief in a "binity," or twofoldness, in the Godhead. Nor was that peculiar to the Fourth Gospel. Paul had told the Philippians (2: 5-11) that it was One who had enjoyed divine dignity who laid aside His high estate and took upon Himself the nature of a humble servant; and in Colossians 1: 15ff. he claims He was prior to all things in the universe and holds all things together, *i.e.* gives meaning to the cosmos. So the author of Hebrews saw Him as One from whom flashed forth the character and reality of God. Evidently before the end of the first century Christians had placed their Lord alongside the One God of the Hebrew faith.

The Greek mind could not rest content with misty outlines of doctrine: it demanded sharper definition. If the Spirit had come to take the place of Jesus (John 16: 7ff.), then what was the relation of that Spirit to God and to Christ? The Greek mind was bold: it did not turn aside from analyzing even the divine nature, but for centuries kept on debating and formulating. False doctrine was all the time compelling the Church to clarify her creed. Jews and philosophers could not be allowed to scoff at Christians as believers in three Gods. When the practical Romans took up the debate, they introduced new terms, and these terms did not exactly translate the Greek. The Greeks had striven to make clear that there was one Being (*ousia*) of God, but within that being were three underlying realities (*hypostasis*). The Romans used the word *persona* for *hypostasis*. What they meant was that the three members of the Godhead were persons in the sense that, as the Scriptures show in passages of colloquy, it is possible for a man to have personal relations with each of them. But *persona* was an unfortunate word in that it could mean the part played by an actor, a rôle instead of a personality: it was thus easier to think of Jesus as but a phase or attribute of the divine. Our translation "person" suggests to modern ears the modern sense of personality, and so we tend to think of the Trinity as implying three separate centres of consciousness. We mean by the term something "less definite indeed than our modern 'person,' but more definite than 'aspect' or 'attribute'; it holds an intermediate place between 'individual' on the one hand and 'emanation' or 'influence' on the other."[4] Human analogies have been brought forward to elucidate the mystery. Augustine suggested that "when the mind knows itself and loves itself, there remains a trinity—mind, love and knowledge. . . . These three are one, and one substance." Or, again, memory, understanding, and will: "These three are one, in that they are one life, one mind, one essence." Again, there is the analogy of love in which there are three—the lover, the beloved, the love that binds. Modern thinkers have argued from the constitution of society. The mind of a society is a real will capable of initiating action and affecting human life: it may be reckoned "on its spiritual side as an individual in a completer degree than the members who constitute it . . . the social mind is, in some sense, a reality which transcends the individuals, though

[4] K. E. Kirk, *Essays on the Trinity and the Incarnation,* ed. A. E. J. Rawlinson, p. 164f.

having no existence apart from them."[5] So in the Godhead there is a society of Father, Son, and Spirit, and yet one real mind over and above all.

These analogies all leave us with a sense of incompleteness, and by their very failure they remind us that here is a mystery that baffles human thought and outreaches human experience. Why should we expect to achieve clarity here? Is this world of ours easily intelligible? Is it not an unsolved riddle? Surely then the Creator of that universe is still farther above the limitations of the human mind.

The absorbing feature of the history of this doctrine is that herein we see the Spirit at work guiding men from grave errors at critical points of the human story. When it was insisted that the Christ was no mere emanation of the divine, but very God, that was like the shadow of a great rock in a weary land of fear. In days when men believed in a multiplicity of angelic powers presiding over the planets, evil powers into whose control you might be delivered by your birth in a certain month, it was a grand message of assurance to be told that high over all malign powers on the very platform of God sat the One who had made Himself known as the friend of frail struggling men. Again, over against the thought of God in Greek philosophy as remote and aloof, it had to be stressed that the Christian God has entered decisively into history in Jesus of Nazareth, and He is known in the Son of Man's activities and self-giving for what He really is: God acted and still acts because He does care for man, whereas the Greek could not sing

> There is no place where earth's sorrows
> Are more felt than up in—Olympus!

There have been times in human history when the philosopher has sought to remove the historical landmarks of Christianity. It is reckoned an offence that God should enter history at a particular moment of time, and attempts have been made to reduce Jesus to a teacher and His legacy to a beautiful but impractical idealism. Against such a dissolution of the historic Gospel into a nebulous philosophy the doctrine of the Trinity has affirmed that Jesus was no mere fleeting human figure, but One in whom God Himself came to visit and redeem His people. Moreover, the teaching of

[5] W. R. Matthews, *God in Christian Thought and Experience,* p. 196ff.

Jesus is not just a series of sayings like the Sermon on the Mount, a closed book of the long ago; it is rather the opening pages of the revelation of God and Judgment that is having fresh chapters written on living souls by the person of the Spirit of God.

The doctrine does not teach that there are three Gods, or three manifestations of God, or three attributes merely made known at different times. Our assertion is that we deal always with God in His wholeness. There is not "a more and a less in the Godness of God," as Barth expresses it. Or, again, "He can be our God, because He is equal to Himself in all His modes of existence, is one and the same Lord." We are misled when we set the inexorable Judge over against the gentle Jesus or picture His Justice as in conflict with His Love. We are confronted by one Person in the fullness of His nature. When Christ touches a man, that is not just God acting on His merciful side. When Christ touches a man, He judges just as He pities. When the woman taken in adultery appears before Him, He does not express His whole mind in the words "Neither do I condemn thee: go, and sin no more." There is the atmosphere created by His embarrassed writing on the ground, His challenge, "Let him that is without sin among you cast the first stone." There is the piercing look, the flash of the eye, the indefinable quality that hung about the whole man, as his contemporaries testify. What appears there is not just a side or phase of Christ or a partial glimpse of the divine. There is there the sense of a Presence real and indivisible. And when we speak of a Person in the Trinity we mean not less than very God, not a mere ray from a distant sun or the faint echo of a far-off voice, but

God's presence, and His very Self,
And essence all-divine.

V. Man and Man's Sin.

We believe that God gave to man, as He did not to the lower creatures, capacity to share His thought and purpose, and freedom to choose whether he would or would not love and serve Him.

We believe that man has used his freedom of choice for low and selfish ends, thus estranging himself from God and his brother man, and bringing upon himself the judgment and wrath of God, so that he lives in a world of confusion and distress, and is unable of himself to fulfil God's high purpose for him.

So we acknowledge man's sin, God's righteous judgment, and man's helplessness and need.

CHAPTER V. MAN AND MAN'S SIN

What Is Man?

"Many a wonder lives and moves, but the wonder of all is man." So Lewis Campbell renders a famous line of Sophocles.[1] The chorus goes on to celebrate the triumphs of man: his conquest of the swelling seas, the subduing of the land to the ploughshare, his skill in capturing and training to his service the beasts of the forest, his power of speech and "windswift thought," and the genius that has created the city and social life. One thing alone baffles man's ingenuity—he has no means of escape from death.

Such is the voice of confident human civilization, the note of a proud and adventurous age like the Elizabethan in England which yields the Shakespearean parallel: "What a piece of work is man! how noble in reason! how infinite in faculty! in form and moving how express and admirable! in action how like an angel! in apprehension how like a god! the beauty of the world! the paragon of animals!" But there too proud man acknowledges his limitation: "And yet to me what is this quintessence of dust? Man delights not me; no, nor woman neither." The Greek and the English dramatists are alike humanists. But each sees his hero haunted by a spectre—death and disillusionment.

And now what has the Hebrew to say? In Psalm 8 the poet pays tribute to the true greatness of the human race: "a little lower than the angels," so very near the divine plane. He has dominion over the created world, all things under his feet, the beasts of the field, of the air, of the sea. And he has no note of sadness at the close, but rather praise: "O Lord our Lord, how excellent is thy name in all the earth!" Why this sustained elevation that neither Greek nor English poet enjoys? Because the Hebrew begins and ends his meditation in God. It is His glory that he sees above the heavens. It is against the splendour of the shining firmament, of sun and moon and stars, that he sets man. It is not by his own wit that man has won dominion over sea and land: it was God who

[1] *Antigone*, line 332.

gave; what glory and honour he enjoys is God's giving to him. So with pride is mingled a most humble gratitude, awe, and reverence: "What is man, that thou art mindful of him? and the son of man, that thou visitest him?" It is not surprising that the Hebrews did not write tragedies: they had the tragic in their history, plenty of it, in a Saul, an Elijah, a Jeremiah; but they did not, like the Greek, find purgation of soul by gazing upon the stage-set drama of another's pain. The only purgation they knew was forgiveness, and that can be given only on a scene where there are two actors, the Father and the prodigal son.

We have just emerged from an era when men were not bothering about their sins: sin was only a falling upward on the evolutionary road of inevitable progress. It was the mood of a scientific age intoxicated with the overflowing splendour of discovery after discovery, an age that had seen man's advancing conquest in so many fields and enjoyed comparative peace and plenty, even profusion. But today we are the scared survivors of the hideous nightmare of unexampled totalitarian war, and we are not so sure that we can pick ourselves up and assert that we have just stumbled upwards. There is a biting ache in the conscience that tells we are but paying the penalty for sins of exploitation and unbrotherliness in international relations, the sin of drawing ourselves apart in self-righteous isolation and callously asking "Am I my brother's keeper?"

Sin in Scripture stands out naked and unconcealed. It is revealed in its true colour of blackness and darkness. But life never ends in the sombre note of Greek or English tragedy—in baffling death or utter world-weariness. Scripture opens with man expelled from Paradise; but it goes on to the restoration of even the nameless penitent thief. "Today shalt thou be with me in Paradise." Genesis confronts us with the fruit of the forbidden tree and all the woe that came from it; but the Apocalypse brings us to the garden once more, beside trees with leaves for the healing of the nations. It is a revelation in which mercy mingles with judgment—never the one without the other, because either alone is a half-truth. It keeps reminding us that it is never wise to look upon the human scene in isolation. We must needs call to mind the injunction of Jean Paul: "No day should close without a look at the stars."

God Gave . . . To Share His Thought and Purpose. Gen. 1: 26 to 2: 7; Ps. 8; Ps. 19: 7-14; Ex. 20; Matt. 10: 28-31; Matt. 12: 10-13; Mark 8: 35-37.

God created man in His own image (Gen. 1: 27). What do we mean by this proud claim? The Psalmist thought he had entered into the meaning of that word when he went out under the stars and "considered" the heavens (Ps. 8: 3). That splendour of flaming glory stirred something in the spirit. He felt the trivial concerns of the flying moments drop from his mind like a pack from his shoulders, and his soul soared out in thought. It was as if a voice out of the glory addressed him and he answered. The beauty that was in the creative mind of the Master artist touched his soul, and he was sure that he understood in some small measure why this firmament was made. That it should so stir his inmost being meant that he had entered into God's thought, he was sharing His love of the glory and light. The great Creator was communicating with His creature. So did Abraham feel that contact when the word came to him to go out from the home of his fathers and seek another country. Moses felt it when from the burning bush there came a command upon his conscience, a concern for the people he had left behind in the agony of Egypt. Ezekiel felt it when the word came: "Son of man, stand upon thy feet!" Man is conscious that he can be addressed by God and that he can answer back. There is a language that comes from the Yonder, a language of the soul, that invades the mind, stabs the heart, strikes the imagination, pierces to the conscience. Far down the centuries the wandering Bedouin had this correspondence with heaven, something that his faithful steed or his passive camel could not share. Even the cave-dweller must have had glimmerings and wonderings as he stood in his rocky shelter awed by the thunder and lightning of some sweeping hurricane or the flaming up of volcano on his landscape; he must have reached out vaguely for help, and the fact that he clung to life and developed the art of living under the passing terrors means that help was given and dim hopes passed into assurance that relationship with the Beyond could be sustained.

The Psalmist looking up into the bowl of night was not just a passive receiver: he "considered"; he followed up his impressions and analyzed his thought about the mysterious universe. This power the other creatures did not have. He was impelled to reach out and penetrate to a meaning in things. As the light steals in at the window of a morning and persuades the eyes to open and the senses to respond to the delights of the sun and air, garden and flowers, so there was a something from beyond the beauty and mystery that touched the mind and quickened the imagination, and led him out to acknowledge a Yonder, a spiritual universe into which he was ushered. There was more than his own will in all this. It was as if an unseen visitor had crossed the threshold and, all unbidden, had constrained him to receive company. There was a Gracious One who had been mindful of him and had visited him with good news from afar. There came about an interchange, a sharing, a feeling of having entered into the will and thought of Another, that Other who in the shaping of things must have intended that out of His handiwork should come such encounters, such joyous quiverings in the depths of His creatures. God had written the poem of the flaming firmament, and man had read it with delight and understanding.

For all behind the starry sky,
Behind the world so broad,
Behind men's hearts and souls doth lie
The infinite of God.

So far we have considered man under pressure of awe and wonder before the splendour and majesty of the outer glory of God—the universe that invades through the gateways of the senses. The mysterious and the terrible smote upon the spirit of the observer, and the sense of an undiscovered Yonder thrilled and troubled him. But that experience must often have been paralyzing, leaving but a vague and undefined awareness of the reality beyond. When and how did reality take shape and character?

Consider an old story from Herodotus. It comes from the days when Corinth was ruled by a few men of a family who married and inter-married. Of these a lame daughter, Labda, had to go outside for a husband, Eetion of Petra. An oracle proclaimed that justice would fall on Corinth through a son of Labda, and so ten men of the clan banded together to destroy the child. They came to the courtyard of Labda and asked for the child, having agreed that the first man who handled the child should dash it to the ground. The unsuspecting princess brought the child and gave it to one of the men. As he took it, "by a divine chance" the child smiled up into his face. Compassion gripped his heart and he hastily handed the little one to the second and he again to the third, till all ten had passed the child on unharmed and back to the mother.

Here we see how the *moral* sense has laid hold of man. How did it come to be? Experiencing the affections of fatherhood, how did they come to extend these affections to another child? How did the defenceless one come by the disarming smile? How did rude and cruel men come by that nobler prompting from within? How did the law of the family come to be the law for those outside? How did the law and custom of the tribe become the moral code in a wider sphere? So many questions we can ask and cannot answer.

But the Hebrew was sure of the answer to this problem. He had in his heritage the line of Moses and the prophets. They had experienced an unveiling of the mystery behind the chain of events: the Word of God came to them. They pioneered—or rather were led—in applying the justice they knew in the national sphere to the universal, the international sphere. The God whom they expected to punish their enemies for unrighteousness must on the same principle punish the favoured nation as well. "You only have I known of all the families of the earth: therefore I will punish you" (Amos 3: 2). There could not be one law of righteousness for one nation and a different law for another. Jehovah the Vindicator of righteousness within their own borders came to be seen as the upholder of justice for all men. Alongside Psalm 8 we read Psalm 19. There by an inspiration from above two poems are woven together into one. The God of creation is sung in the opening section:

> The heavens declare the glory of God;
> and the firmament sheweth his handywork.
> Day unto day uttereth speech,
> and night unto night sheweth knowledge.

Then in the second section the God of the moral law is celebrated:

> The law of the Lord is perfect, restoring the soul:
> the testimony of the Lord is sure, making wise the simple.
> The precepts of the Lord are right, rejoicing the heart:
> the commandment of the Lord is pure, enlightening the eyes.

The inevitable comment on this conjunction is the utterance of Immanuel Kant: "There are two things that fill my soul with holy reverence and ever-growing wonder—the spectacle of the starry sky that virtually annihilates us as physical beings and the moral law which raises us to infinite dignity as intelligent agents."[2]

The Hebrew conception of man as the crown of creation carries over into Christianity. Jesus sets infinite value on man, testifying confidently to God's care over him. "Ye are of more value than many sparrows," He assures us (or, if one might dare to emend the text, "you are on a different plane from sparrows"). And yet even these are treasured by the Creator's love. Not one falls to earth unnoticed by Him. So much more may we have faith that all happenings to us men are of account to Him. The very hairs of our head are all numbered (Matt. 10: 31; 12: 12; Luke 12: 7). Still more startling is the declaration that even the whole world is not to be set in the balance over against the human soul (Mark 8: 36). And though Jesus stands in the tradition of Israel and values her holy institutions, He would set aside the claim of even the hallowed Sabbath before a human need (Mark 2: 27). No teacher ever so unwearyingly gave himself to individuals, as if each single soul was worth His tarrying or journeying.

It is typical of Jesus that He is less the spokesman of God's spectacular glory in the firmament than He is of those more intimate beauties that stir the spirit of man. He speaks of the flowers in the garden or the grass at our feet rather than of the stars. He turns His interest on the common sparrow or the silly sheep rather than on the splendid eagle or the strutting peacock. But the merciful heart of a good Samaritan on the roadway or a humble housewife grieving over a lost coin or a widow at the offering box—these evidences of the moral nature of mankind are the real objects of His concern. For Him these are the witnesses to the godlike in man.

And is not Jesus in His very self the proof, final and complete, of the image of God in man? On what other ground was the Incarnation possible? Before God could come to tabernacle in flesh and blood there must needs have been in our nature the

[2] This section owes much to Rufus M. Jones, *The Testimony of the Soul.*

potentiality of that glory and splendour. In a Hosea or a Jeremiah the candle glowed and went out, and men saw in them the dim and brief foreshadowing. The Word of God shone out and lit the path in crucial moments of history—and that light blazed always from the soul of a man. Then at last Grace and Truth flashed out into history with a radiance that was never to die away. The Word of God became flesh and dwelt among us, and we beheld His glory. The Father found His interpreter in one who was bone of our bone, flesh of our flesh, because from the beginning God had given to man the capacity to share His thought and purpose.

Freedom to Love and Serve Him. Mark 12: 28-31; Matt. 5: 3-16; Matt. 25: 34-40; 1 Cor. 13; Col. 3: 1-4; Phil. 4: 4-9.

What then is the measure and stature of Christ, the mould and temper that expresses the image of God?

1. It is a life that puts God first. It keeps an ear ever open to the diviner harmonies of a higher world, that world where His will is done and His purposes are the over-ruling concern. The soul will be lifted to God in prayer with each dawning day and it will fold up the busyness of the hours before the mercy-seat. God may send health or He may appoint sickness: both can be borne for His glory. He may set us in days of peace or days of war: the place of honour and the concentration camp are likewise calls to witness to eternal truth. There will be choices where the love of home and country will be set in the balance against other loyalties, and we may have to tread the wine-press alone for the honour of a conviction. There will be pressed on us separations from the society of our brethren where we have been nourished, and it may not be clear whether we are playing the part of a Paul or of a Judas: yet there can be only one law for us, the praise of God rather than of man. We are but pilgrims and sojourners, men of unclean lips and living among a people of unclean lips, and yet we must be prepared, if the vision comes, to offer ourselves in causes where we may never see success. Such a life is other-worldly in the best sense—that it reckons not at all on the glittering prizes that men covet and strive for, but seeks always to lift the eyes above the temporal to the far horizon of the eternal beauty, to leave the soul open to those imponder-

ables, the things that cannot be bought with a price and do not die with death. There is a rare serenity given to those who thus concentrate their all to witness to the truth. "Man's chief end is to glorify God and to enjoy Him for ever."

2. It is a life that is pre-occupied with the human and the personal. Jesus lived for the eternal realm, but it was for that end that He took a towel and girded Himself among men and gave Himself, a ransom. Ours is an existence frankly bounded by time; yet surely the tasks of the passing day that God wills for us become luminous with meaning because they fit into His grander universe of personal values. We are not just hithering and thithering on twopence-halfpenny errands; but, just as the trivial services of the apprentice fit into the smooth operation of a large business and gain dignity thereby, so are our citizen's duties in a democratic world seen as glorified by their contribution to the Kingdom of God into which all our national endeavours are combined by the over-ruling providential hand. The Zaccheus who had entertained Jesus saw his intercourse with toll-booths and custom dues thereafter as no mere avenue to one man's comfort and aggrandisement, but as an affair where human beings can testify to the eternal principles of right and justice and grow together in amity and mutual esteem to the well-being of the perfect state. A centurion who built for the Jews a synagogue was doubtless a man who understood that morale as well as brawn and muscle went to the making of a soldier; and after his contact with Jesus we may surmise that there was a temper in his personal relationships with the members of his company that turned a hireling's trade into a vocation of honour and integrity. It is not a mere case of always living as ever in the great Task-master's eye with a suspicion of fear in it all. It implies a recognition of other than temporal measurements. There are but *twelve* hours in the day, but time is not an issue when a great physician has to deal with the soul of a man or a great artist has to set on canvas a vision of imperishable beauty for the enrichment of his fellows. There is an economic side to things; but our world is one where Mary may break her alabaster box just because love bids her. State services depend on income tax; but there are geniuses who can only pay in poetry and impractical generosity and gifts of laughter or consolation. There is virtue

untold in organized religion; but there are souls who become inflamed with the truths of God and prophesy with Shavian eccentricity in circles beyond the orthodox. "Quench not the Spirit" was a Pauline injunction. It was not Jesus who would call down fire from heaven on those who walk not with us. Nothing human is alien to the Christian, because the humanity where once tabernacled grace and truth is ever being used of God as the veil from which His radiance streams again and yet again.

Did not our Lord sum up the whole duty of the Christian man in the two commandments "Thou shalt love the Lord thy God . . . and thy neighbour as thyself" (Mark 12: 28-31)?

But is it not chimerical to set before man such a picture of manhood? Is it not an emotional ideal and not a practical proposition? Man, it is claimed from many quarters, is not free so to love and to serve. Are we not enmeshed in a chain of causality, the helpless victims of the forces and the fevers of all the yesterdays? Does not heredity determine our physical structure and our mental equipment, and is not environment, economic and social, a clamping and entangling power which has fixed our potentialities before ideals and ambitions vainly fire the soul? Does not the psycho-analyst show us that our minds are poisoned by noxious influences from the subconscious, and fears, grown monstrous, haunt us from the hidden experiences of childhood so that today our decisions are rendered impotent by baneful legacies from long ago? Are we not just day-dreamers and opium-eaters playing with fancies and figments of the imagination when we talk of God and immortality? Are not our feet of clay set in an economic universe where the only values are material and our only service is the labour we can give to the common good? Are we not by blood and soil appointed some to be hewers of wood and drawers of water while others are a chosen and superior folk born to rule and to be served? Have not God's eternal decrees pre-determined our lot, some to damnation, others to eternal joys: how can there be a power over us and beyond us, controlling and directing all the forces and figures of history and yet leaving to us the possibility of free choice?

We can only cut ruthlessly through these cobwebs of argument by applying the keen edge of experience. We know that when a certain temptation swept up we *could* have said "No" to it: we *deliberately* spoke to our friend the bitter wounding word while all the time an inner voice appealed against it; we *chose* not to run in that contest because we feared the sweat and the toil and the humiliating defeat (James 1: 14-15). Heredity may have laid a horrid hand upon our shoulder, but we also have seen the awful example of what *yielding* to inherited tendencies can mean: we are fore-warned, and by grace can throw off the hindrance. We are more than the mere sum of all the yesterdays. Abraham Lincolns are not produced with mathematical exactitude from a commingling of heredity and environment. We have more than can be bought and sold in the labour market. We are no superior folk: we are sinners like our brethren, and our own hearts condemn us. We are not placed in this world to be run down like clocks: there are renewing and recreative energies within us that clocks never knew. And the God and Father of Jesus Christ sent Him into places of crisis and decision, into flesh and blood with all its weakness and limitations, and yet He sinned not. Under that same God we pass out into that field of trial and testing where character is made by the very process of striving and overcoming. As the physical man comes to strength and maturity by continuous exercise of all the muscles and functions of the body, so out of the heights and depths of the emotions, out of the flights and fancies of the mind, out of the advances and repentances of the soul, out of the interplay of all the spiritual energies within us, there is a personality growing, and it is only in the atmosphere of freedom that persons know they are more than things. We are free to love and serve Him.

But How Has Man Used that Freedom? Ps. 51; Is. 1; Is. 59; Jer. 2; Rom. 3: 9-23; Rom. 7; 1 John 1: 1-10.

Scripture testifies that in the experience of man sin is universal. "Surely there is not a righteous man upon earth, that doeth good, and sinneth not" (Eccles. 7: 20). "No living man is acquitted before thee" (Ps. 143: 2). "Who can say, I have made my heart clean, I am pure from my sin?" (Prov. 20: 9). From Genesis to Revelation the facts of man's daily fallings are not hidden. The reign of sin begins with Adam, continues with Cain, comes to a first crisis in the flood, only to renew itself from age to age in spite of judgment and warning. It is the tragedy even in the great: the flaw in Saul, the scarlet in the ideal King David. The chosen race remains a sinful stock: "Behold, I was shapen in iniquity; and in sin did my mother conceive me" (Ps. 51: 5). As the vision of God grows more luminous the conscience becomes more laden. It is for pardon that the deepest petition rises, and there is exultant gratitude when it is granted: "Bless the Lord, O my soul: . . . who forgiveth all thine iniquities" (Ps. 103). The very nearness of this people to God but deepens the cleft that sin makes between them. The progress of revelation is the story of God's striving with individual and with nation to warn and to deliver from the thraldom of sin.

And so in the New Testament. Jesus steps upon the national scene amidst hosts of penitents crying for release; His first combat is with the Tempter, and the last cry of dereliction (Mark 15: 34) hints that the conflict with sin is carried on to the bitter end. The ministry of love has to sound finally the stern trumpet note of condemnation against hypocrisy in the seat of piety (Matt. 23); against His innocence and purity the black heart of a Judas, the shiftiness of a Pilate, the cant of a Caiaphas, stand out in dreadful clarity. He who has pled with the Master of the vineyard for patience till the tree had still another chance must needs break out into a "Woe" of sad yet searching doom over the favoured but unheeding city (Luke 13: 6ff., 19: 41ff.). If final proof were needed of the blackness of darkness in the human heart, that Cross on Calvary stands out stark and stern in naked protest against a graciousness spurned and a love unrequited. No wonder that with this depth of iniquity so recently plumbed Paul has no reservation to make: all have sinned and come short of the glory of God. Weighing the forces of flesh against spirit, he declares that these are contraries (Gal. 5: 17) irreconcilably opposed; and the Apocalypse is very sure there is a seat of Satan to be overthrown, a key to be turned on the abyss before peace can come to humanity and victory to God.

Do we need to call witness outside Scripture? What is the vast literature of tragedy but the picture of men fascinated by the sinister, the inevitable flaw in the best? What says any man's conscience as the lid is lifted on forgotten years? What nation can point to history and say, "See! The record is clean"? What about the tragic waste of our time, the incredible horrors wrought in Poland, in concentration camps, in desolate London streets, in the wreckage on the seas, on the plains, hurtling through the air? To this is science fallen, to this has humanity's proud culture descended. Reason given of God is pledged to brutish butchery.

How Does Sin Come to Be Universal? Gen. 3; Rom. 5: 12-21.

The answer is given in the story of the Fall in Genesis 3. That vivid portrayal of the first man set in his Eden before the Tree of Knowledge has a human and arresting quality, and it is by deduction from this that Christian dogma has been constructed. The story itself can be variously interpreted. It has been read as a picture of man's *disappointment over civilization*: "much knowledge increaseth sorrow;" human culture has not brought happiness, but rather disillusionment. We may construct the splendour of a Babylon; but to what purpose since we have lost our Eden of guileless innocence? The most obvious and direct meaning of the story, however, is that all our woe comes from man's sin and disobedience against God: it testifies to the age-old *fact of conscience*. The Oriental mind rejoiced in the psychological penetration of the narrative, but it did not go on to build dogma upon it. In fact the Old Testament has no further direct reference to the Fall, and in describing the activities of men the assumption throughout the sacred books is, not that man is the helpless victim of the fall of his first parent, but that men are free agents, and their sins, from Cain's downwards, are their own responsibility. It is in the later literature of the Hebrews, in books *outside* the canon of Scripture, that allusion and theorising about the Fall appear. In Esdras 4: 30 we read: "A grain of evil seed was sown in the heart of Adam from the beginning." We are not told who sowed that seed, but evidently the evil tendency is thought of as being in Adam before the Fall, in the nature he derived from God. In another passage the writer insists that somehow we all share in the sin and unhappy doom of Adam: "O thou Adam, what hast thou done? for though it was thou who sinned, the evil is not fallen on thee alone, but upon all of us who come of thee. For what profit is it unto us, if there be promised an immortal time, whereas we have done the works that bring death?" (7: 46). Another writer in the Apocalypse of Baruch strikes a different note. "If Adam did sin first and bring untimely death upon all, yet those too who were born of him each prepared for his own soul its future torment, and again each of them chose for himself his future glory . . . Adam is therefore not the cause, save only of his own soul, but each one of us hath been the Adam of his own soul" (54: 15-19). Thus there would appear to be two strands of thought: (1) that we are all somehow involved in the sin of Adam, and (2) yet each man is his own Adam, responsible for his own sin. Jesus does not refer to this conception; but evidently Paul was familiar with it. "As in Adam all die, so also in Christ shall all be made alive" (1 Cor. 15: 22). "As through one man sin entered into the world, and through sin death, and so death extended to all men, for that all sinned" (Rom. 5: 12ff.). But Paul does not there make clear whether all sinned on their own responsibility, each his own Adam, or whether without any act of their own all sinned, each being born into the evil legacy of the race. The Apostle then has no theory of the *origin* of sin; he affirms simply the *fact* of experience that the whole race of men are involved in sin.

There is thus no compulsion from Scripture to accept the traditional doctrine of the total corruption of our human nature: "that we are utterly indisposed, disabled and made opposite to all good and wholly inclined to all evil."[3] It was chiefly Augustine who drew the Church towards this sombre view. There were contributory factors in his own environment. He had memories of his own evil-doing and hopeless struggle in youth; he accepted a line of thought that regarded the flesh as completely evil; he was leaning away backwards from the rival teaching of Pelagius, a monk who took too rosy a view of man's possibilities for good; he wrote in the darkening days of the fall of Rome. There is a similar dark horizon before us today. The failure of man's moral nature to keep pace with his machines, the inhumanity of large industrial combinations that set profits above the welfare of workers, the corrupt practices that raise their heads in our wealthy democracies, and finally the world's lapse back into the horrors of totalitarian war—these and many other evils becloud our time. To read the history of the world between 1918 and

[3] *Westminster Confession*, vi. 4.

1938 is to feel that man's best endeavours are perverted by powers almost demonic: the very movements towards a good like disarmament are factors that hellish forces twist to their fell purposes. Amid the ruin of so much of the world's beauty and the blasting of our fairest hopes it is easy to turn to the view that man is totally corrupt. But what the seeing eyes of Jesus discerned was a world where there was a movement toward penitence, where tax-gatherers who had compromised with conscience were not irretrievably lost, where Magdalenes had their finer moments, where even the rude soldier's trade did not kill out the tender emotions, where there were many fumbling disciples but only one traitor. He had reasons for complete pessimism about human nature on the Cross, yet He prayed for His enemies as men who did not know, not as men who *could* not know any better. Paul lost his Demas, but he recovered his John Mark and he had his faithful Luke, and he went confidently to the synagogue first in every city because there were better elements there, consciences stirred even under Judaism, and he found the stuff everywhere of which "saints" are made. Of course we assign all these works of transformation to the unstinted grace of God, but must not grace find a lodgment, each good seed a potentiality in the soil? It is in the decadent Infancy Gospels that we read of Jesus making clay pigeons live: in the actual ministry it was never dead clay but living flesh on which He wrought His miracles. The prodigal son remains a son even in the far country. To impute guilt there must be in man a sporting chance to do right. In his incisive way Dr. John Baillie[4] has clinched the matter thus: a totally corrupt being would be as incapable of sin as would a totally illogical being of fallacious argument.

Does Evolution Explain? Matt. 15: 10-20; Matt. 21: 28-32; Luke 15: 17-21; Luke 16: 27-31; James 1: 12-27.

The theory of evolution gave a new slant to the discussion on the origin of sin. If we are descended from an animal ancestry, then are not our evil instincts a carry over from the ape and the tiger within us, the growing pains of evolving humanity? We inherit impulses, appetites, before we develop wills and moral

[4] *Our Knowledge of God,* p. 33. Every student should read this most clarifying book.

sense. Thus every human being has in his make-up instincts and passions which in themselves are not wrong, but morally neutral: they pass into sins only when he fails to control them for moral ends. They are the raw material out of which come our virtues as well as our vices.

Objections to this view readily occur: (1) Granted that we have these natural impulses, why is it that we *all* fail to subdue them? Why is it that each man can point to this occasion and that when he slipped, let go the better and chose the worse? (2) Again, though we might dimly see in that line of thought how we stumble into the gross and bestial sins, how do we come by the sins of the spirit? Can pride or Pharisaism be derived from animal nature? (3) But the most serious difficulty is this—that to explain all should be to forgive all. If we are but the victims of the beast within us, why do we not forgive ourselves? Why is there in each one of us a sense of guilt, a conscience burning with the knowledge that we knew better than yield to that appetite, give way to this impulse? The theory does not go far enough. It is like explaining that a child has inherited a father's eyes and a mother's mouth, but not why these eyes flash with sudden anger and why that little mouth should pout.

Against Thee, Thee Only. Matt. 23; Rom. 1: 17-32.

Sin is, beyond all else, a fact of the *religious* life, the black cloud that comes between us and the face of God. It is the spurning of love, the refusing of His righteous way. What stands out in Adam's story is that, having received so much in the loveliness of the garden, he should reach out after the one thing more, putting appetite above God's one wish. What renders inexcusable Israel's making of the golden calf is that they had experienced so lavishly of grace and deliverance and now spurned the hand that gave. What came to consciousness in the prodigal son was the "bread enough and to spare" in his father's house, and yet he had asked life on his own. "Father"—and how much lies in that word of address—"Father, I have sinned against heaven and in thy sight, and am no more worthy to be called thy son." "Son" was a name that summed up the love that had lit up the years, the love that had poured out extravagantly and unstintedly all that a father had, the love that had been brushed aside to gratify a pride and a selfish wish to control one's own. As Dr. Whale[5] sums it up: "Man's 'Yes' was to be a response, not to 'Thou shalt,' but to 'I have created and called thee; thou art mine.'" We are made in the divine image; but instead of gratefully living in the light of that glory, we kindle our own mean little candles and grovel in the semi-darkness of the cave we have hollowed out for ourselves. That men and women and little children today are living, not on the broad open plains with all the breezes from the sea and the mountains blowing in upon them, but in bomb-proof shelters and miserable dug-outs —that is a picture of what sin has done for man. We have seen the little child turn his back on the sea to play in his own small puddle. It is human perversity at an early stage.

Estrangement, Judgment, Wrath.

All this means estrangement from God. He does not change: His love remains towards the prodigal. But sin puts more than distance between God and His children. We shun the eyes of those we have offended. There may be kindness lurking there to smile back upon us yet, but we turn away and stay away. There is a graciousness that might be playing about our lives, but we will not suffer it. We put up a wall of reserve and misunderstanding. The reason for our avoiding a wounded friend is that we know that we have put ourselves in the wrong in his sight. We have set judgment in those rebuking eyes of his. In a moral world when we wrong the one who loves us we pass sentence on ourselves, we place ourselves in the prisoner's dock. So it is in our dealings with our best friend, the God who has loved us with an everlasting love, the God who at infinite cost has redeemed us. Under His righteous gaze we know we stand judged.

The sinner inevitably falls under the wrath of God. As One whose nature is holy, God must be actively hostile to evil. He is aflame with moral passion, and therefore "it is a fearful thing to fall into the hands of the living God" (Heb. 10: 31). The complacent human father may forgive and forget in a shallow-hearted way; but a father of supersensitive integrity confronted by a daughter who has dishonoured his name must needs quiver with pain even though he finds grace to forgive. So, if we may dare

[5] J. S. Whale, *Christian Doctrine,* p. 44.

to liken our human emotions to the divine, the pure and holy God cannot but resent that His creatures should play fast and loose with the moral law. His universe is set in an order in which truth and right must prevail. We can trace His laws in the physical world: to abuse the noble functions of our human bodies is to reap disease and shame. And in the world of the mind we see how pride and swelling self-esteem can breed a madness and confusion in the brain. This sensitive universe He has created is quivering with His own aliveness; the principles of retribution run through the structure like nerves in the human body. When sin jars that universe, there is that quick reaction that declares His wrath. Our God is a consuming fire. It is from Love that cares terribly that wrath flashes out.[6]

Even from the gentle Jesus we have words and moods that declare this terrible wrath. "Be not afraid of them that kill the body, and after that have no more that they can do. But I will forewarn you whom ye shall fear: Fear him, which after he hath killed hath power to cast into hell; yea, I say unto you, Fear him" (Luke 12: 4-5). "Except ye repent, ye shall all likewise perish" (13: 3, 5). "There shall be weeping and gnashing of teeth, when ye shall see . . . yourselves thrust out" (13: 28). What was that suggestion of majesty about Him that made Peter call out "Depart from me; for I am a sinful man, O Lord" (Luke 5: 8)? Was there not a flash of condemnation in "Get thee behind me, Satan: for thou savourest not the things that be of God, but the things that be of men" (Mark 8: 33)? What was it in His glance that made Peter go out and weep bitterly (Luke 22: 62)? What austerity was there in His face on the way to Jerusalem: "And Jesus went before them: and they were amazed; and as they followed, they were afraid" (Mark 10: 32)? In more than one of the parables there is a portrayal of sternness in the end (Matt. 25: 45). There is the finality of the irreparable in His sad "Woe" over Jerusalem "that killest the prophets" (Matt. 23: 37; Luke 19: 41). "If thou hadst known!" And His tears said more than His words. When the would-be accusers brought before Him the woman taken in adultery, He wrote on the ground in a silence that told both His hate of sin and His abhorrence of

[6] Cf. Rom. 1: 18, with note in Moffatt Commentary of C. H. Dodd; Plato, *Laws,* 905.

a cruelty that made men value a quibbler's victory above a human soul (John 8: 6).

Sin cannot be contained and gathered into harmless channels. That is one great reason for the divine wrath. It sunders man from brother man and corrodes the fellowship of the human family. Hebrew thought had a strong sense of the solidarity of the race: what evil one did passed as a poison into the life of the community: the theft of Achan was a blight on the whole army, the act of a bad king made all Israel to sin, the selfish extravagance and dissipation of the rich wrought havoc on the poor (Amos); corruption penetrated the body politic, "the whole head is sick, and the whole heart faint. From the sole of the foot even unto the head there is no soundness in it" (Is. 1: 5f.).

Jesus is never more stern than when He delivers His "Woe unto you" over those who cause little ones to stumble (Matt. 18: 6). The narrow laws of Pharisaism cut into the tender ties of home and aging parents: with *corban* rules "Ye suffer him no more to do ought for his father or his mother" (Mark 7: 11f.); the tragedy of their hypocrisy was that "Ye shut up the kingdom of heaven against men: for ye neither go in yourselves, neither suffer ye them that are entering to go in" (Matt. 23: 13); the sin that sent men to everlasting fire was a self-preoccupation that did not aid a brother's need (Matt. 25: 41ff.): "Deliver him to the tormentors" is the startling retribution that falls on one who had no mercy on a fellow-servant whose wife and children would be involved in ruin (Matt. 18: 23ff.).

Sin tangles up all the delicate inter-relationships of society so that everywhere confusion and distress enter where the divine will purposes harmony and largeness of life. One individual's shortcomings can wreck a home; one obdurate and selfish employer or a reckless labour leader can throw idle men into the marketplace and misery into countless homes with fell results upon the whole community. Our new world unity only carries sin's contagion in wider swathes across the world. A company of men in a city board-room looking at profits rather than human interests can issue decrees that stop the wheels of industry in lands across the sea, and that collapse upsets the balance in some other related trade and casts a shadow across still further lands. Poverty, bankruptcy, shattered lives, disrupted hopes, despair, suicide, moral collapse, mental breakdown—so the vicious circle widens out. The economic disturbance is but the more manifest symbol of a deeper malaise of the soul. Lust and passion, pride and sloth, each send their noxious vapours forth to corrupt and destroy. One man's insane ambition can drag a nation into war, and in our inter-locking international life that war spreads and engulfs a whole universe. And each division breeds bitterness and hate, and misunderstanding darkens counsel. The world drifts into a nightmare of chaos and woe: it is a worldwide black-out where man's tiny candles but accentuate the gloom. Only an action large and luminous can break the pall of spreading evil, and that action must be by the strong right arm of God. He alone can work man's redemption.

VI. Redemption.

We believe that in the greatness of His love for man God has in Christ opened up a way of deliverance from the guilt and power of sin.

We believe that Christ, by living our life without sin, by dying at the hands of sinful men with faith unshaken and unfaltering love, has done for man what man could not do for himself. On the Cross He bore the burden of sin, and He broke its power; and what He did there moves men to repentance, conveys forgiveness, undoes the estrangement, and binds them to Himself in a new loyalty.

We believe that by His resurrection and exaltation Christ stands victorious over death and all evil, and that He fills those who commit themselves to Him with such grace and strength that in Him they, too, are conquerors. His redemption of man is at once an awful mystery and a glorious fact; it is the Lord's doing and marvellous in our eyes.

So we acknowledge the unmerited love and the mercy of our God in giving His only-begotten Son that we might not perish, but have everlasting life.

CHAPTER VI. REDEMPTION

What Man Could Not Do. Gal. 3: 19-24; Rom. 11: 32-36.

"There is nothing that man can desire from the gods, nothing that the gods can grant to a man, nothing that wish can conceive or good fortune bring to pass which Augustus . . . did not bestow upon the republic, the Roman people, and the world." So run the fulsome words of the courtly historian Velleius Paterculus. But a brother historian lets the light in on that same Augustus: there were things he could not achieve in his own household. He had to acknowledge vexation of soul over his grandsons, Gaius and Lucius, because he could not instil into them the virtues befitting members of the imperial house: they were given to luxury and to insolence. It was the story over again of Eli, the aged priest of Israel. Neither priests nor kings can control the waywardness of the human heart. Augustus introduced Gaius to the Senate as the Führer of youth, *princeps inventutis,* but the real leader of youth was already introduced to a most inconspicuous company of folk at Nazareth in a corner of his empire. How little right Augustus had to the extravagant claims of Velleius Paterculus appears in the picture we have of him in his old age, trembling fearfully before thunder and lightning, carrying a sealskin for protection, and at any hint of violent storm diving for shelter into an underground vaulted room. Kings cannot control their own fears, far less protect their subjects from the manifold evils that beset the realm of the spirit.[1]

Reconstruction is the blessed word upon our lips these days. After great upheavals men look with eager expectation to the new order. It was so in the days of Augustus. National barriers were broken down. Greek thought and literature with all their power to stimulate had overflowed the world and given to mankind a vision of the larger, more generous interests of the mind. Over the far-flung battlefields of East and West peace had fallen at last, fratricidal strife had ceased to pour her blood-

[1] Quoted by J. Y. Simpson, *The Garment of the Living God,* p. 255.

offerings upon earth. Under such a beatific respite were induced in a war-weary world hopes that mounted to high heaven.

But architects of great empires are not physicians of the spirit. There are tears in things, as Vergil has it. "I have been made to learn," writes R.L.S., "that the doom and burthen of our life is bound for ever on man's shoulders, and when the attempt is made to cast it off, it but returns upon us with more unfamiliar and more awful pressure."[2] So Aeschylus long ago:

> Taunt follows taunt and things are hard to read.
> The spoiler's spoiled: murders to murder lead:
> And long as Zeus abides upon his throne
> Sure the ill-doer must suffer and atone.
> God set the law. Who out of bounds may throw
> The brood of curses? The race is glued to woe.[3]

Evidently man—modern as Stevenson, ancient as Aeschylus—is persuaded that there are some things he cannot do. There is a sequence that is hard to break, a bondage that demands a divine intervention.

The Lord's Doing. Rom. 5: 1-11; 1 Cor. 1: 18—2: 5.

There is a paradoxical quality in the Gospel story that betrays the handiwork of God. Wishful thinking could not have lit on Jesus as the bearer of the liberating word for mankind. There was so much of the surprising and the unexpected in the manner of His coming and the method of His action that we can only ascribe the initiative to the divine wisdom. To step out of a carpenter's shop for this superhuman task seems fantastic. No good thing could come out of Nazareth, and no exponent of peaceful policies was looked for by revolutionary Galilee, the seat of recurring outbreaks against Rome. A little company of fishermen and tax-gatherers was no formidable invasion army for the setting up of a new order. To combat the sophistries of a subtle world there was no scholar among them. To think that out of that arid period of legalism new life should spring up, that after centuries of spiritual exhaustion in which no prophetic voice was raised new wine should suddenly burst the old wineskins! Who

[2] *Dr. Jekyll and Mr. Hyde.*
[3] *Agamemnon.*

could have anticipated that out of a nation proudly conscious of its own religious uniqueness, a nation that turned deliberately away from other people as contaminating Gentiles, there should issue a movement that gathered mean slaves and abandoned sinners to its fold and welcomed with open arms all sorts and conditions of men?

Was it not strange too that at the very moment when the strong right arm of Rome had gotten her the victory over all nations, when the approval of heaven seemed to be stamped on the efficiency of ruthless forces and masters of the art of war, there should appear that startling notion that by suffering love and a patient humility a Kingdom could be established on the earth, and that a Kingdom without end? And the chosen point of appeal to mankind was a humiliating criminal's cross, the least spectacular of platforms, the most repulsive of all standards. Then to go on to assert that to men who had thus foully done Him to death this man had only forgiveness to offer, that the burden of sin was taken away for faith alone! How could it be suggested that a righteous God could overlook the accumulated sins of that war-crazed and lust-driven world of men? Man could not have the face to imagine so free a gift. The wonder of it stamps it as divine. Only God can deal in such stupendous generosity. The divine initiative shines out from every feature of this moving story.

Marvellous In Our Eyes. Acts 2: 22-23; Mark 8: 31-32; Mark 10: 35-45; Gal. 4: 1-5.

"Him, being delivered by the determinate counsel and foreknowledge of God, ye have taken, and by wicked hands have crucified and slain" (Acts 2: 23).

This is the first recorded pronouncement of the early Church concerning the mystery of the Cross. This is their primary conviction. "It is the Lord's doing and marvellous in our eyes." The Church proclaimed the Lamb slain before the foundation of the world. That death upon the Cross was no human mischance, no accidental miscarriage of justice on the part of a Roman governor. It was a grand design of God in which the human actors were but players fitted into a larger drama than their minds perceived. The God who made man, and sent him into the universe with the perilous gift of freedom, had foreseen the tragic failure, and had made gracious provision for a grand act of redemption. There was One who was to bear the sins of the world according to the divine plan. Wickedness was to guide men's hands, but that deed was to be a mirror in which they would see themselves in their true nature as never before. God was to deliver up, to surrender, that which was infinitely precious, to achieve His hidden purpose. That purpose was to redeem mankind. All through history He had been stirring, provoking, cherishing movements to that end. In the evolving story of Israel His seers had come to trace the working of His hand. Had He not set His seal on Israel and yet delivered her up to torturing spoliation, oppression, and exile? Was it not by her defeats and sufferings that He had striven to woo her from the affections of earth? Did she not learn more from her humiliation than from her victories? Was it not from out of slavery under Pharaoh, from wilderness experiences, that she came first to discern the righteous God of Sinai? Did not the favoured King David and the inspired Elijah and the suffering Jeremiah all learn by buffetings and humiliation? Was this not the divine way, the sorrowful way of the Suffering Servant of God? So the culminating act, the Cross of Christ, was His deliberate purpose, the choice He had made in the beginning of time.

God Has Done. Heb. 2: 17-18; Heb. 4: 14—5: 10; Heb. 7: 26-28; Heb. 10: 24-28; Phil. 2: 6-11; Eph. 2: 4-10.

The way of deliverance for men came in a single decisive act of God. The New Testament rings from end to end with the sense of a "once-for-all-ness" in this deed of God. This is emphasized consistently by the tense of the verb the writers use to describe the coming of Christ Jesus: it is the tense (aorist) that marks an action as taking place at a point of time. It is a fact of history, the Fourth Gospel assures us, that God let His love light on the world: *He made a gift,* the gift of His only-begotten son; and the end in view was that every individual soul setting its faith in Him should not fade out into futility, but should touch life on a new plane of being (John 3: 16). Paul is equally insistent about the historic character of that invasion. When there came the crisis point of time, he says in Gal. 4: 4, 5, *out He sent* His own son, born of a woman, born under the slavery of law, that He might buy out the enslaved of the law to the end that we might get back the status of sons. Again in Phil. 2: 7, He took a slave's rôle and thus in one act of will poured Himself out. Further, in Col. 1: 13 he exalts the Father as the one who made it possible for us to share the lot of the saints in light, who *actually effected our rescue* from the power of darkness and translated us into the Kingdom, the realm of His beloved Son: deliverance has been achieved in one stroke. So in Rom. 3 after describing the human situation—that all men committed sin and so fell short of God's high purpose for their destiny—he declares that God set out in the forefront the Christ as a means of achieving our reconciliation. Striking the same note of affirmation, Peter (1 Pet. 1: 3) blesses the God and Father of our Lord because He really has *brought us to birth* into a new life of hope; and the author of the Apocalypse (1: 5) breaks into praise to "him who *loves us and has loosed us* from our sins with the shedding of his blood," the change into the tense of finished action being significant. In all this testimony the Epistles are but under-scoring the words ascribed to Jesus Himself in Mark 10: 45: "The Son of Man came not to get service, but to give it, and to make the gift of his life as a ransom for many." The author of Hebrews has as his theme the *finality* of the work of Jesus: the occasional voices of the past have given place to the one complete utterance in the Son. The continually repeated sacrifices of the ancient Hebrew ritual were ineffective; now has come by contrast a sacrifice distinguished by its singleness and finality. It was but *one* sacrifice that He made for sin: by a single offering He has for all time perfected those who are under sanctification (10: 12-14). Once and for all at the culmination of the ages Christ has appeared to abolish sin by the sacrifice of Himself. It is appointed to men to die but once and then to undergo judgment. So Christ, after being once and for all sacrificed to bear the sin of many, will appear again—but without any relation to sin—to save those who are on the lookout for Him (Heb. 9: 26-29). Protestantism certainly has here sure and abundant evidence for the faith that there was one complete and adequate self-giving; an event so unique that there can be no repetition.

In this one decisive intervention of God we are confronted by two elements that cannot be taken separately: (*a*) a life lived without sin with faith unshaken, and unfaltering love, (*b*) a death suffered at the hands of sinful men. Too often the death has been considered in isolation as if by one blood-offering a transaction was carried through that mollified an angry God and enabled Him to score off the piled-up debt that stood over against human kind. We must see Christ in His wholeness, in the total witness of His life and death. The death is meaningless unless we see it as the crown and culmination of a spirit and virtue that were poured out without stint upon the earth.

By Living Our Life.

Consider that sinless life. His work and words engendered such bitter hate that, if His contemporaries could have found any shred of evidence against Him, they would have seized upon it and magnified it with the will to slander. The fact that they tried to cast aspersions on His birth, on Mary rather than on the son, indicates how futile was their search for taunts against Him. And the word "sinless" is a weak negative term that should be displaced in our mind by the thought rather of His positive moral power, an elevation of mind and soul and heart that gave to human personality a new glory. It was a phenomenon that had never been known before even in a nation that excels in the greatness of its heroes. A Hosea and a Jeremiah were outstanding men, set on a pinnacle in the national religious tradition, and yet those closest to Jesus were not content to put Him on that high level. Those who were so close to Him as to see magnified any flaw yet counted Him the Chosen One of God, the One fit and ready to open the gates of a new order upon humanity. Men had to stand back and ask questions about such a life. That within a mortal body such as we have life could be sustained without spot or stain; that the evil forces of this world, the principalities and powers that struck terror into other men, should play vainly upon this soul, presenting temptations and Gethsemanes, rejection and a criminal's cross, without breaking a serene confidence in an overruling Providence; that amid misunderstanding and scoffing and deliberate hostility the outpouring of His love and ministry should have been persisted in to the end—that was a new emergence in the human story. Here was one who from the time He stepped out into the open surprised and startled men so that He was a spectacle, the centre of crowds, the focus of popular bewilderment. "Never man spake like this man," and it was about God that He always spoke. Here was a magnitude that human personality had never touched before, and the feature of it all was an undimmed mind in every situation, an unstained purity before God, and an inexhaustible love towards man.

Yet to such a one as this ungrateful humanity dealt out the foulest of deaths, cruel in its brutal torture, shameful in its pitiless publicity, humiliating in that it was plotted by His own people. Such a dark death against the background of such a pure life compels the bystander to ask questions of God and man. God must have had a meaning in this or else His Providence is impugned.

With Unfaltering Love.

Evidently then this deliverance of man from sin was no easy affair. We do not believe like the dying Heine that it is God's business to forgive. Rather we acknowledge, as Paul says twice over, that we are "bought with a price" (1 Cor. 6: 20; 7: 23). Jesus Himself was much preoccupied with the cost of the new order. The Kingdom of God, He said, was like treasure hid in a field, treasure that demanded the sacrifice of all else that it might be obtained, a pearl so lustrous that other values must be cheerfully surrendered that one supreme joy might be possessed. The rich young ruler had to learn to sell all and give to the poor to find eternal life. The poor widow who threw into the treasury her whole wealth of two mites fascinated Jesus because His mind was turning on that great law of sacrifice. So Mary with the alabaster box drew His praise for the magnificence and meaningfulness of her self-giving, as did the sister of Martha who cut out all lesser concerns for the one thing needful. What girded the disciples to Him with hoops of steel was that they left *all* and followed Him. So in His own life there was that completeness of self-giving of mind and heart and soul: the whole goblet was drained. With a true appreciation of where He laid the emphasis the Evangelists have given us Gospels that gather half their narrative about the Cross, and the Church from the beginning saw the emblem of her life in the broken bread. Jesus spent months in Galilee for days He spent in Jerusalem; but the Christian tradition has centred, not on the lake shore where He taught, but in the city where He died: the point of the supreme sacrifice focusses the attention of men.

But this supreme sacrifice only climaxed an expending of virtue that had been going on all the way. Action might appear only in a healing here and there or an agony in Gethsemane, but the burden was for ever on His heart. Beside the sightless and the crippled whom He healed there were the light-headed and the soul-deadened who would not respond. For one rich young ruler who answered his love there were twenty who turned aside with disdain; for one disturbed Nicodemus who came by night there were a score of unmoved hypocrites who flaunted their haughty pride by day. There was an open home in Jericho, and there were warm hearts in Bethany; but synagogues like Nazareth cast Him out, and Bethsaidas and Chorazins threw up ramparts of unbelief. The solid mass of Pharisaism and the entrenched class of Sadduceeism held on stubbornly to their positions in the key points of the nation; and if Israel's elect remained obdurate, how could the waiting world be saved? The world seemed bent on clinging to its sin and to its indifference to sorrow, and the weight and frustration fell upon the one super-sensitive soul and the few vaguely sympathetic about Him. Our hearts are wrung by the tortures and sadnesses of occupied lands of Europe, but we grow jaded and callous under the daily repetition of the horrors. Not so the Son of Man: His Gethsemane was everywhere and His soul exceeding sorrowful unto death. Virtue went out of Him daily and the heart bled. There was no sorrow like His sorrow.

God In Christ. 2 Cor. 5: 11-21; Col. 1: 19-20; Col. 2: 9-10; John 14: 20, etc.

Now all this continuous self-giving of Jesus is the self-utterance of God. It is the Graciousness that is behind all things breaking out into the arena of human history. Here in these memorable months of ministry in Galilee and Jerusalem we are permitted to hear more than a whisper of Him, to see more than the edges of His ways. In the clarion call to the Kingdom we are listening to the declared purpose of God Almighty that from out of the welter of society and the tangle of conflicting nationalisms He is bringing about a new creation, building a spiritual temple of the souls of men, in which He will make His Presence feared and loved. In the Beatitudes and the parables we gain glimpses of His standards and His ways, His estimates and His judgments. The hands of the Good Physician laid on sick folks, the opening of the eyes of the blind, the casting out of demons, the forgiveness spoken to the paralytic and the Magdalene, the raising from the dead—these are practical affirmations that our God is a living God and a redeeming God, a God of righteousness and *therefore* a Saviour. He is the Good Shepherd who goes out after His lost sheep, one whose love seeks after men in their forsaken condition and carries them in His pity to the place of health and healing. What was the history of His people but a long, long shepherding full of sad tenderness? But through all this tenderness there is the strong will that, though it forgives seventy times seven times, yet descends with terrible condemnation on the wicked servant who had no mercy on his fellow (Matt. 18: 21-35). It is a will for righteousness that cannot dally for ever with a Jerusalem that slays its prophets and refuses to discern the day of its visitation. This is a love that finally breaks into judgment on hypocritic Pharisee and calculating Sadducee. The lightnings are to flash and the thunders roar on those who know the good and yet choose the evil: there is an unforgivable sin, a passion for righteousness that is a consuming fire. There is the place of unrepentant privilege over which even redemptive love can but utter a sad "Woe unto you" and break into bitter weeping (Luke 19: 41ff.). Here is a judge who makes no final compromise with sin, and He is minded to declare it unforgettably. But how?

On the Cross. Mark 14: 35-41; Luke 22: 35-37; Gal. 3: 1-5; John 12: 20-33.

The Suffering Servant of God lived out the eternal patience in the ministry of Jesus: bearing men's sins and carrying their sorrows, He cherished high hopes that they would repent, saying that the chastisement of their sin was falling on the innocent. But they did not repent. There is a scorching utterance of Jesus strangely overlooked yet surely full of meaning, menacing meaning. Towards the last hours of the ministry, when Judas has gone out to make his fell betrayal and the darkness is gathering on Gethsemane, the Lord confronts His boldest follower Peter with the weakness behind his bluster, and goes on to look grim reality in the face. "When I sent you without purse, and scrip, and shoes, lacked ye any thing? And they said, Nothing. Then said he unto them, But now, he that hath a purse, let him take it, and likewise his scrip: and he that hath no sword, let him sell his garment, and buy one. For I say unto you, that this that is written must yet be accomplished in me, And he was reckoned among the transgressors: for the things concerning me have an end (*i.e.* reach a climax)" (Luke 22: 35-37).

What end? Why this apparent reversal of pacific policy? Had the way of the Suffering Servant failed? With Israel unmoved and unrepentant what next? God had a further appeal to mankind to make. Beside the Love that bears must be set the Judgment that smites. The optimism that believed that human nature would repent gives place to the fact that human sin is too deeply entrenched to be overcome by a merely patient pacifism. Sin must be *judged* and for ever stand *exposed,* and righteousness must be blazoned forth alongside of forgiving love. The patience of the divine love is consummated in the passion to expose and overcome sin. The Cross is the end, God's final word to mankind. Gethsemane and Calvary tell us that there is no gully too deep or too dark, too lined with thorns, for the saving arm of the Good Shepherd.

He Bore the Burden of Sin. Mark 15: 34.

"My God, my God, why hast thou forsaken me?" (Mark 15: 34). This loud and anguished cry directs us into the darkness and mystery of the Cross. Many attempts have been made to soften its harshness or to explain it away altogether. It has been set down as a quotation from a Psalm (22) that Jesus was recalling for the comfort of His soul. But one does not quote in a loud voice to quiet a troubled heart. Nor is it convincing to suggest that the Psalm goes on to end in a triumphant note. If out of the horror of these hours of torture the sound of jubilation had come, bystanders would surely have recorded their amazement at such courage, and Christian tradition would have treasured it. Some critics have attempted to make out that Jesus expected a dramatic intervention by divine forces to rescue Him from the grasp of His enemies, and that this cry records the bitter disillusionment of hopes unfulfilled: the heavens that Jesus expected to become alive with chariots and angelic horsemen remained dull, brazen, heartless. But how often had Jesus repudiated the popular hunger for a sign from heaven, and surely pain would not make Him turn traitor to His own lifelong convictions. Nor can we think that the cry simply registers His protest and resentment that suffering had filled His cup to the brim and now His courage fainted in the way. Had he not consistently taught from the very hour that the Messianic crown was placed on His head by Peter that for this Son of Man the way of suffering was divinely appointed? Again and again He had acknowledged this as His portion, the cup He must needs drink, the cup that He saw passing likewise even to the lips of His followers (Mark 8: 31, 9: 31, 10: 33-39). He did not regard suffering with Peter's eyes: He had entered into God's thoughts, and so learned that sorrow and travail are greatly used to shake men's souls, deepen their understanding, and so fit them to serve the larger purposes of divine wisdom.

Can it be then that in this saying we see the dark cloud of sin casting its shadow on the Cross and shutting out the gracious face of God, separating the Father from the Son of His love? On such a sombre line as this Christian thought has often travelled out in the hope of probing the mystery, and to this track humanity will return and return to grope again. Yet as we turn over the historic solutions we find much that gives us pause.

(*a*) Could Jesus in that dense darkness of soul have been suffering Himself the shock of God's righteous *punishment* for sin? Could this be Paul's meaning when he says that Him who knew no sin He made sin for us (2 Cor. 5: 21)? Can we say with John Calvin that here He was enduring within His soul awful tortures, the torments of a man condemned and lost? Did the weight of the world's sinfulness snap the cord that had held Him so far in unbroken fellowship with the Father? Is God so much the prisoner of His own laws of retribution that for human sin a more than human heart must break, for human wrongdoing more than human blood must pay?

To such a line of thought protest rises within us. What righteous principle is left in God if He thrusts out into the horror of the pit of pain His purest and best in order that, His sense of justice vindicated, He may now let the undeserving sinners into His favour? Moreover, if Jesus was paying the penalty of sin for others, was that not the very thing He would have rejoiced to do—an experience for Him full of light and not of darkness? There would be no desolation in such pain, at least to the soul of one who yearned to release His brethren from their evil plight. He would have cried out: "Let the darkness cover me if thereby they may have light!"

(*b*) Again, this agony of Jesus has been explained as the anguish required by the *perfect penitent:* as our representative before God, He must know what we in our sad experience know, the emotions of the sinner. Indeed only a pure soul such as His can adequately realize the exceeding hatefulness of sin to God. He alone could plumb the depths of its degradation, enter into its horrid shamefulness, bear its weight upon His conscience for our sakes. With evil thus crushing the soul and crowding out God, He would taste the doom, the estrangement, the "lostness" of the sinner. Only such a deep revulsion as He felt towards sin can create in us the mind that leads to true repentance.

Certainly we count it true that Jesus reached out and took to Himself the burden of our sin. But could one who knew no sin really enter into the consciousness of the sinner? Can anyone but myself repent for my sins? Can any other feel the guilt that is mine alone? Is penitence not too personal a need to be transferable? It was the way of Jesus to identify Himself with His brethren and to enter into their lot. But confronting the sinner did He not rather stand on God's side, rebuking the sin by the presence of His purity and uttering God's word of forgiving? We do not think of Him as entering into Hell with the penitent thief, but rather as receiving him in God's name and leading him into Paradise.

(*c*) It has been contended under many forms of theory that Jesus had to offer to God *"satisfaction"* for human sin before forgiveness could be granted to men. There had been given a moral law, and for human transgressors there was punishment. On the heavenly books there was a vast score of obligation standing against man, and some equivalent must be offered to an outraged God before justice could be done. And so into the scale against the human mass failure was thrown the weight of the God-man's offering of Himself that the heavenly balance might be adjusted. Old debts must needs be paid before a new order could come in.

To this there is one answer that immediately springs out. If to God there is some quantitative equivalent rendered, then there is no such thing as His free forgiveness. He takes His pound of flesh before He lets us go. That is not grace, but legalism. Obviously no such view can hold, and yet here there is a reality concealed under a crude exterior.

(*d*) Was the sense of dereliction due to man's unresponsiveness? Jesus was wont to see God in this fair world of the birds and the lilies and *especially* to mark His active presence in the daily life of men. Can it be that His supreme hour of dereliction came because He felt that God had faded out of the faces of His fellowmen? He had hoped that in response to His proclamation of the good news there would suddenly yet surge up in Israel a mass repentance, an awakening at last of the nation to their true need and vocation. Did He yearn for the Spirit of God to sweep through the nation as the wind courses through fields of standing grain? But as He looked out from these last days, behold, rather a hardening of hearts, a turning away from Him of the national aspirations, and a settling down on their lees of even the pious and the poor (Luke 22: 35ff.). Did he watch with sadness the long-fingered forces of enmity and reaction clutching at the circle He had aroused, drawing them back into paralysing doubt and eventual desertion? He watched a Judas let the vision fade away and slink back to be an easy prey to silver and smooth words. He saw impetuous Peter break under the light badinage and accusing eyes of a maid and courtyard hangers-on. Caught in a common panic, His chosen ones forsook Him and fled. Roman justice that towered up in the world as the strong and inflexible authority over an evil age crumpled ingloriously before fanatic clamour. The religious leaders of His own people, not content with spurning their heritage of faith and hope, had sinned deliberately against the light, committing the unpardonable sin, and in excess of arrogant pride had come to wag their heads and fling their taunts in petty triumph over the one who had disturbed the sleep of their easy consciences. Surely after all the people He had trusted had turned crazed and bloodthirsty; man on whose redeemability He had built His hopes had become possessed. Where was there foothold for the assurance He had given that the Kingdom had come, that the Gracious God was breaking through into a new intimacy with men? Looking round, He felt humanity crowding close with malice and contumacy, hypocrisy and betrayal, fanatic hate and mob violence, derision and blasphemy—like wild tongues of flame shooting at Him, searing Him, stifling Him. Surely He was beset with demons and not humans. The devil was gangmaster and men his utter slaves. "God of mine, God of mine, for what end hast Thou deserted me?" For one swift span He had sensed an utter horror and aloneness, confronted by naught but "the enmity of the carnal mind to God." It had been the joy of Jesus to see in the open countenance of men, in the smile of little children, in the love of brothers and the passionate devotion of women, the very guarantee and evidence of the presence of the Living God; and now it was as if—in the nightmare of the trial, the judgment, the sorrowful way and the agony of Calvary—he had been carried leagues away from the light and glory of the Father's face. Who can measure the cost and bitterness of that hour when sin the estranger set his infinite distance between the Son and the Father?

He Broke Its Power. Rom. 3: 24-28; Col. 2: 8-15; Eph. 2: 11-18.

Can God finally grant salvation from sin without first exposing it and once for all judging it in such a way that all the universe may see and know and shudder before it? Paul seemed to see in the Cross that crisis point in world history. There the malign influences that bear upon the life of man with all their train of law and lust and death met and lost in an epic encounter with the Son of God. Rom. 3: 24-28 pictures Jesus as set forth deliberately as a means of achieving reconciliation. In His forbearance God had for long appeared to be passing over sin: His patience was mistaken for complaisance. So now at this present epoch He intervened to do a something that would leave no misapprehension about His concern for righteousness. He would vindicate the moral order once and for all; and, once the dread deed was done, the way would be open for salvation on the basis of faith alone. Col. 2: 13ff. fills in some details of this apocalyptic drama. There Paul claims that the law, which with all its injunctions stood over men convicting them of sin, was cancelled at Calvary: it was nailed to the Cross and so taken right out of our area of concern. There too the evil powers that menace human life—having had a free hand to do their fell work in the flesh of the Man of Nazareth and having utterly failed—tasted complete defeat; they came out of that combat broken and no longer formidable, like prisoners of war borne along in the triumphal chariot of their conqueror, the Christ.

What can Paul mean by this dramatic language? Evidently when the mists have cleared away from Calvary men are to recognize that the supreme issue has been decided. That act on Calvary had a cosmic effect; it was to alter the whole conditions of the human struggle. There is a wisdom behind the face of things that has at last been revealed to mortal eyes. In the beauty, purity, and graciousness of the human *life* of the Son of Man the life of heaven has been unrolled: what God had intended to be the glory of human existence in the consummated Kingdom was there realized on earth for a brief span. Now that mystery of His purpose had been further unveiled in the *death* of Jesus. The Cross was another and infinitely dramatic piece of "realized eschatology," *i.e.,* it was the Judgment Day anticipated and foreshadowed. The character and method of God's final dealing with sin stood there plain to see. As Principal D. S. Cairns expressed it, "Paul believes that the Cross of Christ stands in lieu of the Great White Throne. Christ by His atoning death on the Cross has done something which makes that Judgment Day unnecessary for all who believe in Him. He has completely vindicated the moral character of God."[4] In what way does Paul suggest that vindication was made?

(*a*) *God asserted His will to overcome every evil power.* In the world of Paul's time, as we gather from Colossians, men tended to believe that supernatural forces were distributed abroad in the universe in a multiplicity of forms: there were powers and principalities of evil warring against the good power, and that conflict was reflected in our human souls in the struggle of good and evil. Over the stars presided many an evil genius, and woe unto him who, born in an unlucky month, fell under the baleful influence of a demon: for such an one the scales of fate were weighted. It was an immoral universe that held such destiny over men—a universe in which sin was inevitable. But Paul insists that there is no power loose in the world that is beyond the control of God's Son. He existed before any created being, natural or supernatural, and, as originator of all, He is Lord of all (Col. 1: 17). The supernatural energies are not distributed at

[4] D. S. Cairns, in *Expository Times,* vol. lii. no. 2, p. 61.

large, but are gathered together in the one Christ: all the potencies of God are in Him (Col. 2: 9). There is no force that can touch us in the realm of experience and destiny that He does not control. That is manifest in His own human life: all the powers of darkness had there the chance to draw Him into evil courses, and they were frustrated: even in the agony and darkness of rejection and the pain of the Cross they had failed to make Him curse God. Indeed the Cross might be likened to a conqueror's chariot in which the Saviour rode victorious with the defeated demons as captive warriors in His train (Col. 2: 15). A life *without sin,* crowned by a cruel martyr's death *without blasphemy,* was a vindication of the character of God and of the worldly conditions He had appointed for human life. When He went on to raise Jesus from the grasp of death, He made clear for ever His will to overcome man's last enemy and every form of evil.

(*b*) *God discharged man's burden of sin.* What of the law that stood over against man, ordinances that he never could fulfil and that therefore condemned him to dire penalties? Did not the law express the mind of God, and was not the character of God bound up with its fulfilment? Could God abolish the reign of law and its dread consequences? Yes, Paul claims. That law was cancelled and was nailed to the Cross like an old bill, symbol of an obligation that had been redeemed. The law, he maintained, was not a necessary and immutable feature of God's dealing with man: it was but a temporary régime, as temporary as guardianship over a boy in his immaturity (Gal. 4); the boy's father all the time is but waiting to institute a richer mutual relationship of person to person. Jesus in His intercourse with God had risen above the law to that richer relationship. He had lived out His life and expounded His principles on a more intimate basis than law and external penalties, a basis of understanding love, and God had blessed that new relationship inasmuch as He had been able to live a life without sin. Jesus had thus exposed before men another side of God's nature; He had bidden men see beneath the sternness of the Judge the face of the Father. That human father is truly righteous who does not hold up all the family delinquencies for a day of rude reckoning, but in intimate personal bearing with and sharing with the erring sons and daughters lifts them above their errors and evil desires, and woos them into a union deep and spiritual: their resultant common mind and affection for the best things demonstrates the victory of love over evil. With a graciousness like His Father's, Jesus had been taking up men's sin as an agony and heartbreak to Himself while imparting to the forgiven sinner a new impulse toward good. That was fulfilling the moral order in a way that imposed pains and penalties could never do. The only ultimate objective of law was to educate man in moral truth, to eliminate the disharmony of sin. The pain caused by sin to the one he loves cuts deeper into a man's conscience than any legal penalty. Such a sin-bearing love touches and transmutes the sinner's soul. The moral order is vindicated by being transcended. God is alive in the law as flesh is alive, but His nature is deeper than the moral sense alone. He is alive in His love likewise as warm blood is alive, and His love animates His righteousness. The true antidote to sin is not wounding penalty, but healing grace. The stream of evil that sin spreads through the social network of life is swallowed up in a counter-stream of good that arises from the springs of love and forgiving. "Where sin abounded, grace did much more abound" (Rom. 5: 20). "The sin of the world is like the waves of an angry sea breaking on the eternal shore, and transformed from its sullen darkness into the gleaming beauty of the breakers. The divine grace, which is the divine will to forgive and to suffer in forgiving, does not only defeat sin, but makes its consequences contribute to the spiritual beauty of the universe."[5]

God's holiness is offended by sin, as the law is intended to witness. Wherever there is sin, there is registered suffering in God. But God accepts that suffering as the outflow of His gift of freedom to man. Nor does He repudiate the responsibility for all the tragedy of sin that freedom has wrought. He holds it as a personal care upon the eternal heart, a burden that no other can bear. In Christ He shows His willingness to accept that load and finally discharge it. As Dr. James Denney puts it in a letter: "I have often wondered whether we might not say that the Christian doctrine of the Atonement just meant that in Christ God took the responsibility of evil upon Himself and somehow subsumed evil under good; . . . I fancy it was something like this Calvin had in mind when he said that God did not make His noblest creature *ambiguo fine,* without knowing what for; *i.e.,* He

[5] H. Wheeler Robinson, *Suffering Human and Divine,* p. 170.

was quite prepared to take all the consequences, and He took them in Christ."[6] Thus it comes about that "the blot is worked into the finished design of the picture, the discord is resolved into an enriched harmony. The sin-marred world, viewed as a whole, is transformed into a realm of victorious and forgiving love."[7]

(*c*) *God exposed and finally judged sin.* After that day of blind unreason man must look up and see there on the Cross the hatefulness of sin in its true magnitude. Against the unexampled purity of the Son of Man the blackness of sin stands out in its stark hideousness. The guile that twisted the evidence against Jesus, the hypocrisy that professed to put away this man for the security of the nation, the vaunted justice that sent the innocent to be scourged in the name of good relations between rulers and ruled, the cruel hands that thrust the cross on His bleeding shoulders, the ruthless unconcern that drove the nails into His quivering flesh, the light-headedness that flung clever taunts at Him, the evil leer of satisfaction that distorted the faces of priestly onlookers—these phases and forms of one sinister power of sin must confront and shame men for all time. That exposure pointed directly toward us men that sin might lose its fascination for us. We must see ourselves as the brothers and cousins of the betrayers and murderers; after one convicting gaze into that mirror of awful truth we must acknowledge sin in ourselves and seek to flee from it for ever. God is not changed, but we are changed. Overwhelmed by the fact that the Son of God had voluntarily suffered in Himself the shock and horror of sin's evil consequence, we are broken in heart and ready to be reconciled with the Father of our spirits.

For Us. Heb. passim; Gal. 3: 13-29; Rom. 5: 12-21; 1 Pet. 2: 21-25; Rev. 7: 13-14.

There is a representative aspect of the work of Christ on the Cross that is hard for the modern mind to grasp. Ancient society was not so conscious of the rights of the individual. Men were more deeply rooted in family and racial groups and accustomed to the idea that what the father or king or leader did availed for the

[6] *Letters of Principal James Denney to his Family and Friends,* p. 187f.

[7] H. Wheeler Robinson, *Redemption and Revelation,* p. 275.

whole community. In much of Paul's thought revolving round our oneness with Adam, and in the conception of Christ's High Priesthood in Hebrews, this idea is dominant. There is no escaping a social solidarity in which we stand for good or ill. The forced regimentation of the Fascist state and the cultivation of the Führer principle indicate that humanity has lost a unity that it would fain recover. There is a real oneness and interdependence and mutuality in human life, a pervasive unity of spirit that seeks to express itself in community. It is significant that just when ancient faiths were dissolving and national kingdoms were disrupting and a false new unity was being superimposed by force of arms and an emperor, just then the Christ appeared with a power of attractiveness and sensitivity and a universal human appeal. Right into the heart of estranging enmities and paralysing fears and disintegrating despair came this dynamic and vital man of love and faith and confidence.

Now within the social network of our living we cannot isolate sin. It injures the doer and the victim and casts its blight upon those whom they touch. Forgiveness does not cancel the evil result though it restores the sinner. There are consequences that have spread outwards and downwards that no individual human can overtake and nullify. Only the advent of a counter-activity of equal force and pervasiveness can restore the social whole. That needs a creative redemptive urge from above. Scripture is never done assuring us that Jesus went through deep and dark waters *on our behalf*. There was a profound depth of affliction that as Son of God and Son of Man He plumbed for our sake. Making men always strangely God-conscious in His presence, He freely accepted throughout the years the burden-bearing of a sensitive heart that feels for every brother's sin and every sister's sorrow, and on the Cross as our blood-brother and God's Anointed One He felt the shame of what sin brings upon man and the anguish that it lays upon God. As Son of Man, the symbol and promise of a new order of humanity, He ever sought to champion the disinherited outcast and to stand with sinners as conscience awoke within them. Having daily lived in deepening fellowship with the Twelve, He could not leave them without making clear how He loved them to the end, giving them the bread and the wine that declared the completeness of His self-giving. He who had taken upon Himself our daily load could not in His final agony be less our brother. Thus here was "One who has realised to the uttermost in His own person all that sin meant, One who has drunk the cup our sins had mingled, One who has felt all the waves and billows break over Him in which God's reaction against sin comes home to us sinners."[8] So Jesus by love had achieved an identification of His life with mankind that constituted Him king in a realm closer than an earthly kingdom (Col. 1: 27, 3: 3). That ceaseless knitting of heart to heart and the final gathering of us all into a sin-bearing deed of love form mankind into a new spiritual whole. Our sense of indebtedness and answering devotion are as the nerves and binding muscles of a spiritual body (Eph. 4: 6). The spirit of the living Christ possesses and animates each member. Thus when Jesus breaks the evil entail of sin, we too in that living interlacing are set free; when He has fulfilled the law, we sharers of His hidden life are under its terror no more; when He has proved His supremacy over the demonic forces of the universe, we too, who are linked to Him in the moral bonds of the Kingdom, are redeemed from fear, more than conquerors through Him that loved us. The Cross becomes luminous only when we realize that there hangs upon the tree the Christ appointed before the foundation of the world, who has made Himself one with the sin of man, and it is in intimate union with the victorious Lord of the Resurrection that we are called on to live out our human lives. Calvary is a foretaste and anticipation of the final overthrow of evil in the world.

He Moves to Repentance. Acts 2: 22-42; Acts 4: 10-12; 1 John 1: 9-10.

What thoughts well up within us as we look upon this strange man upon the Cross? Could we stand beside the mourning women or the frightened disciples, what would they betray of their emotions? How would Peter feel, the frankest and most human of all His followers? Already Peter had betrayed foreshadowings of the tempest in his soul. When the Lord turned and looked upon him in the Judgment Hall, He was really ascending the steps of the Cross; the furies of human hate and passion had

[8] James Denney, *The Christian Doctrine of Reconciliation,* p. 159.

gathered about His head and already fashioned an unseen crown of thorns for His brow. His coming fate was clear—the forsaken and abandoned leader upon whom the shades of death were closing. The Lord turned and looked upon Peter. And Peter went out and wept bitterly. These eyes so full of understanding love and pity smote to the depths of his soul. It was a Love like that he had denied, a loyalty like that he had failed to emulate. Penitence flooded Peter's heart. Tears alone could utter his emotions, and the tears were not salt enough to express all he felt. And the centurion who stood by was heard to mutter: "Truly a righteous man." As if he were saying: "It is I, a man of blood and violence, who should hang there and not this innocent man." That startling purity rebuked the conscience of the soldier and, pagan though he was, he needed only to have known the Crucified a little better and he would have been mastered by an emotion like Peter's—penitence that he should have a part to play in such a foul deed. Dr. James Hope Moulton has suggested that this was the soldier who heard and later passed into the memoranda of the Church the words, "Father, forgive them; for they know not what they do." Was it that forgiving love that amazed the plain blunt soldier? Did that touch him to shame and evoke his testimony—the first stage towards a Christian penitence? And there is the word of the dying thief to his taunting fellow: "Dost not thou fear God, seeing thou art in the same condemnation?" (Luke 23: 40)—as if upon this rude bandit, hero of many breathtaking encounters, there had fallen an awe such as his soul had not known, an awe that betrays how the reality of God was forcing itself upon him in the presence of this Jesus. He knew he was confronted by a purity that spoke of the Unseen Holiness. And if only one of those women looking on had written an autobiography, how much deeper the note she would have struck! But all would testify to the same effect—the sense of shame and rebuke that by human machination such an one should die like a criminal. Penitence is the primary response in any human who considers this cruel Cross. Bound together in the bundle of life, we are guilty. Like Peter we acknowledge His leadership, profess to follow, and go on to deny. Men of the world like the centurion, we know beside His holiness that we are unrighteous. Caiaphas sent Him to His death; but so do our compromising policies. Pilate let Him die to keep the peace: so do we evade our responsibilities and play for security. A city welcomed Him and then forgot to guard Him. Such are our cities—professedly Christian, but crucifying Him nightly in our places of ill fame. The daughters of Jerusalem and of every city are constrained to weep when they consider how readily they adore Him and as easily forget Him.

Forgiveness. Eph. 1: 3-14; Eph. 2: 1-18.

Forgiveness is the supreme gift we are given from the Cross. The love that said in the midst of the bitterest agony, "Father, forgive them," is the Love that never faileth. Forgiveness was a gift that the saints of the Old Testament claimed: "As far as the east is from the west, so far hath he removed our transgressions from us" (Ps. 103: 12). And in a very real sense they must have known release. But the forgiveness that the Cross conveys is richer, deeper. It is not a mere overlooking of sin, but the entering into a living union with the God who has stooped and suffered to save us. We are fast held by love of a new degree—the love of a shepherd who goes out after even one lost sheep, the love that pursues and pleads and stretches patience to the uttermost, a love that has not even waited till we in our penitence sought it out, but took the initiative, entered the human scene, lived and suffered with us, and died for us. We see the soldier march past in peace time, and we know he is pledged to defend us, our homes and our fatherland. But in war time he comes back with tattered battle dress and crippling wounds and the face of a man who has looked into the eyes of death, and now we know that he has written his pledge in blood. The Cross is the proof that forgiving is more than forgetting. It speaks of a heart that has been grieved by every act of rebellion and yet has taken to itself and consumed the evil entail of our sin.

Under pressure of so generous a love estrangement must die away. Counting himself fortunate if only he could become a hired servant in his father's house, the prodigal finds himself at a banquet table like a guest of honour and received as a son again. Estrangement lingers only in the jealous heart of a brother where sin still rules. Surely even there the heavy sulky brow must relax under the compelling love that protests: "All that I have is thine."

A New Loyalty. Gal. 6: 14-16; 2 Cor. 5: 17-21.

The bond that binds us to the eternal world is a new and finer tie. It is the bond of gratitude, of responsive love. "Who loved me and gave himself for me" is the phrase of Paul, indicating his sense that it was no mere general amnesty that God gave men, not the opening of prison doors that has sometimes symbolized a new monarch's accession to power, but a love that in person turned the key in my own cell. There is in this experience the richness of a personal discovery. In the parables Jesus frequently makes the individual stand out: one prodigal son, one brother who says "No" to his father and repents, one servant who receives ten pounds—as if to emphasize that forgiveness is the opening of a single experience, an encounter with God that is unique to each soul and that leads out into a physician's care for each particular life. But to come to the Father is at the same time to come to His household, the community of His saints. We may enter through a single portal, but the room we enter is large and generous and peopled by a great multitude. The father of the prodigal summoned the whole household to share in the festal return. When one sinner repents it is all heaven that rejoices. The Apocalypse that depicts the heavenly courts resounds to the praise that is a rich deep chorus: the fellowship we enjoy is wide as the multitudes that compose it.

Victorious Over Death and Evil. Rom. 6: 3-11; Phil. 3: 8-16.

If the story of Jesus came to a dead halt at the Cross, there would always be honour for Jesus, but misgiving of the gravest about God. On Calvary we would see only another dreamer come to a grim awakening, another idealist fallen from his dizzy height to the cruel rocks of earth. So far from vindicating His righteousness, God would be declaring an Olympian aloofness; so far from manifesting His love for men, God would be pilloried as the one who did not care.

> If Calvary had no aftermath
> When Christ had struggled up the path
> Of pain and death and tenfold woe!
> If earth had closed upon the flow

Of matchless ministry and love
With naught of answer from above!
If God had rested in His wrath
And Calvary had no aftermath!

But Calvary had its aftermath—
Christ risen walked the garden path,
And bade sad Mary lift her eyes
And greet her Lord in glad surprise:
The time had come to cease from tears
And cast aside all mortal fears,
For God disdains to speak in wrath
And Calvary had its aftermath!

If Calvary had no afterglow
When Christ had suffered long to show
That Love could tread a darkening road
And Patience bear a heavy load
Of human hate and bitter days
Yet still in faith uplift God's praise,
Then human hands would cease to sow
If Calvary had no afterglow.

But Calvary had its afterglow
When fishermen set forth to row
And toiled all night till Jesus spake:
"See! Cast on yonder side the lake."
Then laden nets and hearts deep thrilled
Forecast sea harvests He had willed.
Praise God! For all Christ's brethren know
That Calvary had its afterglow.

Jesus had never asked for a sign, but God had given a resounding sign unasked. The Resurrection came as a grand affirmation of the life of faith and love sustained deep into the night of gloom. Men had proposed a political murder, but God had transformed it into a heavenly benediction. Caiaphas had played for narrow national stakes, and God had answered with the breaking of an alabaster box that filled the whole world with the odour of the ointment. That act of resurrection was a foretaste of the victory of the eternal will to righteousness. Man's deepest evil can be transmuted into the high purpose of God. So must all the forces of darkness fade away before the legions of the light.

Such Grace and Strength. Col. 1: 24-27; Eph. 1: 15-23; Eph. 4: 4-16.

Moreover the Cross is charged with a power that passes into human penitents with a renewing energy. A deliverance so great has a momentum that carries a Stephen to a martyr's crown and Paul to a worldwide mission that has not yet ceased to find new frontiers. The breaking of the thraldom of sin releases potentialities in mankind: under the impulse of the Resurrected One men can face the ordeals before which they once quailed, and come out more than conquerors. Faith and love have their victories that only the impetus of the Cross can explain. The weight of the world's sin is heavy; encased in the meshes of our social life we share burdens and carry inherited loads. It is ours to fill up what is lacking of the suffering of Christ.

VII. The Church.

We believe that the Church, the society of the redeemed, was brought into existence by God Himself through the work and risen power of Christ, Who in calling men into fellowship with Himself calls them by the same act into fellowship with one another in Him.

We believe that the Church is the organ of Christ's mind and redemptive will, the body of which He is the Head. Under Him the Church is called to the proclamation of the everlasting Gospel with its offer of salvation, to the worship of God, Creator and Redeemer, to the loving service of mankind, and to the care and nurture of the flock.

We believe that all members of the Church are one in Him, and that the life of the Church in every age is continuous with that of the first apostolic company. The groups commonly known as "churches" are called to share in the life of the whole Church, of all ages and of all lands, entering freely into the full heritage of thought, worship, and discipline, and living together in mutual confidence.

We believe that for the fulfilment of her mission in the world God has given to the Church the Ministry, the Scriptures and the Sacraments.

So we acknowledge one holy, catholic, apostolic Church, the Body of Christ, the household and family of God.

CHAPTER VII. THE CHURCH

The First Apostolic Company.

"And it came to pass in those days, that he went out into a mountain to pray, and continued all night in prayer to God.

And when it was day, he called unto him his disciples: and of them he chose twelve, whom also he named apostles" (Luke 6: 12-13).

When Jesus thus called to His side twelve men to share His thought and His destiny, He was foreshadowing the Christian Church. And the circumstances attending that decision are enlightening. (1) The group arose in answer to worldly hostility that was hardening into bitter hate: "And they were filled with madness; and communed one with another what they might do to Jesus" (Luke 6: 11). Following the will of the Father who is Love, Jesus had put human need above venerable tradition, and so had aroused that unreasoning opposition that only a long process of patient testimony could hope to undermine. (2) That call of the Twelve moreover was no snap decision, no petulant counter-thrust. All night long He had wrestled on the mountain top, seeking to assure Himself that this creative act was the will of God. That association that was to take final shape as the Christian Church issues from the counsel of the All-wise God. Jesus would fain have worked with the established orders of the day, using the synagogue and the Pharisee as His instruments in the forwarding of truth; He would rather have expressed His mind within the forms and institutions of Judaism. But superstitious fear and professional jealousy had banged and bolted the door against Him, and He could none other than form His own society of friends. (3) The men He chose to share His high enterprise in living were simple unlettered men from the fishing grounds and the customs office, pessimists like Thomas and ardent men of action like Zelotes, ordinary men of varied moods and classes; for His way of life was a vain offering to the world if it could not capture and hold and sanctify the common folk of every rank and condition. (4) Moreover the place for Christ's people is right in the midst of needy humanity: "And he came down with them, and stood in the plain," and immediately it was in a great concourse of folk "out of all Judea and Jerusalem, and from the sea coast of Tyre and Sidon" (Luke 6: 17) that the first contact of the incipient Church was made—contact that offered the Word of God with healing and release. And that contact must never be lost though the world may strive to break away. "Blessed are ye when men shall hate you, and when they shall separate you from their company, and shall reproach you, and cast out your name as evil" (Luke 6: 22). Not that there is any merit in thus being cut off from the community and detested; it must be for an end—for the Son of Man's sake. The task of the Church is to be one of persistence in well-doing. Love, give, judge not: such are the imperatives that chart the course of the future for this new community. But these heights of living can be scaled only if the highest draw us heavenward: "Be ye merciful, as your Father also is merciful" (Luke 6: 36).

God Who at Sundry Times. Ex. 19: 3-6; 1 Pet. 2: 9; Rev. 1: 6.

This movement that Jesus had initiated was not altogether new: it was but a continuation of an urgent demand that the Spirit of God had ever been pressing upon the human sphere. God had never left Himself without a witness: always in the souls of men there had been an awareness of a divine invasion, the pressure of a Presence that would not be denied. The Eternal Creator had never ceased to separate for Himself a people: "You only have I known of all the families of the earth," said the Word to Amos (3: 2). The people of Israel, conscious of an act of great deliverance, had made covenant at Mount Sinai, acknowledging the hand that had been stretched out to free them from oppression and absorption in Egypt, and in the Ten Words and in the call to life as a free people they had recognized One who was disclosing Himself and claiming them as His own by virtue of His mighty Act and righteous Will. Surrounding peoples might stand on the same or higher levels of culture, they might enjoy broader lands and vaster power and riches, and be raised to dizzier heights in the changing landscapes of history and experience; but because at the heart of her social structure there were ever those who kept tryst with the Eternal Justice, Israel the people was different. Other folk were like beasts of the jungle threading the forests in search of prey and, having found repletion, returning again to their lairs, circling eternally in the semi-darkness of the woods; but the Hebrew, fascinated by the music of the waters, kept pursuing them through bog and marsh to clear stream and open country, and kept ever marching on under open skies to the sea. It was the pilgrimage of faith that Abraham began when he went out not knowing whither he went, but, because he was divinely led, seeking a city whose builder and maker is God.

By the Saving Remnant. Is. 1: 9; Is. 8: 16-18; Is. 10: 20-23; Is. 2: 2-5; Is. 9: 5-7.

Not all of Israel were faithful. Rather the temptations and allurements of the encircling world made graves for the many, and only the few kept pushing on in the spirit of the true pioneers. The forward march of Israel was possible only by the saving of the elect remnant: "Except the Lord had left unto us a very small remnant, we should have been as Sodom, and we should have been like unto Gomorrah" (Is. 1: 9). Men's sluggard hearts grow fat, their ears are dull, their eyes drop shut: they will not change their ways and turn towards God to be healed (Is. 6: 9-10). But the prophet does not lapse into the lethargy of the majority. He sees in the stupidity of the many the challenge to the faithfulness of the few who face and acknowledge moral facts. What Winston Churchill said of the work of the Royal Air Force over Britain in 1940 might be said of Isaiah and his remnant.

The assembling of this spiritual band marks an epoch in human history. The prophet rightly saw in his God-given insights teaching to be sealed and guarded as a treasure in the keeping of his disciples. This minority, Isaiah taught, must learn to await the Lord who is hiding His face: they must regard themselves as hostages of the Spirit, signs and symbols in Israel from the Lord of Hosts who keeps watch above His own in Mount Zion (8: 16-18). While the masses may not know or consider, the elect must face the facts of life with unflinching eyes. They will mark and share the divine sadness over the vineyard of Israel that brings forth wild grapes. Their Saviour God "looked for justice, but behold oppression; for righteousness, but behold a cry." They will share the dream of a day when men shall beat their swords into ploughshares and their spears into pruning-hooks (2: 4), and when the blood-stained war-cloak shall be food for the fire. But well they know this wished for spring time will issue from no war-weariness or parley of peoples: it starts from a fresh miracle of grace: "For unto us a child is born, unto us a son is given: . . . and his name shall be called Wonderful, Counsellor, The mighty God, The everlasting Father, The Prince of Peace" (9: 6). The remnant had the sustaining confidence that God had His hand upon the world and the shape of history, and He was yet to manifest Himself anew in the advent of Immanuel.

The prophet rebukes scornfully mere temple-treading, and appears to hold his society together by no institutional bonds, but relies only on an inner loyalty to the divine Spirit. Yet the source of all his inspiration is a vision that comes to him in the Temple, in the shrine which had for so long proved itself as the spiritual home of his fathers (6: 1-12). It was in the midst of worship, in the seeking of the Divine Presence, that the call came to him. And there too came the assurance upon which he based his community: though the judgments of history may see the oak tree of Israel shattered and prostrate, yet the broken stump may sprout again; the vital tenth within the nation may win it a new lease of life (6: 13). And again that call came to him because his heart's concern was deep planted in the politics of his time: it was in the year that King Uzziah died that he sought and heard the Divine voice. Neither prophet nor divine community could function except in so far as they were rooted deep in the nation's life and interests.

And in Divers Manners. Jer. 31: 31-34; Dan. 7; Is. 42: 1-4, etc.

The idea of a spiritual core within the nation that will save the whole found expression again and again, notably in Jeremiah, in the Suffering Servant songs, and in Daniel.

Jeremiah (31: 31) pictured a new covenant that God would make with His people marked by three notes: *inwardness,* "I will put my law in their inward parts"; *individualism,* "they shall all know me"; and *forgiveness,* "their sins I will remember no more" (31: 33f.). It brings a new and closer fellowship with God. And it is all His gracious doing: for it is the act of forgiveness that floods mind and conscience with a new knowledge of the Divine nature and inspires a grateful eagerness to do His will. Thus the prophet strikes a new note in insisting that what makes a man a member of the community is the direct action of God on each individual, a forgiving act that awakens each soul within. And Jeremiah was here indulging in no mere spinning of fancy, but applying in the large what had been his own experience. Caught in the gruelling disasters of the Exile and faced by what seemed the dissolution and cruel wrecking of his beloved nation, he himself had reached out and found a God who chose the darkness in which to draw nearer.

The poet of the Suffering Servant songs (Is. 42: 1-4; 49: 1-6; 50: 4-9; 52: 13 to 53: 12) extended his vision beyond Israel to other nations. Brooding on the inexplicably heavy suffering of his people, he breaks out into a new conception. It is not for their own sins but for the sins of others that the holy people are suffering: they must be vicariously bearing the sins of the world. But therein is a divine mystery, for there will be an awakening among the tyrant peoples, a conscience quickened to convict them of their sins and moving them to contrition and repentance. Thus salvation will come to the many by the mute unprotected suffering of the servant nation of God. It may seem a fantastic hope in a mind unacquainted with life's grim realities. But no! the prophet was driven to his extravagant dream because he was rooted in history: he was held by his love for his people and by the equally sure conviction that God could not be without purpose in what He allowed to fall on Israel.

Again it was in times of national anguish that another seer had his vision of the Son of Man (Dan. 7). A dictator was striving to wrench Israel from her traditions and force her into acceptance of an alien culture. In her own strength the nation had no future. Over against the brutal empires of the past, fittingly symbolized by savage beasts because of their bestial cruel policies, Daniel conceives an empire of another sort, marked by ways of reason and humanity, the kingdom of the saints of God. While persecution is still raging on earth the prophet sees in the timeless sphere above a mysterious figure brought before the Almighty on His throne and invested with royal dignity. That figure was like unto a Son of Man and he came on the clouds of heaven, signifying that it was by the power of God that there would come this reign of the saints of God. Thus again it was revealed that the only way out of this troubled world that the sin of man had made was by the Divine intervention, and that through the instrumentality of those whose lives He had fired with His Spirit.

Hath Spoken By His Son. Matt. 16: 13-19; Mark 11: 17; Mark 14: 58.

When John the Baptist by the banks of Jordan began his mission of repentance, he may have thought of himself as calling into being such a company of the saints of God as might fall heir to all these prophetic hopes. The Day of the Lord was at hand—a great and terrible day of judgment that would see the wheat separated from the chaff. The rite of baptism was the winnowing-fan sifting out the finer souls who heard and made response to the voice of God. Jesus came forward and made Himself one with His brethren. But in the course of that experience He was called to be more than a member of that community. It was revealed to Him that He was to be Israel's ideal king, the agent and representative God had chosen to inaugurate the Kingdom without end. In the power of that call He went out and preached the Word that proved like a dividing sword, cleaving the living from the dead that must be left to bury the dead. In the Twelve whom He chose to share His work and mission He saw the nucleus of the new Divine order.

But did they recognize Him as He truly was? When the Galilean ministry drew to its close, He felt the time had come for mutual understanding. Hence the questions at Caesarea Philippi: "Whom do men say that I am?" and "Whom do ye say that I am?" It fell to Peter to make the historic declaration "Thou art the Christ." To Jesus this meant that another than Himself now shared the conviction that God had chosen Him to bring into actuality on the earthly scene the universal Kingdom of the saints. As such Jesus was more than a prophet: what the prophets had yearned for *He* was to realize. And that utterance of Peter was no mere human guess or calculated appraisal. It was an insight given by God. "Flesh and blood hath not revealed it unto thee, but my Father which is in heaven" (Matt. 16: 13-17). As the seers who forecast the true community had been spokesmen of a

Word given of God, so the recognition of its Messiah was an inspiration. Jeremiah had recognized that membership in the new covenant implied divine operation on the human heart. Peter was being borne into that new knowledge of God and was having a new moral sense awakened in him before he could see in the carpenter of Nazareth the Son of God. With the law written in his heart he was to become able to "bind and loose," discern the values of the Kingdom. But he had yet much to learn. When Jesus began to teach that the Son of Man must needs suffer, he protested and was rebuked. The Spirit had not yet come to abide in him: it came but fitfully as to the prophets of old. But in that high moment of inspiration when he had hailed his Messiah, the Church had been foreshadowed. He was historically the first to make the grand confession, and on this revelation granted to him as on a rock that had for a moment risen above the stormy waters Jesus saw the foundation for His community.

NOTE: This primacy of Peter was a matter of historical priority. It was not something he could transmit to his successors in office any more than Christopher Columbus could hand on his discovery of America or James Watt his invention of the steam engine.

When Jesus came finally to Jerusalem, He was well aware that hostility and intrigue awaited Him and that His days of active ministry might be few. What He chose to do on borrowed time were surely acts of calculated meaningfulness. It was His deed of temple-cleansing and the *teaching* uttered there that stung the authorities to action. What was that all-important teaching? Evidently that part of it that was quoted at the Trial had been startling to orthodoxy: "Destroy this temple made with hands and in three days I will raise another made without hands." This word has been taken to refer only to the Resurrection. But it was only when He was raised from the dead that that meaning was applied, the Fourth Evangelist tells us (2: 22). Commercialism and malpractice were destroying the Temple, emptying it of meaning. The Temple was the place where God revealed His Presence. In the blood bath of animal sacrifice and the accompanying priestly spoliation that Presence could not be manifest. But God was not thereby defeated. Jesus would raise up a spiritual temple in the hearts of His followers: the

Church would be His body. In His community of devoted disciples the Presence of God would be bodied forth. The Church is the extension of the Incarnation. The Presence of God manifested itself in the life of the new community. People coming into contact with its members felt a power, a reality that was not of earth. With Jesus came the release upon the world of a new spiritual potency, revolutionary as an element like radium in the physical world. As foretold to Nathanael, the heavens had now been thrown wide open, and remained open so that the ministries of God's graciousness kept coming continuously upon men. The Divine Presence was available now in no mere temple of stone and lime, but in a house of flesh and blood, a society of faith and love, sweetness and light.

Through the Work and Risen Power of Christ, Luke 22: 15-30.

On the night in which He was betrayed Jesus drew His disciples about Him in the Last Supper, a rite that was the sealing and designation of these first members of the new community. The bread and wine given and received along with the words of ardent expectation and promise set a glory within these lives that was never extinguished: for they then began to experience that self-communication of the Divine that has ever since then proved the strength of the Church. "I appoint unto you a kingdom," said Jesus. The joys, the privileges, the responsibilities of the new order were to be theirs. Christians are called to a sovereignty of the spirit which they exercise not from arrogant assumption, but by reason of a new insight that the Christ mind bestows: they bring standards and values into the moral life that fit them to be the judges of the New Israel. Jesus saw in these His companions through many testing months an illumination of soul that enabled Him confidently to tell His judges at the Trial that from henceforth they would see taking shape the Kingdom of the Son of Man as pictured by Daniel.

It was the experience of Pentecost that revealed to the community the reality of the spiritual contact now open to them. Seven weeks had passed since the crushing blow of the Crucifixion, and from farm to fishing-ground and from fishing-ground to farm there had flashed the news of strange happenings, disclosures of the loved presence of their Lord such as the Resurrection stories tell. There had been questionings and long, long silent thoughts on the part of many, and then, perhaps in that hallowed upper room amid familiar scenes, came together for the first time a considerable assembly of adherents of the Crucified One. Could so many dare to hold on to their hopes in Him? They looked round in wondering surprise. Then speech broke forth. Testimony incited testimony till faith blazed into a flame and burned away all doubt and fear. Enthusiasm and holy gladness rose to fever heat and there came the verifying proofs of the Spirit. Now they knew a power was active upon them, that power that had centred in Jesus and now had come to settle upon them; His Church, His spiritual body, had come into being.

That company at Pentecost must have been strangely startled people. They had not come to Jerusalem to found a church. They had come as the spirit bade them, expecting vaguely that they would carry through the ancient ritual of the Jewish Feast of Pentecost—to record their gratitude to the Giver of all at the close of the grain harvest. That there would be a gathering of believers in Jesus many might have hoped for, but perhaps few expected. And when they did come together, it was to enter upon an experience that was altogether beyond their calculations. Their world was turned upside down. And even when they started on their way homeward they were quite unaware of the magnitude and significance of that grander harvest of which they had tasted the firstfruits.

Brought Into Existence By God Himself. Eph. 1: 3-23; John 15: 1-17.

And so it had been down through the centuries. Men had been caught up and borne along by a tide of mysterious urgency. When Isaiah went to the Temple he probably went simply as a mourner with bent head; he came away enlightened and exalted. Could Jeremiah know that in the intensity of his seeking after God and in the intimacy of the resultant experience he was shaping a covenant relationship that was to be the foreshadowing and type of a new spiritual society? When the seer portrayed the Suffering Servant of the songs and Daniel saw in his vision one like unto a Son of Man, they showed by their vagueness and dimness of outline that they were not sketching a human reality that their eyes had seen, but rather an ineffable wonder and glory that their eyes would fain see. When John Baptist pictured the coming one, the wielder of the destroying axe and the winnowing fan, he was far, far away from the divine reality that did step forth: a voice was speaking to him in accents that he but faintly comprehended. When Peter and Andrew, James and John, went out to mend their nets one day, they had no notion that other and finer nets would be substituted in their hands. And we can assume that the counting-house Matthew was quite astonished to find himself embark on a venture where calculations were all thrown to the winds, while hesitant doubting Thomas was the most surprised of all men when he emerged on to a platform of deliberate affirmation, "My Lord and my God!" The Church was never a matter of human planning and premeditated choice. It was God's doing throughout the centuries that all the outlines were finely drawn, and it was through the work and power of His Son that the Church became a thing of history in flesh and blood. When it did take shape, it was not the meticulous planning of a committee in Jerusalem, but a spirit-filled company that overflowed and scattered under the compulsion of persecution. That power that had descended upon the company was scouring the roads beyond and laying hold even of an enemy and persecutor like Saul of Tarsus. That timid and hunted folk should receive into their friendship an avowed enemy like Saul, that a rich man like Barnabas and many others should sell all they had and share their wealth with those who had nothing, that former revolutionaries should sit down with once orthodox and sober Pharisees and with the tax-collectors whom they had counted traitors to the national cause, that proud Jews who had always reckoned themselves a chosen race should find themselves in a society into which were welcomed Gentiles of every nation and every class—that was proof enough that the God who called men into fellowship with Himself one by one was calling them also into fellowship with one another.

The Society of the Redeemed. Ephesians 2: 1-10.

If we could mingle in that first company of the Church and begin to ask each one how he came by this new life, there would be but one answer: it came through contact with Jesus Christ who, as St. Paul puts it, "loved me and gave himself for me." Gratitude for a graciousness that was wholly undeserved was the tide that carried man after man into the Christian circle. Paul never ceased to marvel that as he was engaged in a headlong career of hate and persecution against all who bore the name of Jesus he was "arrested," captured, led into that society of friendship and light; those whom he had persecuted kept heaping coals of fire upon his head, ministering to his needs of body and mind. That he could be forgiven his past and set upon the new road must mean that *someone* had intervened between God and his deserts, *someone* had taken his sin upon himself, and won release from all the shame of it. *That one* must be none other than Jesus Christ. So Paul's love overflowed towards his Saviour Christ, and there and then began an association that was to last all through life and beyond it. "It is no longer the old self that now rules my mind and affections: Christ has taken control of my whole being" is Paul's testimony (Gal. 2: 19f.). So completely were all his willing and desiring now centred in Jesus Christ that he was not any more just Saul the Pharisee or Paul the Roman citizen, but rather the slave of Christ completely and indissolubly commissioned for His service.

The Body of Which He Is the Head. 1 Cor. 12: 12-27; Eph. 2: 11-22.

Paul thus thought of himself as "in Christ," incorporated in a spiritual organism of which Christ is the head. As the head directs every movement of the limbs, so Christ controls all the members of His society, His body (1 Cor. 12: 12). Or, as John records the same truth: "I am the vine, ye are the branches" (John 15: 5). That does not mean that we are related to Christ as branches growing out of the stem of the tree, but rather that we are drawing from and are dependent on the life energy that flows through the whole and makes the whole a vital and fruit-bearing creation. Close fellowship with Him is the source and condition of Divine life in us. Moreover, God has made us the necessary supplement and completion of His life. In a startling phrase the Apostle calls the Church "his body, the fulness (*pleroma*) of him who is being filled or completed" (Eph. 1: 23), as if Christ were an inclusive personality who cannot reach final fulfilment or development without the Church. The Divine purpose in the Incarnation awaits its crown and culmination in the Church. The body by which Jesus of Nazareth had expressed God's love and will to self-giving was no longer to be seen on the streets of Jerusalem or Capernaum; but now that same Spirit had in the Church an instrument that could exercise His will in wider fields than Palestine. His life flowed into every receptive member of the community as the sap of the vine penetrates to the tips of the remotest branch. His love and mercy and vital energy ever seek outlet, and in the far-branching Christian society He has renewed and extended as it were the touch of His hand, the glance of His eye, the beat of His heart. The Incarnation which began in Galilee had now become amplified and prolonged in the ever-deepening life and outreaching ministries of the Christian Church. Or, to use that other metaphor that Jesus Himself had first used, the Presence of the Living God had now come to dwell in an ever-rising and ever-extending spiritual house, Christ Himself being the corner stone, the apostles the pillars, and believers of every age and time the living stones that are continually taking their place in the cathedral that God goes on building throughout the ages (Eph. 2: 20-21). The seer of the book of Revelation saw no temple because the Lord God and the Lamb were themselves there, the living Presence and final reality.

Called to the Proclamation of the Everlasting Gospel. 1 Cor. 1: 23-32; 1 Cor. 9: 16; Gal. 3: 1-5; Rom. 10: 11-15.

Jesus came preaching and continued preaching even in the final testimony of the Cross; and when His disciples awakened to His living presence, the first impulse was to preach. It was the fine edge of his preaching that brought Stephen to the first martyrdom, and it was the call to "bear my name before the Gentiles, and kings, and the children of Israel" that claimed Paul on the Damascus Road and kept him voyaging over land and sea to the end. The Church owns a New Testament that is the testimony of the first preachers, and she can hardly turn the pages without hearing the woe laid upon her if she preach not the gospel. Christ crucified is good news that will not keep, a fragrance that must cover the earth. Evangelism is an inner necessity laid upon us all as members of Christ's body. To listen to a pulpit voice without that passion is like "drawing in your chair to an oot fire," as a Scots mother phrased it. "The church exists by mission, just as a fire exists by burning."[1]

To the Loving Service of Mankind. Mark 10: 45; Luke 10: 25-37; John 13: 14-15; Rom. 12: 19-21; Col. 3: 12-17; James 1: 22-27.

Jesus came not to be ministered unto, but to minister. He took a towel and girded Himself to the most menial of services. The healing of the sick of body or of mind was the theme of His first manifesto at Nazareth; and such was the pressure of His spirit upon the first disciples that they not only healed the sick but sold all that they had and shared their goods with one another. Take a page from Paul's first contacts in Europe (Acts 16). One of the first fruits he experienced was the Christian grace of hospitality: "If ye have found me faithful to the Lord, come into my house and abide there" (Acts 16: 15). He is moved with pity for the damsel possessed with a spirit of divination and heals her. Immediately Christianity finds itself up against inhuman greed, for she brought her masters much by soothsaying. But the release of a soul comes before private gain. So a new conscience is born in Europe. A runaway slave finds himself in the Apostle's company. The result is a plea that the master will receive back his slave as a son (Philemon). How came to men the first hospitals, the first homes of mercy? Was not the Church a pioneer in education, in agricultural advance? How does the Church make its witness in Africa or China or India? The widow and the orphan, the sick, the depressed classes, the victims of the slave trade, can bear testimony. Social service follows preaching as the right foot follows the left in the process of making headway.

To the Worship of God. Heb. 12: 18-29; Rev. 4, 5.

But Jesus came preaching and ministering because He had first listened to the voice of God in the hour of John's baptism. And He went to that experience in Jordan because He was always about His Father's house and He went to the synagogue as was

[1] Brunner, *The Word and the World.*

His wont on the Sabbath day. It was in the sanctuary that He found His first hearers and proclaimed "This day is this scripture fulfilled in your ears." It was the sadness of His heart that the Temple was a place of merchandise instead of a house of prayer for all nations that moved Him to challenge finally the authorities in Jerusalem—the challenge that brought His arrest and crucifixion.

How much the world owes to the continued service of Christian worship can never be told. Enough that we catch a few fleeting glimpses of its spirit and fragrance. We recall Paul at Philippi, beginning his work in Europe, going out of the city to a quiet place "where prayer was wont to be made" by the riverside. "We sat down, and spake unto the women which resorted thither" (Acts 16: 13). So out of a Jewish prayer-meeting emerged the first Christian service in the Western world. "On the Lord's own day gather yourselves together and break bread and give thanks, first confessing your transgressions that your sacrifice may be pure." So runs the second-century manual, the *Didache*. From Asia Pliny writes to Rome to the Emperor Trajan (*c*. 111 A.D.) of the Christians there in days of persecution: "It was their habit on a fixed day to assemble before daylight and sing by turns a hymn to Christ as a god; and that they bound themselves with an oath, not for any crime, but not to commit theft or robbery or adultery, not to break their word, and not to deny a deposit when demanded. After this was done, their custom was to depart, and meet again to take food, but ordinary and harmless food." Tertullian (*c*.200) gives his testimony: "We are made a body by common religious feeling, unity of discipline, and the bond of hope. We come together in a meeting and assembly, that we may as it were form a troop, and so in prayer to God beset Him with our supplications. . . . We pray also for emperors, for their ministers and for them that are in power, for the welfare of the world, for peace therein, for the delay of the end. We meet together for the reading of the divine writings . . . with the holy words we nourish our faith, lift up our hope, confirm our confidence, and no less make strong our discipline by impressing the precepts. At these meetings we have exhortations, rebukes, and a Divine censorship." We mark the notes of these assemblies—the song of praise, the searching of the heart, prayer for the world's well-being, the hearing of the Word, the making of covenant, the nursing of hope.

In hallowed upper rooms, in the catacombs, in churches mean or stately, in grand cathedrals, on the moorland when persecution came again, in manifold forms, with simplicity often, with gorgeous ritual in other days, the worship of the Church has been maintained down to modern days. Let us but pause to sense the joy of a typical Easter Day, 12th April, 1868. "The day has opened solemnly and religiously. There is a tinkling of bells from the valley: even the fields seem to be breathing forth a canticle of praise. Humanity must have a worship, and, all things considered, is not the Christian worship the best amongst those which have existed on a large scale? The religion of sin, of repentance, and reconciliation—the religion of the new birth and of eternal life—is not a religion to be ashamed of. . . . The Gospel has modified the world and consoled mankind."[2]

The Organ of Christ's Mind. Matt. 11: 29; 1 Cor. 7: 6, 10, 12, 25; Phil. 2: 5; Rom. 12: 5-21.

When disputation arose in the band of disciples, Jesus took a towel and girded Himself; when Judas objected to the costliness of Mary's gift, He replied with a penetration that commanded acceptance. His was a moral authority that was irresistible: even His judges felt His silent power. The Church which is His body knows allegiance to Him alone as its head; therein there can be no divided authority. Yet the Church has its life to live in the human sphere, and its members are beset by contending authorities of state and class and party. Can allegiance ever be divided?

Jesus Himself recognized the human perplexity of living in two worlds, the spiritual and the material. "Render unto Caesar the things that are Caesar's; and unto God the things that are God's." That wise word recognizes that even the imperfect institutions of earth render their service and may therefore claim their dues except where they conflict with a higher demand. The early Church caught that emphasis, and even in the face of a world that was cruel and growingly hostile continued to insist: "Submit yourselves to every ordinance of man for the Lord's

[2] Amiel's *Journal,* p. 140.

sake: whether it be to the king, as supreme; or unto governors . . . Fear God. Honour the king" (1 Peter 2: 13-17; cf. Rom. 13). States in wartime, the totalitarian states at all times, make claims on the whole life of the subject, and the dilemma must often arise of loyalty to Christ or country. There can be but one supreme allegiance, and that is to Christ. But there are dangers to avoid. The individualist may forget that he cannot live to himself: the democratic state faces a situation that his vote and defective citizenship may have helped to create and towards which therefore he has a responsibility. And to cry "conscience" is blasphemy when that word is but a screen for evading the pressure of uncongenial moral demands. He who turns a deaf ear to the urgent cry of the social whole from which he draws his well-being must be very sure that the other voice he hears is that of his one and only master Christ. The precepts of Jesus must not be used as dogmas, shibboleths that will procure an easy crossing of difficult waters. The moral sense would die if it had the simple task of merely quoting the apt saying: it is quickened by the continuous weighing of the issues in the complex situations of modern national and international life. The word of God for the man in Christ must be prayerfully sought until revealed in the individual crisis.

To Share the Life of the Whole. Eph. 4: 1-16; 1 Cor. 16: 1-4.

As we look round upon the Church today we see that she is widely scattered and deeply divided. Her far-flung frontiers are a matter of pride and joy, but her divisions and inner antagonisms are our distress and shame. Differences of interpretation as to the essentials of doctrine and practice have made deep clefts in the history of the past, and national enmities and racial jealousies have often deepened and perpetuated these misunderstandings. The life of the Church is coloured by the character and tradition of the people who constitute her membership, and often her policies become more national than Christian. There have been times when the Church was rather the promoter of her own wars than the peacemaker seeking the unity of all. And within a nation religious suspicion and animosity have often destroyed true national unity.

Yet even in our time we have seen the linkage of the Church

hold across the clefts of war. Pastor Niemöller and the German Confessional Church have more affinity with the Church in England than with the Nazi rulers and policies of their own land. Chinese Christians can hold out hands of reconciliation even to Japanese Christian soldiers whose mission among them is for domination and suppression. The Roman Church continues to function on both sides of the armed camp of Europe. Humane ministries like the Red Cross operate across closed frontiers—and such an organization is essentially a creation of the Spirit of Jesus.

Thus we must recognize that there is a real unity of all Christians in Christ Jesus, a unity that is increasingly able to withstand the strains and tensions of international life. And behind the rivalries of the various communions there is a growing ecumenical movement. After all each branch of the Church asserts its loyalty to the life and creeds of the early undivided Church. Roman and Protestant treasure the same Scripture and the same central Sacraments though they may differ profoundly in their interpretation and practice. Really we are one in Christ Jesus and we each carry our lineage proudly back to the life that sprang up round the Master in Galilee and Jerusalem.

The grand conception of the Church Catholic throughout the world did not come by a federation of local churches. There never was a time when the Church thought of itself as simply a local organization. Had we asked Peter or John or Philip to what association they belonged, they would never have described themselves as members of a Christian synagogue in Jerusalem. "Ye shall sit on twelve thrones judging the twelve tribes of Israel"—that implied that they thought of their membership as in the New Israel, in the new people of God, a community already having existence in the Divine mind and drawing its associates from every nation and every class.

Paul writes "to the church of God which is at Corinth," and goes on to define further: "to them that are sanctified in Christ Jesus, called to be saints, with all that call upon the name of our Lord Jesus Christ in every place." The writer of Hebrews speaks of the general assembly and church of the firstborn. Finest of all descriptions is that of 1 Peter 2: 9: "But ye are an elect race, a royal priesthood, a holy nation, a people for

God's own possession." Elsewhere they are described as "the remnant" forecast by Isaiah, "not from Jews only, but also from Gentiles" (Rom. 9: 24-27); sons of Abraham, Abraham's seed (Gal. 3: 7, 29), the Israel of God (Gal. 6: 16); a colony of heaven (Phil. 3: 20); "sojourners of the Dispersion" (1 Peter 1: 1); "the twelve tribes of the Dispersion" (James 1: 1). Believing themselves to be the inheritors of the proud promises made to Israel, these first converts inevitably thought of their membership in the whole worldwide community, and to them each local church was, like a synagogue, but a microcosm of the whole.

Paul was the great planter of these early churches; and, beginning with a lofty conception of the catholicity and universality of the Church, he was at pains to impart that notion. His great collection scheme, to which he seems to have given some two years of his active life, was probably intended to deliver local churches from a narrow provincialism. It was just possible for an isolated little community set down in Beraea or Colossae to lose touch with the larger community. But Paul saw clearly how the annual contribution to the Temple at Jerusalem made the local Jewish synagogue conscious of its membership in the larger whole, and he coveted for his Christian communities in far-away Macedonia or Galatia a similar reminder of their share in a great worldwide movement pivoting on Jerusalem where their Lord had made His supreme testimony on the Cross. Hence his scheme to link all his churches in a common offering to be made annually to the poor saints at Jerusalem, those who had borne the first shock of the world's hatred of the new faith. For Christians in Corinth to remember the faithful in Jerusalem and for the faithful in Jerusalem to be cheered by the freewill offering of fellow-believers whom they had never seen—that was like a blood stream coursing through the body of Christ, an evidence of life and abundant vitality.[3]

One in Him. 1 Cor. 1: 9-15; Eph. 4: 1-16; 1 Pet. 1: 1-9.

Churches arrogate to themselves the right of determining the conditions of membership: for order and discipline there must be such scrutiny. Yet we must confess ours are but tentative standards, and it is Christ alone who can say who are truly His.

[3] Cf. G. S. Duncan, *St. Paul's Ephesian Ministry,* p. 229ff.

We see the Church visible, but His clearer eye sees also the Church invisible of the saints on high, the redeemed of all ages. And there are those who, like the surprised folk in the parable, have done the Christlike thing unknowingly (Matt. 25: 37ff.). Our boundary lines are like the dividing wall in the old Temple at Jerusalem: they would shut out many who are true children of Abraham saved by a faith and love we cannot discern. It is not for us to unchurch one another, but rather to rejoice to own as fellow-members all who truly love the Lord Jesus Christ and seek the ends of His Kingdom.

The Church that acknowledges one only Lord and insists on a spiritual unity beneath the cleavages in doctrine and practice must ever strive to break down the barriers of division and move towards an incorporating union. A faith that can remove mountains must not suffer frustration before little things. A kingdom that is divided against itself cannot stand. Christ cannot be parcelled out (1 Cor. 1: 13). The forces of unrighteousness have won many victories because the defenders of the faith have been divided among themselves. With a wider tolerance, a larger charity, a deeper love one towards another, and an intenser devotion to Him who is the head and a holier reverence for the eternal purposes of God we would win the battle for unity, and then victory over the world. We can stop short of nothing less than victory, for that means the coming of the Kingdom of God.

The Church offers but the foretaste of that consummation to come. We churchmen are but pilgrims, staff in hand, wending our way up the valleys; sometimes the clouds lift and we have glimpses of the heights beyond. We have in our hearts the dayspring of that larger life, and we sing the songs of the City of God, and in our deeper moments of silent waiting we hear echoes of a grander music. But the glories of the Kingdom in its fullness are not for our time-worn eyes.

VIII. The Ministry.

We believe that God has appointed a Ministry in His Church for the preaching of the Word, the administration of the Sacraments, and the pastoral care of the people.

We believe that the Church has authority to ordain to the Ministry by prayer and the laying on of hands those whom she finds, after due trial, to be called of God thereto.

We believe that, for the due ordering of her life as a society, God has appointed a government in His Church, to be exercised, under Christ the Head, by Ministers and representatives of the people.

So we acknowledge the Holy Ministry appointed by God for the spread of the Gospel and the edification of His Church.

CHAPTER VIII. THE MINISTRY

For the preaching of the Word, the administration of the Sacraments, and the pastoral care of the people.

"And he goeth up into the mountain, and calleth unto him whom he himself would: and they went unto him. And he appointed twelve, that they might be with him, and that he might send them forth to preach, and to have authority to cast out devils" (Mark 3: 13-15 R.V.).

In these words the first Evangelist records the foreshadowing of the Church and, more intimately, of the Christian ministry. This was a step Jesus took when the hostility of the official religious leaders was hardening against Him. Luke insists that it was the sequel to a night spent in prayer with the Father, a decision based on the will of God. The actual choice was made by Jesus Himself: it was no popular election. Jesus had been taking stock of His followers and He had read their hearts and saw there the promise and the potency. The ministry is never a way of life into which any man may casually stumble: His servants are chosen (John 15: 16). The elect ones were first "to be with him." (*a*) Jesus saw from the first that His own personal endeavours must be supplemented and completed by the labours of His fellowmen: He was but the first of the succession of fellow-workers with God in the service of the Kingdom. That is high privilege indeed. (*b*) And more: they were to form the society that on His human side He craved, His intimates to whom He would communicate His thoughts and with whom He would share the sometimes unbearable loneliness in a growingly hostile and misunderstanding world. (*c*) But still more significant was this: "They were to give up their lives to being with him—a thing which not every one could be asked to do."[1] The ministry calls for absolute dedication: it is a task so great and dominant that all earthly ties are cut; it is a life vocation: ordination is not for a few years like a garment to be lightly worn and cast aside when some lesser call or worldly attraction beckons. (*d*) Moreover, this being with Him is an enriching experience. From the beginning men, even enemies,

[1] Menzies, *The Earliest Gospel*, p. 97.

recognized the transforming and renewing power that came to men who had been with Jesus (Acts 4: 13). No one is ready for the work of the ministry who is not much and oft and long in communion with the great Master. Only when that intimacy has deepened into a real understanding and a warm affection is the servant prepared for the next stage. (*e*) The primary practical task is the preaching of the Word. As He was predominantly in the Galilean days the Sower, so is His minister first and foremost a disperser of the Gospel of God with all its germinating power, a Gospel that may encounter much disappointing soil, but the seed that alone can win the spiritual harvest to the hundredfold. (*f*) Further, these ex-fishermen and tax-gatherers were, in spite of all their meekness and humility, to have authority, an authority that came from the knowledge that their words and their powers were not their own, but the manifestation of a God who breaks into human life to cast out demons and all forms of fear and folly. The preacher of the Gospel ought to know that his barque is borne on the wave of an incoming tide—a Kingdom that has never lost movement and is finally irresistible. Strange that Christ's ministers have often been paralyzed by timidities and hesitations, with all the futilities that mock the half-hearted, when all the time they are compassed about with the omnipotent forces of the unseen. Did not Jesus Himself bear testimony as He heard His seventy disciples report on their preaching and witnessing that He watched Satan fall from heaven like lightning? Is there any other authority that can cast the devil from his place of pride?

The earliest Christian mission when Jesus sent out His disciples two by two found its climax in the supper by the lakeside. It was the first ingathering from the work of His "ministers." In spite of the amazing message they had carried abroad and the tumultuous response they saw in that expectant five thousand, their faith burned strangely low. Five barley loaves and two fishes! What are these among so many (John 6: 9)? Their unbelieving hearts were rebuked, and by that mystic sacrament so uplifted that with the excited throng they wanted there and then to crown Him king. Jesus had to separate them from the crowd (Mark 6: 45), and sent them into the disillusioning storm-tossed lake before they came together again and knew each other in the real world. That first sacrament had tested and challenged His "ministers." Then came that solemn hour under the deepening shadow of the Cross when the table was spread and He sat down with the Twelve. "With desire I have desired to eat this passover with you before I suffer" (Luke 22: 15). The Master had willed this supper and His eyes were fixed on them with affectionate longing. One of their own number who dipped with Him and with them in the dish went out, "and it was night." Could they ever forget that lingering shadow on their table? Again the sacrament tested and challenged His ministers. But it did more: it sent a great shaft of light forward into the darkness: "I will not drink henceforth of this fruit of the vine, until that day when I drink it new *with you* in my Father's kingdom" (Matt. 26: 29). He made these plain men realize that the hope of the new covenant focalized on them. They had made a tryst with Him in the eternal mansions. And they would not come there alone: He had set a rainbow of promise over their faith and labours: "Many shall come from the east and the west, and shall sit down with Abraham, and Isaac, and Jacob" (Matt. 8: 11).

The Supper Discourses in John elaborate and confirm the inexhaustible legacy our Lord passed on to His ministers, too rich an inheritance for weak men to carry did we not have the assurance, "Ye have not chosen me, but I have chosen you, and ordained you, that ye should go and bring forth fruit, and that your fruit should remain" (John 15: 16).

No marvel that the Supper has ever been an occasion when His believing folk are delivered from their sad communications and find their hearts begin to burn within them; for He tarries with us there, and it is in the breaking of bread that our eyes are opened and we come to know Him (Luke 24: 13ff.). His ministers must ever return to the Upper Room; for surely it was there, when the door of the world's hostility was shut, that He spoke Peace to their souls (John 20: 19ff.). There too first came to His ministers the Holy Spirit and authority to release men from the burden of sin: "whose soever sins ye forgive, they are forgiven unto them; whose soever sins ye retain, they are retained." That is the place where a Thomas finds his doubts vanish away before the print of the nails and there breaks forth the full confession: "My Lord and my God." Surely above all His ministers have a charge and a responsibility in the perpetuation of the tradition of the Upper Room.

Jesus Himself had the pastoral heart. "When he saw the multitudes, he was moved with compassion on them, because they fainted, and were scattered abroad, as sheep having no shepherd" (Matt. 9: 36). Again He assures us and exhorts us: "The harvest truly is plenteous, but the labourers are few; pray ye therefore the Lord of the harvest, that he will send forth labourers into his harvest" (37f.). His mission as defined at Nazareth was to bring release to the poor and the oppressed; His active ministry was an unresting concern for individual souls, a lingering often over those the world would count insignificant, and a peculiar care of the sinner and the outcast. He lived out day by day His own portrayal of the Good Shepherd. The Twelve He bore very close to His heart. He included them all in the words of Peter: "Simon, Simon, behold, Satan hath desired to have you (plural), that he may sift you as wheat." For the one who needed most He prayed specially: "But I have prayed for thee that thy faith fail not" (Luke 22: 31-32). Among the Resurrection scenes stands out that heart-searching encounter between the repentant Peter and his living Lord. Against the background of the miraculous draught of fishes, symbolic of that sea harvest of men that was to be, and beside the fire that had prepared the simple sacrament of bread and fish, there comes that probing of the soul that befits every minister of the Master: "Lovest thou me?" It is only when our Lord has pushed past lightly spoken first answers, past hesitations and comparisons and evasions, that there is found the essential ground of sincerity on which alone the work of the ministry can rest. Then and only then is the commission given: "Feed my sheep."

It is curiously interesting to pause for a moment over the metaphors that Jesus used in relation to the work of the minister. The fisherman's task is one to be carried on in difficult waters often and under fickle conditions: there are times and seasons when we cast in vain. Such too is the lot of the sower. The preacher's task of wooing and winning men is in the realm of the unpredictable. There is here something that counts more than the human factor: results depend on movements we do not initiate and control; but we can always cast out the nets, scatter wide the seed. But the other task of feeding the flock is a steady unceasing one. Here there is the call for all our human powers of foresight, constancy, unresting affectionate daily and hourly care. There is the closest of ties between the Good Shepherd and His sheep: He knows the "blackface" and the "crooked horn"; utter dependence and affection and individual interest make a most intimate bond between pastor and people. But it has its perils like the fisherman's, and even the laying down of life (John 10: 15). Perhaps we read too much into these metaphors. But it is well to remember that, while it may not be in the preacher to win men, it is at least much more in his human field of duty and consecration to hold and cheer and tend those who have been won.

When the book of Acts unrolls the opening chapters in the story of the Church, the first Christian assembly hear the proclamation of the Word (2: 14). God had shaken all souls there, and Peter rose to declare the meaning thereof. The *Word* had its first triumphs then at the hands of the chosen apostles. And the secret of their sustained power in that life of witness was the house-gathering when they recalled their Lord in the *breaking of the bread* (2: 42). And how soon the *care of the flock* emerges as a responsibility outgrowing already the power of the Twelve: they have to enlarge the number of ministers and appoint seven men (Acts 6: 5).

The Epistles of the Apostle Paul mirror the early Church in operation. His most urgent care is always his Gospel with the exposition of doctrine that that involves: the *Word* is primary. But each letter moves on to practical exhortation where the missionary shows himself a shepherd of the flock: the *pastoral care* of the people is ever on his heart. Not as often as we might expect does he deal with the *Sacraments*. But that their proper adminstration weighs on his soul is clear from the solemn character of the charge he laid upon the Corinthians (1 Cor. 11: 23ff.). It is after the fashion he had received from the Lord that he gives direction. Clearly he feels a charge laid upon him here, an inescapable obligation towards the right and proper administration of the Holy Supper. One other indication of the immense concern he has for that act is hidden from the casual reader. But it lies beneath the historic rebuke that Paul delivered to Peter (Gal. 2: 11). When Peter withdrew from eating with Gentile Christians because of scruples born of the Jewish law, he was making it impossible for Jewish and Gentile Christians to meet at a common Lord's Table. As the celebration of the Supper was associated with a common meal, there could be no one-minded society where one half feared to eat what the others might put on the table. Only because he sensed that this was dividing the Lord's body did the Apostle rebuke publicly his brother in the service. Clearly anything that brought division to the holy Sacrament was anathema to the sensitive minister of Christ. This then is a measure of his care for the right administration of the Supper.

A Ministry. Mark 10: 42-45.

The ministry has a stamp upon it that marks it off from all other vocations. Jesus by His own words and acts defines its unique character. He took a towel and girded Himself and washed His disciples' feet: "I have given you an example, that ye should also do as I have done to you" (John 13: 15). That incident probably crowns the contention of which Luke tells us(22: 24) as to which of the disciples was to be accounted the greatest. "The kings of the Gentiles have lordship over them; and they that have authority over them are called benefactors. But ye shall not be so: but he that is the greater among you, let him become as the younger; and he that is chief, as he that doth serve." The passion to govern has no place in the Christian minister: his is the will to serve. "The Son of Man came not to be ministered unto, but to minister." The only pre-eminence His servants should covet is that in which the verse culminates: "to give his life a ransom for many." Place-hunting, the worldly scramble for office and distinction, are ruled out of the Christian circle. Yet that does not imply any dead level. In the company of the Twelve even Jesus had His peculiar intimates, those who came nearest to Him because they had the insight, and those who led because they had the talent to lead. But the characteristic type of pre-eminence is willingness to "spend and be spent" in the service of mankind.

Such willing service claims nevertheless its own homage and reward. There is no greater champion of the rights of that homage than the Apostle Paul. "We beseech you, brethren, to know (*i.e.* respect) them that labour among you . . . and to esteem them exceeding highly in love for their work's sake" (1 Thess. 5: 12). Members of the Church are to recognize the authority of those who have set themselves to the service of the saints and of everyone who shares in the work and in its toilsomeness (1 Cor. 16: 15). Gal. 6: 6 declares that there is an obligation to share life's good gifts with the preacher of the Word. That is sowing to the Spirit and reaps eternal life. First Peter 5: 1ff., after defining the obligation of true shepherds of the flock of God (not to hold off till pressed into the service, not to allow mercenary motives to enter in, and not to be domineering), appeals to the younger members to reciprocate by due acceptance of the authority of the elders. Indeed all must put on "the apron of humility."

Called of God. Gal. 1: 1, 15-16; 1 Cor. 12; Eph. 4: 11-16.

The primal form of ministry in the early Church did not spring from human contriving, but from divine inspiration. Christ was manifestly alive in the Church: His body was vibrant with His quickening spirit. Each individual life was open to the inflow of the divine, and each had his gift, or *charisma*. "There are diversities of gifts, but the same Spirit," as Paul expressed it (1 Cor. 12: 4). Some had practical gifts and some had spiritual, and all had their function in the living organism as our members have in the human body. It had been foretold that in the age of the Messiah there would be an outpouring of the Spirit: as Joel had it and Peter affirmed it, "Your sons and your daughters shall prophesy, and your young men shall see visions, and your old men shall dream dreams" (Acts 2: 15ff.). It was not surprising that in Palestine with its noble prophetic tradition there should be such a rebirth. But in Hellenic and Roman lands as well, wherever the Christian message took root, the wonder of the good news broke down the barriers of reserve, and lives became athrob with a creative power. The Living Christ seemed to have an immediacy of touch with His own, and personalities overflowed with a richness of life not explicable in human terms.

The prophetic power marked three different classes—apostles, prophets, and teachers (1 Cor. 12: 4ff.). Their gift was the supreme one, that of the Word, the direct product of the Spirit, never dependent on any ecclesiastical form. The Word was the revelation of the mind of God, its interpretation and application in the concrete situations of experience. It was a return to that directness of divine guidance which the prophets of the Old Testament had known in "Thus saith the Lord." Only now it was the living spirit of the Risen Christ that was the interpreter of the mind of God.

The *apostles* were first those disciples Jesus Himself chose and sent out; then Matthias, substitute for Judas; Paul, called by the Risen Christ; others such as Barnabas and Silas, the name being more loosely used as time went on. The kernel idea was that they were "sent out," "under commission," lifted from the common ties and set apart for a lifetime, "not from men, neither through man, but through Jesus Christ" (Gal. 1: 1), for the preaching of the Word. Their field was the world, wherever the Spirit might call them to preach and persuade men to hear. Typical was Paul, the one who recognized no frontiers, who never intruded on the sphere of another man, but was ever pressing on that every human being should hear the Word that saved. Inevitably he was organizer and teacher as well as the inspired prophet declaring the mind of God and the preacher of the Gospel. But primarily he was the bearer of the Word. He ever kept first things first. His example in setting the ministry of the Word in the chief place can be ignored by no living Church. But there were consequences of his activity: he was, *e.g.,* the unifying force behind all the churches he created. In fact he showed by his collection scheme that churches needed to be linked together in practical ways as in spiritual. The Apostle was thus the creative and pioneer force *par excellence.*

But there were also the *prophets,* men who had the gift of the Word and yet were called not so often to missionary activity, but rather to the edification of the local community. The power-house of the Church is its worship service, and there for the praise and the reading of the Word was needed the man with the gift of exposition and unction, one who could so utter the divine mind as to build up and enrich and encourage his brethren in the faith and by prayer lead into the divine presence. The acts of God in the ministry, death, and resurrection of Jesus had not only to be told, but to be brought to bear meaningfully on the tragic human situation. The words of Jesus had to be pondered and interpreted in new phases of our manifold experience. The prophet was a man who must have reflected much. But also he had his visions and revelations. Such a man naturally led in worship and in the supreme act of the Eucharist, where he could be trusted to transcend the normal forms and lead in inspired prayer (*Didache,* 10: 7). The Spirit is no respecter of persons, and, in spite of the conservatism of tradition, the Church learned to welcome women as well as men among the prophets (Acts 21: 9). The prophet need hold no office: his prestige rested on his gift. In fact, so great homage was paid to this spiritual quality that there was the danger of the prophet turning autocrat and unduly affecting discipline, administration, and election to office. Wandering prophets became a problem later in the Church, and tests had to be applied by local leaders to distinguish the genuine from the spurious: "Not every one that speaketh in the spirit is a prophet, but only if he have the ways of the Lord" (*Didache,* 11: 8). If a prophet uses his gift to order a meal at will or to demand money, he is a charlatan. "No man speaking in the Spirit of God saith Jesus is anathema" (1 Cor. 12: 3 R.V.)—so counsels Paul, wise as he is spiritual.

A third order were the *teachers,* men who excelled in knowledge, as of the words of Jesus and the truths of God, and had the gift of teaching catechumens. Their opportunity lay in the local church, where new members who came in would need instruction. There never has been a time in the Christian Church when we could leave everything to the inspired ecstatic. Always there is a body of sifted knowledge and experience that has to be passed on. Doctrine has to be taught and explained. The rites of the Church have to be interpreted. The story of Revelation in Israel, as in the life and death of the Master, has to be re-taught to each generation, not merely recited, but set forth in its meaning and power.

There is a permanent value for the Church of today in this free untrammelled movement of the Spirit of God. We *all* may see the heavens opened and the angels of God ascending and descending upon the Son of Man. There stands open before each man an unobstructed path to the Throne of Grace. The Divine Presence is not the prerogative of the few. There is a sense in which all true believers are prophets and priests. Certainly that Church is strangely untrue to the Apostolic Church in which channels of communication with the divine are reserved for the officials and accredited clergy. The Reformation Church set great store by the priesthood of all believers, and so must any living Church today.

After Due Trial.

This dependence on the movement of the Spirit was all the more complete in the early Church because there was a vivid expectation that any day a supernatural order would descend upon men with the second advent of their Lord. It was only as that lively hope faded into the further distance that thought settled down to a long term organization. Yet even throughout this ardent first period there were steadying influences—the conservatism in human nature and the testing process of actual experience. Jews passing into the Christian ecclesia carried with them a liking for the familiar moulds into which their lives had been cast under the law. That life was patriarchal in type, society finding its centre in the head of the household, or in such a pillar man as a king or high priest, and all authority was derived from him. Thus primacy in authority fell to the disciples who had been chosen by the Master Himself. And when they sought to fill the blank caused by the desertion of Judas, they looked for one "of these men which have companied with us all the time that the Lord Jesus went in and out among us, beginning from the baptism of John, unto that same day that he was received up from among us, of these must one become a witness with us of his resurrection" (Acts 1: 21-22). In this way the revelation of the Spirit was balanced always by practical knowledge of the tradition and that discipline that Jesus had recognized in those "who continued with me in my temptations" (Luke 22: 28). Before they depended on the Spirit in the casting of lots they had made a realistic sifting out of men, *e.g.*, Joseph and Matthias. So, as Jewish practice in the synagogue set high value on the testing of the years that makes a man an elder, or presbyter, so the Christian society looked up to its seniors, the elders (i.e. presbyters). Thus emerged perhaps the first officials in the local group.

By Prayer and the Laying on of Hands.

When the original disciples found themselves no longer able to give adequate care to the interests of the growing community, they chose the seven men, usually called deacons, though that name is not given in Acts 6. Here appears the prototype for ordination to the Christian ministry: "when they had prayed, they laid their hands on them" (6: 6). This laying on of hands was a case of Jewish procedure (*e.g.*, at the setting apart of a Rabbi) adopted in the New Israel; but it was a ritual found in many ages and countries. Perpetuating the ancient conception of power or responsibility passing from person to person by contact, it was conjoined with prayer, showing that faith really rested in the unseen transmission of spiritual potency from on high. This became the recognized form in the life of the Church, accompanied often by fasting as well as by prayer (cf. Acts 13: 3). Society needs a mode of making visible to its membership the delegation to office or responsibility. The supreme gift of the Word was not regarded as passed on in this rite.[2] A man could discern the Word: it was self-authenticating. But other forms of service, like the practical duties of the seven, were conferred by ordination. Thus the ordination of a minister today carries us back in imagination to the first days of high adventure when the Mother Church at Antioch was sending out Paul and Barnabas to their historic missionary journey.

For the Due Ordering of Her Life. 1 Tim. 3-5; 2 Tim. 2: 14-26; 2 Tim. 4: 1-6; Titus; 3 John.

No society can long sustain its existence without developing some forms of organization. Even the Spirit-filled Church had need of the guidance of grave and experienced men; for inspiration sometimes burns low, and some means must be provided for bridging periods of dullness and apathy. The Jerusalem Church had in the circle of the apostles a governing body which drew its prestige from their direct association with Jesus. Peter was at first the natural leader and, later on, we find James the Lord's brother the accepted head of the Church, perhaps because he had more obvious administrative gifts than the impetuous Peter, perhaps because in ancient society blood-relationship to the Master gave him an undisputed priority. As Paul passes back through South Galatia on his first missionary journey "confirming the souls of the disciples, exhorting them to continue in the faith" (Acts 14: 22ff.), he does not leave before "they had appointed for them *elders* in every church." By the time he is writing from prison to his beloved Philippians he names specially *bishops* and *deacons* (1: 1). The difficulties that arose in a church like Corinth when emissaries came along claiming to be super-apostles (2 Cor. 11) showed the need for strong local leadership: the missionary founder could not always be at hand to bring order out of a chaos of parties (1 Cor. 1: 10). A great Church movement like the collection for the poor saints in Jerusalem needed officers to arrange

[2] Bartlet and Carlyle, *Christianity in History,* p. 294.

it and guarantee its financial soundness (1 Cor. 16). The Pastoral Epistles are evidence of the growing importance of leaders of competence and probity.

It is impossible to pronounce definitely on the forms of government that arose in the Church. Local circumstances probably called for different organizations. But the Jewish synagogue was an obvious model to follow, and the earliest local government was probably through a council or synod of *elders,* otherwise called presbyters. These evidently were chosen and set apart by the whole Christian community: in the choice the influence of a missionary like Paul, if present, or of an outstanding prophet would count. "Let those elders who preside well be deemed worthy of double honour, especially those who labour in word and teaching" (1 Tim. 5: 17). Thus elders might vary in the function they discharged in the Church: some would excel in the leading of worship, some in the conduct of business.

No clear distinction emerges between the elder and the *bishop* (*episcopos*) of earliest times. "In the New Testament," wrote Dr. Hort,[3] "the word *episcopos* mainly, if not always, is *not* a title, but a description of the Elder's function." Paul, addressing the elders of the Church of Ephesus (Acts 20: 17), calls them bishops (v. 28): "Take heed unto yourselves, and to all the flock, in the which the Holy Ghost hath made you bishops, to feed the church of God." These bishops were to be true teachers. At other times they might be leaders of worship and generally take a position such as was held by the priests of the Old Testament Church (1 *Clement* 44, 4). The government of a whole area by one supreme bishop was a gradual development. The dominant position of James at Jerusalem did not influence the Church at large as immediately as we might expect. Quite clearly local churches enjoyed a real measure of freedom to develop according to the situation and necessities of the case. Distance and circumstances divided them from one another, and the practice of an Ephesus in the Asiatic sphere might differ widely from the Roman. The living spirit and no dead hand of conservatism held control. From a letter of Polycarp to the Philippians we learn that as late as A.D. 120 a college of presbyters and deacons still functioned there in Macedonia, and even in Rome apparently the same

[3] *The Christian Ecclesia,* p. 228ff.

system held.[4] The rule of the one bishop really came about in the Church generally to meet the need for the control of heresy. In the cities where Greek culture flourished and Greek thought coursed freely there was a danger of losing the Gospel in a flood of speculation. In the interests of order and uniformity the Church had to make clear its essential truth. A canon of scriptures was evolved and the outlines of a creed began to be formulated. As part of this same process the authority of one over-ruling bishop was found the most effective means of securing unity of discipline, practice, and belief. His prestige was derived from no theory of an unbroken and exclusive succession from the apostles. The theory of apostolic succession is a later idea barely supported by the facts. Rather the bishop was the visible symbol and organ of the unity of the Church and as such the chosen of God.[5]

Thus no modern church can claim by appeal to the apostolic age that it has any greater authority for its orders than any other. Dr. B. H. Streeter summed up his investigation into the facts in these words:[6] "Among these, the Episcopalian, the Presbyterian, and the Independent can each discover the prototype of the system to which he himself adheres. . . . Indeed, if my hypothesis is correct, then, in the classic words of *Alice in Wonderland,* 'Everyone has won, and all shall have prizes'."

What becomes clear from the history of the first Christian centuries is that God has guided His Church to many forms and blessed each one as it met the peculiar need which called it into being. The marvel lies in the diversity and adaptability of the organ of the Spirit. The Church declares her vitality in the way she has chosen her instruments in each crisis, and today by seeking spirituality as well as unity in her manifold diversity she will best declare her faithfulness to her one Lord and Master.

[4] Johannes Weiss, *The History of Primitive Christianity,* p. 818ff.
[5] Bartlet and Carlyle, *Christianity in History,* p. 306.
[6] *The Primitive Church,* p. ix.

IX. The Holy Scriptures.

We believe that the great moments of God's revelation and communication of Himself to men are recorded and interpreted in the Scriptures of the Old and New Testament.

We believe that, while God uttered His Word to man in many portions progressively, the whole is sufficient to declare His mind and will for our salvation. To Israel He made Himself known as a holy and righteous God and a Saviour; the fullness of truth and grace came by Jesus Christ. The writings were collected and preserved by the Church.

We believe that the theme of all Holy Scripture is the redemptive purpose and working of God, and that herein lies its unity.

We believe that in Holy Scripture God claims the complete allegiance of our mind and heart; that the full persuasion of the truth and authority of the Word of God contained in the Scripture is the work of the Holy Spirit in our hearts; that, using Holy Scripture, the Spirit takes of the things of Christ and shows them unto us for our spiritual nourishment and growth in grace.

So we acknowledge in Holy Scripture the true witness to God's Word and the sure guide to Christian faith and conduct.

CHAPTER IX. THE HOLY SCRIPTURES

Revelation. Jer. 1: 9; Gal. 4: 9; Phil. 3: 12.

As I look out from my window I see before me a lovely college quadrangle with lawn and scattered trees. The central building, Victoria College, carries the mind back past the present structure to an older one, a hundred years old and more, which spells the name pioneers. It is inseparably associated with the toil and struggles of the men and women who came to this land on a voyage of discovery—seeking new homes. They sought and found. They cleared the forests, cast in the seed, and their successors dug deep in the earth and discovered untold mineral wealth. From the days of Christopher Columbus onwards this whole continent has had *discovery* as its incentive and watchword: onwards to the Pacific, northwards to the Arctic, downwards into the earth in quest of coal, iron, silver, gold, oil. It has been an epic of human endeavour, personal venture. No wonder such a land has preached the gospel of strenuousness, the religion of humanism. Discovery is a human word: it emphasizes the wealth and knowledge that man goes after.

But there is a knowledge that we do not go after, that presses in upon us. As I so reflect the air grows strangely heavy around me. Thoughts refuse to come. There is a vague feeling of discomfort. There comes an unnatural darkness, then bursts of choppy wind swirl up the leaves. Now the explanation of it all —the thunder rolls and the lightning flashes. The storm had been making me gradually aware of its imminence; there came a sense of something after which I had not gone out in search: there was an invasion of my consciousness from without. So movements stir around my personal world, events gather over my head, experiences culminate in a crisis, and I realize that in the complex God has declared His will for me in a command unsought and unsuspected.

Then my eye falls upon a photograph of a friend of forty years' standing. There he is looking down at me and his presence seems to fill the room. I think away back over the years in school, in college, on summer holidays in long conversations as we walked across the sands or along the winding roads. And the impression is one of a great indebtedness—a thousand lessons I have learned from him all these years. Of course I sought his company and tried to probe his mind. But chiefly I am aware of a steady *receiving,* gathering, harvesting, not of knowledge only, but much more of friendship, of help, of inspiration, comfort, and all the graces that lie in personality to give. There was always something more to learn. A person may be discovered so far by probing; but from the depths of his nature come the imperishable things—and these we get by his *self-revelation.* "Revelation" is a richer word than "discovery." It tells of more than lands to be settled, more than mineral wealth to be dug up, more than knowledge and abstract truth to be received by the mind. Revelation tells of another personality reaching out towards me, anticipating my needs and forestalling my thoughts, strengthening my will, giving of the manifold gifts of friendship, solace, hope and love.

In the sphere of religion we have often misused the word "discovery." We have pictured the great prophetic souls going out and finding the truth of God in experience. But that is never their way of speaking. As the lamp of God burned in the Temple and Samuel was laid down to sleep, the voice came to him as it had come to Abraham and to Moses. "The Lord took me as I followed the flock," said Amos (7: 15). "Before thou camest forth out of the womb I sanctified thee, and I ordained thee": so Jeremiah (1: 5) assures us he was called. The Psalmists bear witness to this divine initiative: "O Lord, thou hast searched me, and known me . . . Thou understandest my thought afar off. Thou compassest my path and my lying down. . . . Thou hast beset me behind and before, and laid thine hand upon me" (Ps. 139: 1-5).

It is doubtful indeed if "discovery" with its emphasis on human achievement is ever rightly used. When Columbus set out on his historic voyage, was it not because forces and influences planted in his mind *drew* him and *persuaded* him? Our pioneers in this new land had hardly built their log house and cleared their little strip of forest before they were kneeling down to thank God for *leading* them to that goodly land; and they did not rest content till the new settlement had its house of God in the midst: they knew their efforts were not their own. Before men found silver in the earth, before Newton discovered the law of gravitation, before the scientist discovered the secret of nature in the laboratory, before Euclid worked out his propositions, the divine mind had been there. But if we do make a distinction, it is clear that impersonal things are discovered and personal beings reveal themselves. God is personal, and it is the testimony of Scripture that He has ever been revealing Himself. We are made in His likeness, fashioned for fellowship with Him; and so, if our hearts are open, we may receive His communications. Some would say that since the Fall our natures have been so totally corrupt that we are unable to receive the Divine Word: only by miracle, by sheer supernaturalism, can revelation come; there is no way from man to God, but only a way from God to man. But others will hold with the prologue of the Fourth Gospel that there is a light that lighteneth every man: even the prodigal in the far country remains a son of God who has but to come to himself. At least we have the assurance that God is a self-revealing God, and by His grace His Word has ever been reaching out and finding men, convicting them of sin, and calling them into communion with Himself. To this great truth the Scriptures of the Old and New Testaments bear witness.

Communication of Himself. John 1: 14-18.

What is communicated by God to man? To answer that let us reflect on the unveiling of friend to friend. What does a friend convey to us? A mother teaches us to walk, to speak, to give names to this object and that, but is that all? Is it not the giving day by day of herself? Even in the realm of knowledge the teacher whose business it is to instruct—to convey knowledge of mathematics, literature, history—has failed if he has not given something more: the inspiration of his personality, the uplift of his example, the effect of a character and a life that means more than all his knowledge. So in Scripture we find that what God offered to man was not just the truth of His righteousness or the wonder of His majesty. It was that: one aspect of reality came home to this prophet and another to that—to Amos His righteousness and to Hosea His love—but it was never the truth by itself. It was God Himself speaking, the Presence behind the word which was invading the life. What God communicates is never less than Himself, and it is only our sinfulness and obtuseness that keeps us from grasping that gift in its completeness. Love and the understanding that comes with the years open the secrets of the soul, and knowledge of persons grows from more to more. The climax of fellowship is complete self-giving, and as with the human so with the divine fellowship: God reveals *Himself,* in the rigour of His righteous will, in the richness of His grace, in the depth of His love.

Great Moments. John 12: 27-32; 1 Cor. 2: 1-2.

If again we may compare lofty divine realities to the human, we must expect that this self-revelation of God will have its great moments. In intercourse between persons we have encounters that linger in the memory for ever because in the intimacy of some solemn hour the barriers of reserve were let down and we were permitted to see our friend in a fresh light, in some unsuspected richness of character. Perhaps it was some sorrow that came to us, some need of comfort, some touch of self-pity. And our great-hearted friend drew aside the veil and told us of an episode in his own life that had left a scar; then we knew him in a tenderness we had never suspected. We felt rebuked, ashamed, grief-stricken; and somehow in the mutual sharing we touched a deeper depth of understanding than ever before. After such moving contacts a friend is treasured as a richer possession. So in the divine intercourse there have been glowing points, splendid hours when God showed His name and nature in its strength or compassion. When God made solemn covenant with His people on Sinai, when He confronted Isaiah in the Temple, when He claimed Jeremiah, these were days luminous and awesome. But chiefly in the coming to earth of Jesus Christ, in His life, death, and resurrection, the glory of the Lord shone forth upon man: these are supremely the great moment of His self-revelation.

His Word Only in Scripture? Phil 4: 8-9.

Has God revealed His presence elsewhere than in Scripture? Has He not disclosed Himself in nature and in other faiths? Is there not a general revelation to men in the physical world and in history as well as the special revelation that all Christians know and recognize?

Paul, according to Acts 14: 17, declares that God has not left Himself without a witness "in that he did good, and gave us rain from heaven, and fruitful seasons, filling our hearts with food and gladness." In the many-templed Athens he saw the upsurge of the divine in the reaching after an unknown God: He who gave life and breath and all things is not far from any one of His creatures. He reminded the Romans that the pagan world had evidence of His presence: in the work of His hands His everlasting power and divine nature shone before human eyes from the beginning. They have a law of conscience written in their hearts (Rom. 1: 20ff., 2: 12ff.). Following that line of thought (cf. Heb. 1: 1), we have been ready in these latter days to recognize in the faith of the nations, in Buddhism, in Confucianism, in Hinduism, and in other religions the self-disclosure in imperfect forms of the living and true God, foreshadowings of the perfect revelation in Christ Jesus—an "antechamber" of faith. But we have failed to realize with Paul that these ethnic faiths have often been the futile speculations of darkened minds, evidence of the pride and purblindness of men, perversions that have shut out the glory of God: religious systems have often been a defence mechanism against the will of God rather than a revelation of it. Is it not true that Jesus Himself, in spite of all His largeness of heart, had to condemn in blistering terms the pretensions of Pharisee and Sadducee, that the early Church had to definitely contend with and break away from law and Temple that it might assert its freedom and spirituality? So may it not be that we have as Christians the obligation to present, not appreciation and commendation, but judgment and condemnation of what are half-truths and deceitful make-believe in contrast to the truth and reality of the Gospel? Is that not to be true to the "One who cleanses and consecrates . . . human and national heritages and aspirations and then gives them back . . . infinitely enriched"?[1] If in Christ God did something for men that was utterly unique, there cannot be many ways to salvation, but only one.

As for the seeing of God in nature, how much of that is a sentimental ecstasy over gorgeous colouring of sunrise and sunset, an emotional upsurge that is more beautiful than deep? God's world is terrible as it is lovely, nature is "red in tooth and

[1] Dr. Nicol Macnicol, *International Review of Missions,* July, 1938.

claw," and carries in her lap typhoons as well as summer breezes, hissing serpents as well as blue birds. He is nearer God who has looked with awe and horror into the mystery of things, and has had to fight his way to a faith that can see the hand of God in all that fascinating darkness. Only he who has grasped God in a Gethsemane of sorrow and come to walk with Mary in a garden of Resurrection is able to see with clear eyes the God who made the light and shade of the universe. The lilies of the field had glory in the eyes of Jesus because He knew in a more intimate context the Father in heaven. To those who have come to know the self-disclosure of God in the Cross of Calvary nature is not merely beautiful, but sacramental. Experience in a field beyond beauty makes even loveliness more meaningful. How much more grand the sunset to a man who has seen its soft light falling on the mystery of a crucified life passing out into peace at last! How much more radiant the sunrise to a Peter who, having toiled all night and caught nothing, sees the outline of a figure on the shore!

> Birds with gladder songs o'erflow,
> Flowers with deeper beauties shine,
> Since I know, as now I know,
> I am His, and He is mine.

In Many Portions Progressively. Heb. 1: 1-5.

The Old Testament is the record of an ever-enlarging, ever-deepening knowledge of God. The God who walks familiarly in the Garden of Eden is very different in aspect from the terrible God of Mount Sinai, or the God who contends with Jeremiah. There is a great stretch of experience between the demand that Agag be hewed in pieces before the Lord and the call to the Servant of the Lord to suffer vicariously for sin. The God who begins as the protector of a single nation comes to be known as the righteous Jehovah who must be Lord of all the peoples. The jealous and avenging God of Nahum who devours the bloody city with fire and sword and canker-worm is one aspect of truth; very different is the graciousness revealed to Jonah: "Should not I spare Nineveh, that great city, wherein are more than sixscore thousand persons that cannot discern between their right hand and their left hand; and also much cattle?" (Jon. 4: 11). God uttered His word in portions and progressively. There were times when people needed a stern Elijah as God's spokesman, times when the consolation of an Isaiah were opportune. There were dissolute times that needed the menacing Day of the Lord of an Amos, times when the hard-pressed people were cheered by the vision of the Son of Man of Daniel. Men are not able to receive the full glory of God; the brightness of the light must sometimes be softened and dimmed.

The Barthian school of theologians are concerned to let the specifically New Testament revelation shine out in all its splendour; that might seem to take from the glory of the Old Testament revelation. They recognize that God was there in the life of ancient Israel: the consuming fire passed that way and the evidence remains. "The law is the compression of divine revelation left behind in time, in history, and in the lives of men: it is a heap of clinkers marking a fiery miracle which has taken place, a burnt out crater disclosing the place where God has spoken."[2] All revelation, they maintain, must be read in the light of the resurrection of Jesus Christ, when the Eternal decisively broke through into time. Is not that precisely how the Old Testament must be viewed? The Jew reads the Old Testament, and for him it is supreme, the changeless standard. Our eyes must regard it differently: it is to us the avenue of torches that casts the light on the face of Jesus Christ. The Old Testament finds its completion in the New. The ten words given on Sinai are the virile sturdy stem from which spring the flowers of the Beatitudes. The firm lines of the law are the rude sketch over which the artist paints in the finished picture: it is the Gospel that speaks in soft yet strong colours. The righteousness which punishes for three transgressions and for four is but prelude to the love which forgives seventy times seven times. The Day of the Lord that brings vengeance upon the enemies of Israel gives place to a judgment that separates the sheep from the goats, not on lines of nationality, but on principles of humanity. The restored kingdom of Israel broadens its gates to receive many from the East and the West to sit down with Jacob. Thus did Israel come to know throughout the years of travail God the Holy and the Righteous; but grace and truth came by Jesus Christ. To approach the Holy God of the Old Testament there were proprieties and conditions to be observed as before an awesome Presence, and there were a

[2] Barth, *Romans*, p. 65, Eng. tr.

contractual element and naturalistic limitations attaching to the law of the Righteous One. But with the coming of the Gospel the barriers were down: God was seen as coming out after His own, a Father calling His sons one by one into an intimate and absorbing fellowship.

Holy Scripture. Is. 55: 10-13; 2 Tim. 3: 15-17; 2 Tim. 4: 13.

But both Old and New Testaments have one dominating hope and theme—salvation. No one can read the Psalms without realizing that the saints of the Old Testament were lifted out of earth's sin and failure and found peace and pardon with a forgiving God. His will might lay heavy tasks upon them, but they delighted to do His law. The New Testament is lyrical with a sense of an astonishing deliverance: a graciousness men had not deserved had thrown open the prison doors and led the way to higher levels of existence; those who have been to gaze on Calvary have a new song to sing. That truth that thus waxed from dim to glorious light throughout the generations lies before us in the Scriptures. It is testimony to, and experience of, the mind and character of God—His Majesty, Holiness, Justice, Patience, Long-suffering. It is the record of His will for righteousness among men and nations—a will that steadily shines more clear and directs itself inexorably towards the good of men. It presents itself to us as the way of salvation. We see there that the specific demands of God must vary: a Gideon has a different task from a Paul, but both have a saving faith. The path is dark for the Psalmist many a time; to a John it is bathed in light; but it is the same mercy that greets both at the end of the journey. Jonah flees to Tarshish, and the rich young ruler goes sorrowfully away from Jesus; but the same pursuing love and judgment hang over their decisions. Throughout the chequered story of the saints there are experiences that gladden and testings that chastise, encounters that uplift and calamities that threaten; but the wisdom from above mingles the bitter and the sweet and proffers the cup of salvation. Surely there we too who run may read the mind and the will of God and be guided in the way everlasting.

The Old Testament is a library in itself, the library of the chosen people of God. It is a sifted library. Throughout the centuries there must have been other poets and historians and prophets. But a religious people was concerned to cherish those books that had nourished their religious life, and so these were preserved. The Spirit of God brooded over them and led them to hand down those books which now make up the Divine library that we know as the Canon of the Old Testament.

Luke 1: 1-4; John 20: 31; 1 John 5: 13; Col. 4: 16; Rev. 1: 11.

The New Testament explains itself. As the Apostle Paul pushed on in his missionary career, he kept touch by letter with the churches he had founded or that his followers had established. Problems arose on which his young converts needed instruction. They wondered what would happen to those who died before the Lord came again, whether it was right to eat meat that had first been laid on the altars of heathen gods before being sold in the market, whether it was right to go to law before heathen courts. Such questions were constantly arising, and a Spirit-filled man like Paul was the one who could give guidance. He wrote answers, and they were so valued that they were passed on to other churches; copies were made and preserved, and gradually central churches came to have a whole collection. When Paul died, others like Peter had to continue the work of keeping touch and giving guidance. As the first disciples died off the need arose for putting down in writing the knowledge of Jesus and His sayings that had at first been passed on orally. So collections of His sayings, stories of His encounters with enemies and enquirers, narratives of His healing miracles, especially all that was remembered of His later ministry and the moving episodes of His death and amazing resurrection—everything indeed that preserved a memory or a glimpse of Him, or any pronouncement that could throw light on the needs of the growing Church—were written down, and so there came into being Gospels. As the Church became mature it wished to depend less on travelling gifted prophets and more on settled ministers and officers, and so the wisdom of a leader like Paul was sought to guide the local churches in the selection of right men: hence arose pastoral letters. The expansion of the Christian movement was a story so amazing that an educated man like Luke felt the urge of the Spirit upon him to write it down: hence the Acts—a book which might have been needed to explain to Paul's Roman judges what Christianity was and what it stood for. As the Jews had loved to picture the end of things, the final punishment of evil and the triumph of the good, so the Spirit fell upon the author of the Apocalypse and he wrote down his gorgeous visions and messages to the churches in Asia.

There were other books than those that we have in the New Testament today: *e.g.*, we still have small fragments of other Gospels and stories of the infancy of Jesus. But these did not have the appeal of the Gospels we know. There were other epistles and books of lesser insight, compilations for teaching. But, though some of these were included in early collections used by the Church, there was a sifting out of the finest of the wheat and, when heretics began to cause confusion, the selection had to be definite: it was called the Canon—the rule, *i.e.*, that which set the standard. This process took place between the second and fourth centuries. We have only to compare the rejected books with those included in the Canon to see that the Church was guided by the Spirit in making its final choice.

As the coming of Jesus was seen as the fulfilment of the hopes expressed in the long history of the chosen people and especially in the visions of the prophets, it was inevitable that the Old Testament should be treasured alongside of the New. It was from Isaiah that Philip made a convert of the Ethiopian eunuch. It was from the Old Testament that Paul began his arguments in preaching. Indeed in the earliest days, when the leaders were Hebrews like Paul and Peter, they looked on the Old Testament as their Bible, the book that told the story of the promises, the book that fed their souls with the faith of the Psalmists and the prophets. While the New Testament was only in process of being written what could be used to cherish the life of the saints but the books of the Old Testament that looked forward to that salvation the Church was now enjoying? The Church would have been unfaithful to its heritage if it had failed to preserve the Old Testament along with the New.

Herein Its Unity. Acts 8: 26-35; Eph. 4: 3-7; Rev. 21: 5-7.

Wherein lies the unity of all Holy Scripture? That charming writer, Dr. L. P. Jacks, tells us in his autobiography that he set about reading the New Testament to find out what it was all about, and he came to the conclusion that the theme of the whole was immortality. That no doubt is a hope of grand moment, but do we not probe deeper when we ask on what ground that hope was based? Journey's end is there in the eternal Presence, but what by the way? Jesus said, "I am the way"—but not only the way, but the truth and the life also. It is the New Testament conviction that it was Jesus Christ who opened up the eternal world for men; and this came about by what He accomplished in His life and death. That life and death was a setting forth of the mind and will of the Eternal, the manifesting of a Love at the heart of things that willed to save: that was reality—that God had a redemptive purpose and had brought it to pass. And now there was available to men life as God had planned it, life on the level of the Kingdom, life that could be realized by men only through the power that the Christ imparted. Thus the unity of the New Testament would seem to lie there—in that which put a new song into men's hearts, the fact that God had visited and redeemed His people.

The Old Testament is one long straining forward towards that grand day of visitation and redemption. Jesus summed up the tragedy of Jerusalem in this—that the day the city people had dreamed of and lived for had dawned in that very hour and was rapidly passing to its sunset unrecognized. That was the irretrievable that He wept over. The story of the nation really began in the deliverance from Egypt—but deliverance to what? Sinai pointed to the God who alone could enable them to choose between life and death. The period of the Judges was the seeking after a real liberator. The kings were a long succession of makeshifts for the true king. Exile and dismemberment and the yoke of tyrant after tyrant was a prising the people loose from their earthly affections. In all the frustrations and chastening of the years was the discipline with a purpose to it—the will of a God of righteousness to be also a Saviour. The prophets and the seers were for ever pointing to the unseen figure in the shadow, the Potter who had His hand on the clay and moved the wheel of refining. The one thing that gave meaning and unity to the chequered history of the race was that God was working His purpose out, moving the nation towards a day of redemption, the day that came upon Jerusalem unrecognized: "Thou knewest not the time of thy visitation."

Thus the theme of all Holy Scripture is one, the redemptive purpose and working of God towards that end. The culmination of the Old Testament expectation may be seen in the vision of Dan. 7—the coming Kingdom of the saints which the Son of Man received from the hand of God. The long-looked-for divine commonwealth is actually real: it has but to take shape upon the earth. The New Testament declared the Kingdom *has come:* its gates are open and many of the unexpected are pressing into it. This is not a prerogative of any nation, but here all the peoples of the earth merge their identity in a common humanity. What constitutes this common humanity is an indebtedness to the work that Jesus Christ has done: He made all sorts of men new creatures. Redemption has passed from dream to reality: now is the prince of this world cast out. The Now of creation's long travail has come: the New Jerusalem comes down from heaven upon earth.[3]

Complete Allegiance. Gal. 1: 6-9; Heb. 4: 12.

"Thou shalt have no other gods before me." That demand for undivided loyalty lies deep down in the ancient tradition of Israel: it is bound up with Sinai and the hour of sacred covenant. And the claim behind that demand is this: "I am the Lord thy God, which have brought thee out of the land of Egypt, out of the house of bondage" (Exod. 20: 2). Elijah and his successors in the prophetic line maintain this call to a unique obedience, and Jesus places the first commandment as still binding: with heart and soul and mind, with the completeness of our being, we are to own the one true God.

With equal decisiveness the New Testament speaks: there is one Lord Jesus: "For there is none other name under heaven given among men whereby we must be saved" (Acts 4: 12); there is salvation in none other. And again the demand is based on a claim that a great deliverance has been wrought: "God commendeth his love toward us, in that, while we were yet sinners, Christ died for us" (Rom. 5: 8). Many would hold the Epistle of James the weakest link in the New Testament, the "epistle of straw"; yet even there the double-minded man is condemned: we are to waver not at all, but look to the one God. The Apocalypse lifts the veil at the close of history to show all worship and praise concentrated on one: "Thou art worthy to

[3] Mozley, in *Expository Times,* Aug. 1939.

take the book, and to open the seals thereof; for thou wast slain, and hast redeemed us to God by thy blood out of every kindred, and tongue, and people, and nation" (Rev. 4: 11, 5: 9).

The Organ of Persuasion. John 16: 7-15; 1 Cor. 2: 7-16.

When Jesus spoke a parable He was accustomed to close with the words, "He that hath ears to hear, let him hear." It was not enough to utter the word of truth: there must be the receptive heart, the understanding mind. That which was true even of the limpid clarity of the stories told by Jesus is true of all Scripture. The Word of God is not just the sum of words that make up the Bible. But Scripture is God speaking to the understanding through the words.

The voice that sings across the night
Of long-forgotten days and things—
Is there an ear to hear aright
The voice that sings?

The Old Testament is rich in human situations of infinite diversity, and often in the narrative we must re-live the experience of David before Nathan: we listen to a moving story, standing outside it all the while, and then suddenly a voice speaks in our ears: "Thou art the man!" In reading a Psalm we warm to it because there our mood is expressed and the healing words come home to us: there God finds us. In the Gospels particularly, where the penetrating light of Jesus floods the human scene, we often have a sensation like looking into a mirror and gazing at ourselves: I am convicted there as the Pharisee of the parable or as the boastful Peter; the Divine challenge confronts me.

How is it that Scripture thus thrusts home past our defence mechanism? These narratives come from the long ago telling on the face of them how God consoled this saint or stirred that prophet by a living word. But how is that ancient word made living again to me? How does a message from the past become contemporary to me? It is not by the mere study of the historical situation, though that helps to make the past vivid and real; it is not by the exercise of reason, for the clever man may remain cold where the simple mind catches fire; it is not by the glow of the imagination, though that may turn the prose into poetry. The Christian has only one explanation: the Holy Spirit brings the truth to light. The great Spirit who confronted Elijah in his despair reappears in a new context to confront you and me. Dry bones are re-animated, dead words leap to life, and the creative Spirit has done what the genius of a Shakespeare cannot do with the past—set me down there face to face with God. The Cross is a moving spectacle, a martyr's tragic death; the dramatist can re-enact that before my eyes. But the Holy Spirit takes that story and involves me in it, convicts me as among those who drove the nails and flung the taunts; it strikes deeper than mere drama, a spectacle that purges me by pity or thrills me with horror: it forces me to my knees, to contrition, and to pleading; for it is not pity or horror that grips me, but guilt and shame and personal dishonour. And how to men in that plight the voice of forgiveness should come—that is beyond all reason's explaining: it is a conviction that must be born from above by the actual operation of the gracious Spirit of God.

Especially is it true that the Holy Spirit takes the things of Christ and shows them unto us. In the life of the early Church and all through the centuries that fact has been made manifest. The Apostle Paul met new situations rarely by quoting the words of Jesus, but by following the guiding of the Holy Spirit. Men like Peter knew more of the actual words of Jesus, but that did not keep them from playing false to Him by refusing, for example, to eat at the same table with fellow-Christians just because they did not observe the Jewish scruples about food. Paul, inspired by the Spirit, interpreted his Master's will, and insisted on clearing away wrong ideas that frustrated brotherhood (Gal. 2: 11). The pronouncements of Jesus made in the slave state of Galilee two thousand years ago under the simple conditions of Eastern life do not *automatically* apply to all the problems of our modern complicated industrial organization: to use them in that way is to make His teaching like a new law book or a set of dogmas—the very evil He had to fight against in the legalism of the Pharisees. But the Spirit can and does reinterpret for us the principles that Jesus set forth, and these must be applied in our complex civilization if men and women are to be treated as souls and not as machines.

The truths of the Gospel that were to the Jews a stumbling-block and to the Greeks foolishness will not find ready entrance to our minds today, for we too are hidebound in our pre-conceptions like the Jews and schooled in scientific ways of thought like the Greeks. But Christ crucified must be placarded before men's eyes as in Paul's time, and that will be found a power unto salvation. That God should come to earth in the likeness of a man, that He should intervene in the middle of history and do a thing once for all that affected all history, that death should be for Jesus not the extinction of life, but its emancipation—these are truths that the human mind does not find credible by the ordinary laws of thought. But from the beginning of the Christian era intellectuals like Paul and poor slaves like Onesimus have been apprehended by the same power and led to make the same confession—not by argument, but by a persuasion from within which can only be explained as the working of the Holy Spirit of God. The Cross of Christ offends our proud human reason, but it yields its truth to simple faith. Forgiveness seems a contradiction of the laws of retribution, but in the light of experience we come to know it is a fact which transforms life and makes the saddest life strangely glad.

The Church of Christ today owes much to Karl Barth for his recall to the study of the Word of God. Behind Scripture and the Church's preaching is not just a dynamic man, a rare human of charming and commanding personality, but *The Word;* not a somewhat divine, but the Son of God Himself. "Christ being raised from the dead *dieth* no more." Eternity has broken through into time, and is ever at our door. We are confronted with a momentous choice here and now. We are addressed: "God has something quite special to say to each man which concerns him alone. This word . . . says to us always a new thing, which we have never heard from any other one. It is the rock of a 'Thou' flung in our way." "The Word of God needs no Act to complete it; it is itself an Act. . . . If our hearing of a sermon, or our reading of the Bible, does not bring about a corresponding event, it is certain that in the sermon, and in the Bible, we have not heard God's Word. We have only heard human words. For the Word of God always makes history. . . . 'For he *spake* and it was done.' . . . In the event of Revelation time falls away, and what happened in the there and then is spoken to us in the here and now." "Unless the Word of God is understood as decision, it is not understood at all."[4]

[4] Cf. John McConnachie, *The Barthian Theology and the Man of Today,* pp. 63ff. These phrases are intended to direct the student to the whole exposition.

X. The Sacraments.

We believe that the Sacraments of Baptism and the Lord's Supper are effectual means through which, by common things and simple acts, the saving love of God is exhibited and communicated to His people, who receive them in faith.

We believe that in Baptism men are made members of the Christian society. Washing with water in the name of the Father, the Son, and the Holy Spirit signifies God's cleansing from sin and an initial participation in the gifts and graces of the new life. The children of believing parents are baptized and nurtured in the family of God so that they may in due time take upon themselves the yoke of Christ.

We believe that the Lord's Supper perpetuates the fellowship between Christ and His disciples sealed in the upper room, that at His table He is always present, and His people are nourished, confirmed, and renewed. The giving and receiving of bread and wine accompanied by His own words signifies the gracious self-giving of Christ as suffering and living Lord in such wise that His faithful people live in Him and He in them.

So we acknowledge Baptism as God's appointed means of grace at initiation into the Christian fellowship; and the Lord's Supper as His appointed means of maintaining the fellowship in health and strength, and as the act of worship in which the whole soul of man goes out to God and God's grace comes freely to man.

CHAPTER X. THE SACRAMENTS

By Common Things and Simple Acts. Matt 2: 11; Mark 14: 3-9; John 13: 1-15.

When life moves on the level amid the commonplace, talk is easy and flowing. Raise it a little to the plane of emotion, and sentences become broken. Lift it to the heights, and broken words die away, and all we have for self-uttering is the look, the gesture. Thoughts at their loftiest break into symbols. A grip of the hand, a glance of the eye, a shrug of the shoulders, and we sense the movement of the spirit within. So in the realm of religion, where the Eternal mystery has His unmeasured magnitudes to communicate to feeble understanding, there must needs be the sign or the symbol, the picture language of thought too deep for speech.

The Eastern mind was specially productive of sensitive imagery. The Old Testament has many an example. The mourner barefoot, with ashes sprinkled on his head (2 Sam. 15: 30; Ezek. 24: 17; Jer. 6: 26), the keys upon the steward's shoulder (Is. 22: 22), the mantle thrown over the woman in protection (Ezek. 16: 8), the sowing of a city with vegetation-destroying salt (Judg. 9: 45), and the crown placed upon the king's head—all these speak meaningfully and memorably. The incense rising from the altar (Ps. 141: 2), the stretching out of hands in petition for divine mercy (Ex. 9: 29; 1 K. 8: 22), the frontlets upon the forehead and arm marking out the people under the divine care (Ex. 13: 16), the blue of the cloudless sky, the colour of revelation, on the curtains of the sanctuary (Ex. 26: 1) and the fringe of an Israelite's garment (Nu. 15: 38)—these indicate how readily religious ideas and yearnings found expression in symbols. The Sabbath broke the succession of common days to remind men of how God completed the work of creation. Above all, the Temple itself was a symbol, the sign of the divine Presence, to which when the worshipper looked up he knew that no evil could befall his city. The prophets directed attention to the truths that they bore upon their souls by dramatic actions. When Ahijah wishes to declare that the kingdom of Israel is to be divided, he tears his garment into twelve pieces (1 K. 11: 30); Ezekiel outlines on a tile the plan of the city, girdles it with mound and battering-ram, and gazes on his handiwork with uplifted hand, thus betokening Jehovah's impending judgment on Jerusalem; he reduces to scantiness his food and water to indicate the stern rationing that a siege brings (Ezek. 4). So in those who come in the Hebrew tradition we expect this love of the dramatic symbol with its double appeal to the mind and senses.

When we come to the New Testament we see in Jesus Himself the great symbol of God. He is the Word, the one by whom and through whom God utters Himself, declares His mind towards men and their salvation, the will to redeem. And that Word of His is no mere adventure into history on the part of the Eternal, no sudden whim or makeshift device to set right the maladjustment of the human race with Himself. That Word defines for us what He essentially is, what He inevitably is as the Righteous and Loving Father of men. Jesus is the disclosure of the mystery of God. In God there is that splendour of holiness, that grandeur of purpose, that depth of mind and range of interest that no common words can tell with adequacy. Between the magnitude of God and the littleness of man an intermediary was needed, an interpretation of the Eternal to the creatures of time. That interpretation took the form of a man, bone of our bone and flesh of our flesh; that man of Nazareth was God uttering Himself in moving pity and acts of tender healing, in words of light and of judgment, in deeds of power and depths of agony, an exhaustless panorama of the divine will projected on the screen of time. He is the living symbol of the majesty and glory of God. His every parable presents a facet of eternal truth, His precepts and paradoxes sum up the issues of our human destiny, His challenges bring all men everywhere to the bar of judgment. And it is curious to note how every crisis in His evolving story stands out before men today as charged with a universal significance. That He should take His place with sinners in a baptism for repentance, that God's call should confront Him with temptations such as we know in the conflict between the higher and lower appeal, that He should have His moments on the Mount and His agony in a Gethsemane and His irrevocable steps towards Calvary —all these are symbols of the divine meaning in life and signposts on the way everlasting before us.

In the later stages of His life, in the last appeal to men in Jerusalem, He deliberately resorts to symbolic actions, as if He would fain sum up His message in accents unforgettable. He elects to play out the final scenes where human eyes must see Him. What are the focal points of an ancient city's life? Are they not the city gate, where all must come and go, and the Temple of God, the Holy Place of His Presence, where all must draw near in reverence? Here He entered of set calculation, humbly riding on an ass, declaring that He came offering to win His sovereignty by the ways of peace; and there He cleansed the Temple of its empty ceremonialism and commercialism and opened up the one clear avenue to God, the way of prayer.

Peace and Prayer: could His accent fall on finer words? Peace is the dream long deferred of the citizens of this war-torn world, and prayer is the gateway that gives despairing man entrance into life again.

And what are the focal points of a home? Are they not the door by which all come and go and the table where all gather for sustaining and fellowship? At the door stood the water-pots of cleansing water, and who can forget how He took a towel and girded Himself and washed the disciples' feet, declaring for all time that the Christian home is founded on mutual willingness to serve in the humblest capacity? And at the Table He took bread and broke it and gave, and likewise a cup after supper and said: "Drink ye all of it," so setting before us the exhaustless symbol of all human need to receive and the divine love that satisfies to the uttermost.

Towel and Table—fit emblems surely of the unstinted completeness of the divine self-giving.

"Symbol" is a general term for a significant action in the whole wide range of human life, a handclasp between friends, the tattered flags that once led armies into battle and find their place as memorial emblems in a cathedral, the seals that guarantee a legal document. But "sacrament" is a term we have come to apply specially in the religious sphere. It is a Latin term and was used of the soldier's oath of loyalty. But that word states the practical Roman's view of things, the human side of the question. Much richer is the Greek word that *sacramentum* translates: *mysterion*—mystery. That proclaims the divine side of the sacrament. It is a truth of God, a momentous word about His eternal nature and purpose, a declaration of communication that the divine makes to mortal men. Our sacraments of Baptism and the Lord's Supper are handed down to us by the Church as divine appointments wherein by common things and simple acts the will of God to save men is set dramatically forth and His love is communicated to His people who come in faith to receive that gift.

It is our human way to talk of going to church and celebrating the sacraments—as if these were matters of our own decision. But before we go forth God has made manifest His presence there in the sanctuary and waits to meet us, and before we take our place at the table of the Lord He sits there as Host. Grace ever goes before our human response. That is what lies behind the claim that these sacraments are effectual means. When Peter in the first days of the early Church set the seal on the admission of Cornelius and his household by baptizing them, he was not just following the happy inspiration of the moment or unthinkingly taking over into the new movement an old piece of ritual. He was acting by the leading of the Spirit, as is shown by the fact that with the rite came the Spirit. Already there was evidence in the solemn life-changing that accompanied the rite, the hallmark of the divine approval. It is not ours to look round and find other ways and means of expressing the bond and solemn pledge between man and God. The fact is there that under the divine leading these symbols have been handed down from Christian age to Christian age as proven acceptable sacraments that God has been pleased to use and make effectual throughout the long history of the Church. Young people in camp, in love with the open air and the fellowship of like-minded associates under the spell of conference life and worship, may gather on Sunset Point and feel that there in the glory of the reddening sky is fitting symbol of the beauty of God. True, that is a sacramental experience, and the emotion of that hour is of God. But it is the common things and simple acts that have been hallowed by the piety and love of the generations that will prove to us the most effectual means of entering into the meaning and the mystery of the divine self-giving.

"It is irrational to attempt to decide on the strength of general metaphysical theory how God must act in bestowing good gifts on His creatures. The one question we can ask with sanity about such a matter is the *historical* question how in fact God is found to deal with us."[1]

Baptism . . . in the Name of the Father, the Son, and the Holy Spirit. Matt. 3: 1-17; Matt. 28: 19; Luke 3: 7-14.

The rite of Baptism is rooted in the life experience of Jesus. He came to Jordan to the baptism of John. There on the threshold of His ministry He chose to stand with sinners as in the end He died with sinners. His call and ministry are inextricably bound up with the need of men for their supreme deliverance, the deliverance from the thraldom of sin. There is never any suggestion that Jesus felt in Himself the consciousness of sin except the enigmatic question, Mark 10: 18. But He had the unique sensibility that made Him one with His brethren, and it was that compelling sympathy that drew Him from the quiet uneventful life of a carpenter in Nazareth. The trumpet had sounded throughout the land in the commanding voice of a prophet, and that call was to repent, for the Kingdom of God was at hand. It was never the way of Jesus to think that He could cultivate a religious intercourse with God and yet stand outside the common life of His people. He knew that it was in the heritage of Israel that His lot was cast, and the God of His fathers did not enter into personal relationship even with Him apart from other human persons. Within the complex of the social whole of which He was a part God was moving with ominous power. God was shaking the nation by the sound of the axe at the trembling tree and the sweep of the winnowing fan, and His place was there among the awakened penitents of His own people. If an Isaiah or Jeremiah had not felt the tension of their nation's loss and imminent peril, they would never have heard the call of God; and it was because Jesus was bearing His countrymen on His heart that He came with them to Jordan, and, humbling Himself with them in the hour of contrition, He was startled by a divine intimation. Baptism may seem like the singling out of an individual to a lone encounter with God, and in a measure such it is. But there is this other essential aspect: it is within the nation, within the family, that God descends upon the individual.

[1] A. E. Taylor, quoted in Riddell, *What We Believe*, p. 308.

Again, that baptismal rite of John was not an isolated piece of ritual. John was a preacher, and the rite was but the culmination of the impact of the Word upon the souls of His hearers. Such was the keenness of the moral challenge that even publicans became uneasy about their compromise with conscience and soldiers lost their callousness towards their violent vocation. Now both publicans and soldiers were concerned with a national situation, the tax-gatherers being Jews who had become quislings accepting service under the hated alien oppressor, the legionaries being drawn from other subjugated peoples and probably having a fellow-feeling for the people they were policing with methods sometimes of cruel terrorism. Did John's proclamation of the Kingdom lay upon citizens and people a new sense of international honour and justice? At least there was the sharpness of the sword of truth in his declamation: it penetrated to tender consciences and stabbed them to life. But the total effect of the message was not towards revolution, but towards the changing of the inner man, a moral transformation rather than a civil upheaval. Baptism came as the consummation of this awakening, carrying into the presence of God who alone could give release to those who had become burdened with the weight of their sins.

The next thing to be observed is the divine response. The heavens were opened and Jesus heard a call. It was not such a voice as greeted the ordinary penitent. With the nature of that voice we are not here concerned. What is conspicuously plain, however, is that a divine surprise was unfolded. This was not what John Baptist had looked for when he opened his mission under the pressure of the divine Spirit. We have no knowledge that to Jesus under His human limitation any prior intimation was given. It was a clear case of the divine initiative above and beyond all human expectation. For this day God had planned. Before the urge seized the Baptist and before the penitents felt the prompting to come to Jordan, the Providence of God had marked this day for the coming of no ordinary penitent, but for the anointing of the Messiah of God for His healing and liberating ministry. Here is something to be remembered when we prepare to hedge about the ritual with faithless belittling of its possibilities. Who knows when the higher destiny may be laid upon the head even of a child in a mother's arms?

What God appointed that day for Jesus was not a call merely, but that power that makes possible the execution of the call. The Holy Spirit descended as a dove and continued to abide upon Him, empowering Him for ministries manifold and for the untold tasks and agonies in the conflict with wicked earthly potentates. In the strength of that Spirit He went on to open up new truth, to cast light upon human blindness and obstinacy, to combat to the end in Gethsemane and on Calvary the forces of darkness and of death. That is the sort of aftermath the Church came to associate with the rite of Baptism: it was usually marked by the coming of a new spirit with power to lift up the hands which hang down and to strengthen the feeble knees on the ways of spiritual endeavour.

Now what was there on the human side that made possible the strong rousing trumpet call of the Baptist and the wide response of the people of God? Was it not that they all, preacher and converts alike, shared the heritage of faith, faith in a God who with a mighty hand had led their fathers out of Egypt and through the days of a triumphant Babylon and a swaggering Sennacherib and the half-madman half-genius Antiochus had continued to restore and sustain His own? The legacy of a Moses and an Elijah, a Hosea and an Amos, an Isaiah and a Jeremiah, had passed into the culture of this nation, so that, though tossed often into the maelstrom and welter of pagan corruption and superstition, they had a saving something that kept them conscious of their uniqueness and so made them unquenchable and unafraid. And that faith had been quickened by the Baptist's bold heralding of the Kingdom. He spread the assurance that the Almighty Deliverer was on the march again, and soon He would appear on Mount Zion with His legions of the Spirit. "Lift up your hearts, O Israel! Your redemption draweth nigh!" Under the spell of such a conviction nations are reborn and the Spirit of God descends upon the Son of Man. It is upon Nathanaels poor in guile and rich in faith that the angels begin to come and go.

Cleansing . . . and an initial Participation in . . . the New Life.
Rom. 6: 4-11; Col. 2: 11-13; 1 Cor. 10: 1-13.

Baptism then under John marked the admission of men into the company who set their faces with hope towards the coming

Kingdom. The door was held wide open for all who would hear and repent, but the effect of the rite was to constitute the remnant within the nation who were to save the whole. They definitely turned away from the evils of the past and sought the forgiveness of God with His strengthening for the new life. The rite set its seal upon that decision. They held fast together, those followers of John, though many entered into the larger fellowship of Jesus. Paul found the adherents of John still in being at Ephesus (Acts 19: 1-5) long years after John was martyred, and on the banks of the Tigris and Euphrates today live a people, tinsmiths and silversmiths, differing from the races around, who still honour John Baptist as their prophet and practise the ancient ritual of their founder. These are known as Mandaeans or Sabians. But Paul found that these men had suffered the penalty of those who refuse the larger light of the Gospel: they lacked the gift of the Spirit.

The early Church evidently took over the rite and cherished it from the beginning. That is reflected in the concluding injunction of the Risen Christ in Matt. 28: 19. The Fourth Gospel assures us that Jesus Himself did not baptize, but His disciples (4: 2), and we have evidence of its wide acceptance where it is assumed in, for example, the conversation with Nicodemus: "Except a man be born of water and of the Spirit, he cannot enter into the kingdom of God" (3: 5). After Pentecost Peter calls for repentance and baptism in the name of Jesus Christ for the remission of sins (Acts 2: 38). "See, here is water," cries the Ethiopian eunuch, "What doth hinder me to be baptized?" (Acts 8: 36). Peter, seeing the Holy Ghost fall on his hearers in the house of Cornelius, "commanded them to be baptized in the name of the Lord" (Acts 10: 44-48). Paul's personal experience of the Risen Christ does not render unnecessary his baptism: "Arise," said Ananias, "get thyself baptized, and so wash away from thyself thy sins, invoking his name" (Acts 22: 16). The fact that proselytes on admission to Judaism were baptized as well as circumcised would make it natural, almost inevitable, that the disciples should adopt the rite for admission to the Church. It was so utterly appropriate as a symbol of cleansing, renunciation of the old false allegiance, acceptance of the new Lord and His way of life. They would be confirmed in their use of the rite by the manifest approval from on high in the gift of the Holy Spirit (Acts 8: 17; 19: 6).

We see then ample warrant in our tradition for this rite of Baptism. We recognize it as a rite which the Spirit of God has taken and blessed in the past history of the Church. It is a form in which we may look for the divine initiative, even the divine surprise. But its value normally depends on a mental preparation in ourselves. There must be concern for the soul within, a grief for and hatred of our sin, and a turning definitely away from it. And that concern of ours is most alive when we are caught up in the life of our nation and times and realize that we are part of a social whole in the corruption and folly of which we are deeply involved and for which we accept a measure of responsibility. But here is a step that we must take in faith. It is then, in the mood of our sincere contrition, that the Holy Spirit can lay hold on us with power and, continuing with us, can give us of the gifts and graces of a new life. It thus marks our admission to a new life. But it is not a life that we can live alone. It is admission to the Christian society which by its common worship and fellowship will lift up our souls and sustain our goings. Thus it properly takes place in a Christian church before the face of the Lord's people, or, if that be not possible, in the precincts of a Christian home where are members representative of that larger company of the faithful.

The Children of Believing Parents. Mark 10: 13-16.

Baptism under John's preaching and in the early Christian missions would be chiefly of adults, just as it must be today in the foreign fields. The first appeal naturally is made to mature men and women, and for such coming into the Christian community was a real life change, the abandonment of Jewish or pagan practices, and the swearing of allegiance to a new master and a new standard of conduct. Immersion seems to have been the form of initiation in the first Christian church as in the case of Jewish proselytes. That is the implication when Paul speaks of being "buried with him by baptism" (Rom. 6: 4). To him the plunge beneath the waters fittingly pictured the parting from all the old life just as Jesus in death separated from His life in the flesh; while rising from the waters the convert emerged to a new existence as Jesus rose to a new life at the Resurrection. But what of the case of children? "The idea that a parent should enter a religion or covenant-relation with God as an individual merely, *i.e.* by himself as distinct from his immediate family, would never occur to the ancients, least of all to a Jew. There were no 'individuals' in our sharp modern sense of the term. All were seen as members of larger units, of which the family was the chief in the time of Christ."[2] With any change in the faith the household also changed, so that children would pass into the Christian Church in the same act as the father. Thus when Peter received the household of Cornelius (Acts 10: 47), or Paul the household of Stephanas (1 Cor. 1: 16), that would mean that the children also passed under the care of the Christian Church. Just as a little proselyte was baptized into Judaism without his intelligent consent, so this feeling of solidarity would warrant the baptism of a Christian child. And so today in the close social unity of the Christian family the child is under the influence of the Spirit of Christ from the beginning, and that fact is only receiving its just recognition in the act of baptism. But it is not only in the solidarity of the family that the child lives and grows, but in the wider fellowship of the Church, and in acknowledgment of that fact the proper place for the rite is the community church. We cannot be "in Christ" unless at the same time we are in His Church. Thus the whole congregation of His people receive and accept responsibility for the nurture of the growing child. The Sabbath School and the worship of the sanctuary as well as the home training and the beauty of the family altar will make an atmosphere in which the Christian gifts and graces of the Spirit will appear.

The Lord's Supper perpetuates the fellowship between Christ and His Disciples sealed in the upper room. Matt. 26: 17-29; Mark 14: 22-25; Luke 22: 14-30; John 6; John 13-17; 1 Cor. 10: 16-22; 1 Cor. 11: 23-34.

Should we not, then, recall the historical situation and probe as far as we reverently may into the thought and purpose of Jesus when He held the last supper with His closest followers?

It was the night of His betrayal. By the act of one of His own chosen ones He was to be handed over to the authorities. For love of man He had ministered daily and was ready to give His all, and yet one of His intimates on whom He had lavished

[2] J. Vernon Bartlet, *ERE* vol. ii. p. 379.

His sweetest and best gift of friendship had turned traitor and for a handful of silver was throwing back His love tokens in His face. Black ingratitude was confronting Him, and even priests, those reared and appointed for the service of the God of His fathers, were waiting with malignity and proud triumph for His destruction. The human family He had served with ceaseless love and devotion spurned and despised Him, and yet He went on to the end. "With desire I have desired to eat this passover with you." When He might well have turned away and had no more dealings with His kind, He sought the face of men. He hungered for their presence with Him. He drew them closer to Himself. This supper was on His initiative: He had planned and sought it, and it was with gladness that He saw it realized before His enemies struck Him from His last chance of intercourse with His own. This will of Jesus to hold men to Him to the last was not a weak human's clinging to a last spar of hope. This was God's will, the divine determination to accomplish a saving act for an ungrateful race. It was Passover time, and every pious Israelite was looking back over the long years of the faithfulness of God who led them out of Egypt and in hundreds of crises since had never failed them. Through Jesus God was declaring His desire, His passionate desire, to keep the Passover with them still, and this time to astonish His people with a new and more effective deliverance than they had ever known. This was the act of a love that will not let us go. At every communion let us realize that it is on the Lord's invitation that we come. He spreads the Table and He is the Host, the ever present gracious Head of the Table.

His own words.

1. "This is my body broken for you" (1 Cor. 11: 24). Before the cruel cross claimed the frail body it was given and that freely. The Good Shepherd of His own accord gives His life for the sheep. "No man taketh it from me, but I lay it down of myself: I have power to lay it down, and I have power to take it again" (John 10: 18). "For their sakes I sanctify myself" (17: 19). Of His own accord Jesus rose from supper, laid aside His garments, and took a towel (13: 4). Herein is the supreme glory of the Atonement: not in its pain or humiliation or cruel suffering, but in this, that *voluntarily* He gave Himself up. God Himself had inter-

vened again on the human scene: not in far off Egypt and not away down the years, but here in this room and in this age and for us his unworthy and undeserving people He gave His only son. This is the supreme surprise and mystery of all time, that God so loved the world that between us and the inevitable doom our sins brought upon us He interposed Himself. God who sends His rain upon the just and the unjust consummates His love in this that for the ungodly the Righteous One lays down His life. Whereas of old men thought to buy the favour of a capricious God by heaping high His altars with their sacrifices, lo! He sweeps away these tokens of a fitful and imperfect penitence and on the altar the Christ lays Himself, a full, perfect, and sufficient sacrifice for the sins of the whole world. As Dr. W. B. Selbie[3] has put it: "In a world where everything has its price and gifts are measured by their costliness, it seems impossible to believe that—

'Tis only God who is given away.
'Tis only heaven may be had for the asking.

Yet this is indubitably the core of the Christian gospel."

2. "This cup is the New Covenant in my blood" (1 Cor. 11: 25). A compact in ancient days was sealed by blood. By sharing in the sprinkled blood of a victim the two contracting parties were made one. So Moses had sprinkled blood on the people and on the altar of God (Exod. 24: 4-8), and thus the Old Covenant was ratified. Now the New Covenant dreamed of by Jeremiah was being inaugurated not by the shedding of alien blood, but by the voluntary self-giving of the Son of God. That New Covenant meant *forgiveness*: all the evil entail of sin was taken away for ever. And the new relationship with God was one of *inwardness:* no formal bond cemented by external rites like circumcision and the works of the law, but a fellowship so near and intimate that Paul could say: "It is no longer the old selfish ego who exists in me, but Christ liveth in me" (Gal. 2: 20). "The life I now live in the flesh I live by the faith of the Son of God who loved me and gave himself for me." With silver cords, light as air yet strong as iron, the bonds of love with which a Peter and a John

[3] *God and Ourselves,* p. 66f.

were bound to the Master, so are we bound to God the Author of our salvation in everlasting gratitude. It is a union that is created by perfect understanding. The great heart of the Eternal that keeps nothing back is manifest in the life and dying of Jesus: and our love answering that cleaves to the love that gave itself. It is a covenant of knotted hearts: the God who is personal receives and sets His affection on each individual person who comes to Him in humility and contrition of soul. And it is a covenant that is marked by *universality:* it is wide open to all. As Jesus let His love go freely out to a Samaritan woman and a Roman centurion, to a rich young ruler and an outcast Magdalene, to a guileless Nathanael and a much-stumbling Peter, so this covenant of the soul with God is open to every prodigal son who awakens in the far country and betakes himself to the Father's home. Here is no place for the pride that counts itself worthier and, drawing itself up in anger, will not go in, for that but brings the Father to the door pleading: "All that I have is thine. It was meet that we should make merry and be glad" (Luke 15: 31f.).

3. "Verily I say unto you, I will drink no more of the fruit of the vine until that day when I drink it new in the kingdom of God" (Mark 14: 25). Jesus would not have it that His friends should merely look *back* with sadness on a life that was closed, a death that He was dying for their sakes. He would have them look *forward* to the glorious consummation to come. Great as was the cost and the pain of parting and self-giving, it was not in vain. The sacrifice must be seen in the light of the joy to come. The typical festive occasion to the ancient mind was a banquet—for banquets were few and only given on great occasions like the marriage of a king's son. So they pictured the Kingdom to come under the image of a banquet. And Jesus points forward to that glorious climax of history: the reign of God finally a reality in human hearts, the long story of creation and human sojourning ending at last in God's purpose being fulfilled in a society of men and women redeemed to a glad and exuberant life—like drinking wine of a nobler vintage than earth had ever known. "Ye do shew the Lord's death *till he come*" (1 Cor. 11: 26). There is this note of triumph in our communion celebration. Christ did not die in vain. That purposefulness of God that did not spare His only son is ever marching on through the

defeats and the frustrations of life to an ultimate resounding vindication. Calvary is no tragedy, but a stage in the process by which love captures the heights. "I appoint unto you a kingdom" (Luke 22: 29), He assures His bewildered followers. Could they have seen the victories of the Christian faith throughout the ages, would not their dark foreboding have been rebuked? So before our equally bewildered eyes He opens up this vista: man's last enemy is overthrown. God *has come* to rule over mankind. The fact that twenty centuries after Calvary we sit at His table and take the cup means that the final emancipation of man is at hand, that that transfiguration must dazzle human sight:

"When Thy face looketh out from all men's faces."

4. "As this broken bread was scattered upon the mountains but was gathered together and became one, so let thy church be gathered together from the ends of the earth into thy kingdom, for thine is the glory and the power through Jesus Christ for ever." These words occur in the account of the original Eucharist given in the *Teaching of the Twelve Apostles,* a second-century manual of Church instruction, and conserve a thought that is expressed incidentally in our Gospel narratives. The loaf was evidently interpreted at times as a symbol of the *unity* of the Church. And in the act and words of Jesus there was the call to close the ranks, to cement the fellowship, to make real the unity of heart and mind implied in the common sharing of the bread and the cup of the Covenant. The Kingdom in its glory and complete consummation is still on the horizon of our time, but meantime we have foretaste in the Church of the life God wills for us. It behoves us to seek the unity of the body of Christ. We are as branches in the One vine, drawing from the same source of vital self-giving. If He unites us at the centre, how can we suffer aught of earthly origin to separate us at the circumference? When Paul stood up against Peter (Gal. 2: 11) and rebuked him to his face, it was because Peter, by withdrawing from eating with Christians who did not keep the Jewish food laws, was making it impossible to observe a common Lord's Supper—and a Church divided there is divided indeed. Paul was aghast at the peril of such disunion; and surely at our common memorial meal it is our unity in Him that we should cherish.

5. "A new commandment I give unto you, That ye love one

another" (John 13: 34). "If I then, your Lord and Master, have washed your feet, ye also ought to wash one another's feet" (John 13: 14). It is a peculiarity of the Fourth Gospel that it has no account of the institution of the Lord's Supper. It attaches a sacramental discourse on the Bread of Life to the Feeding of the Five Thousand (ch. 6). It may be that the author wishes to insist that the gifts we enjoy flow from the stupendous fact that God became man in Christ Jesus, and not only from the fact of His death. Then at the point in the narrative where we expect the account of the institution of the Supper we have the story of the feet-washing, as if he wished to declare that it was only too easy to remember Jesus in a ritual act: there must be another and a deeper remembrance, a willingness to give ourselves in unstinted service to our fellow-men. People of John's day had a childish faith in the mere performance of a rite, believing that the mere doing of it had a magical effect, and so he pushes into the foreground a practical act of Jesus that taught the lesson in an unmistakable way. In sharing the bread and the wine, the disciples were called on, not merely to recognize how much they were receiving at Jesus' hand, but also to pledge themselves to the same spirit of self-giving. Could they receive from one who gave all without feeling the obligation to go out and do likewise? That is certainly the charge of Paul when he says: "I beseech you therefore, brethren, by the mercies of God, that ye present your bodies a living sacrifice, holy, acceptable unto God, which is your reasonable service" (Rom. 12: 1). While the dominant thought in the act of communion must ever be how certainly God has given without measure for our salvation, yet there is the inevitable consequence: "Freely ye have received, freely give." At the table we are like good soldiers who renew the *sacramentum,* the oath of loyalty to our King and Lord.

6. "This do in remembrance of me" (1 Cor. 11: 24). Two of the narratives of the Lord's Supper, those in Matthew and Mark, omit this distinct injunction of our Lord, and there are those who claim therefore that there was no explicit command to keep this memorial rite. But it would only be more wonderful if the rite sprang *unasked* out of the needs and inspiration of the first believers. The injunction then came irresistibly upon the early Church from the Risen Lord, for from the beginning it was in this act that they cherished and renewed their spiritual

life. "He was known of them in breaking of bread" (Luke 24: 35). "And they . . . breaking bread from house to house, did eat their meat with gladness and singleness of heart" (Acts 2: 46).

He is always present.

It is doubtful if our words "This do in remembrance of me" do justice to the Greek phrase used. Dr. Anderson Scott argued strongly that the meaning is rather "with a view to recalling me."[4] Christ was called back into such vivid nearness by the action that His presence was actually felt by the worshippers. Whatever the exact meaning of the phrase may be, there is no doubt about the testimony of Christian experience: there, as on no other occasion, when we handle the memorial bread and wine, when our thoughts rest on the almost incredible completeness of His self-giving and our hearts are stirred at the fact of our own unworthiness to receive, we are aware of a living touch upon our souls, the pressure of a Presence overwhelming in its intensity. The old Scots preacher, Robert Bruce, put it with rare power: "Speers thou quhat new thing we get in the sacrament? I say, we get Christ better nor we did before: we get a better grip of Christ now. That same thing quhilk thou possessed be the hearing of the word, thou possesses now more largely. For be the sacrament my faith is nurished, the bounds of my soull are enlarged, and sa, quhen I had but a little grip of Christ before, as it were betwixt my finger and my thumb, now I get Him in my haill hand: for aye the mair my faith growes, the better grip I get of Christ Jesus."

The Protestant thought of Christ's presence is to be sharply distinguished from the Roman Catholic idea. There the presence is at the call of the priest: "One word out of his mouth compels the Creator of the Universe and of Heaven to come down to earth, strips Him of His greatness and hides Him under the form of the Bread."[5] In the consecration of the elements it is maintained that the bread and wine are changed into the very body and blood of Christ, and these the priest offers to God as a sacrifice: this sacrifice has propitiatory power and is regarded as a means of winning graces and blessings from

[4] *Christianity according to St. Paul,* p. 191.
[5] Quoted by C. A. Scott, *Romanism and the Gospel,* p. 132.

God. Such claims the Protestant does not make. God's grace comes freely, he believes, and needs no constraint of any form. By the elements he sees pictured dramatically forth the gracious self-giving of Christ made once and for all on Calvary, and as mind and imagination kindle in contemplation of what God thus did for men in Christ Jesus, he receives true benediction. But that receiving is by no mysterious change in the bread and the wine, but by the opening of his soul in faith to the God who has thus drawn near offering forgiveness to the penitent and peace to the troubled. It is a mystery only in the Pauline sense that the grand purpose of God for man, long hidden, was made finally and demonstrably clear when Jesus came and consummated a life of ministry by giving Himself up even unto death. In His infinite compassion God had pity on men enslaved to sin and powerless to break the evil entail. Argument or human speculation could not discover the mind of God; so He took action, and made revelation once for all of a love so generous and unrestrained that it could be made credible only when One came in flesh and blood and lived out the reality and intensity of that love. The bread and wine bid us come to such a love in faith, and coming we are at that table nourished, confirmed, and renewed. Such outflowing love commingling with our faith and gratitude makes a spiritual union so close that it can be said that "His faithful people live in Him and He in them." Stirred in mind by the most momentous truth ever made known to man, and touched in imagination by the simple yet telling emblems of the passion of our suffering and living Lord, we are lifted to an elevation of worship "in which the whole soul of man goes out to God and God's grace comes freely to man."

XI. Christian Life and Duty.

We believe that the Christian life is the life lived in fellowship with Christ and His Church. It begins with repentance and faith. In repentance men turn from sin to serve the holy and forgiving God with new and glad obedience. In faith they entrust themselves to Christ and rest upon Him alone for salvation.

We believe that by the teaching and example of Jesus the Holy Spirit shows men the way and the end of the Christian life, what it means to love God with all the heart and soul and mind and strength, and to love their neighbour as themselves.

We believe that Christian men are called to abide within the fellowship of the Church, to maintain its peace and unity, and to give diligent heed to prayer, to the reading of Scripture, to common worship and the sacraments.

We believe that they are likewise called to live as those who are of the Kingdom of God, and to seek His righteousness both in individual and social life, serving their fellow-men in love for Christ's sake, and striving and waiting in prayer for an ordered common life where the will of God for the well-being and peace of men shall be done over all the earth.

We believe that in denying themselves and in following Christ men are enabled by the spirit of God more and more to die unto sin and live unto righteousness; that they are, under the hand of a faithful Father, in labour, love, and duty, in suffering, sorrow and defeat, renewed in the inner man after the image of the crucified and victorious Christ; and that they receive in this life a foretaste of the final redemption, assurance of the divine favour, peace and joy, and the confidence that He is able to keep them to the end.

So we acknowledge the Christian life as the life lived within the family of God, with the graces and privileges, the duties and discipline, through which the Christian man grows up in all things into Christ.

CHAPTER XI. CHRISTIAN LIFE AND DUTY

In Fellowship with Christ and His Church. John 15: 1-5; Col. 3: 1-4; Eph. 2: 18-22.

"Be ye perfect, even as your Father in heaven is perfect." That is the Christian ideal of conduct. But it is a formidable, indeed an impossible, challenge. That, however, is not where Jesus sets us to begin the race. He does not leave us to toil and moil at the oars unassisted. There is a sail at the disposal of the Christian, and it is with a power that blows upon us out of the unseen that we have to make the venture.

Jesus does not open His message with the words of command, "Repent ye!" That might be John Baptist's way; but Jesus has a prelude: "The time is fulfilled, and the kingdom of God is at hand" (Mark 1: 15). Grace is always in the field ahead of Christian endeavour. The unseen forces of the King of kings have taken the field before the Christian hears the call. The Beatitudes do not frame a command to *be* lowly, meek, peace-loving: they describe the fact that those upon whom the Spirit of God has come with benediction are and shall be lowly and meek and peace-loving. We share a life that opened with Christ and continues in His fellowship. In his magnificent letters Paul does not launch out into a flood of exhortation: he first reaffirms his joyous faith in the God and Father of the Lord Jesus Christ who has already done great things for men, breaking from their shoulders the yoke of sin and death, and leading many into the light and liberty of the Gospel. It is in view of what has been accomplished once and for all on the Cross that the Apostle summons his converts confidently to leave behind them the dead delights of paganism and set their affection on things above. Even in the Epistle to the Galatians, where he is pursuing a heresy in hot haste, he pauses first to exult in the God who has called him to be an apostle, and in Christ who gave Himself that He might deliver us from the present evil world. So Peter, writing to exhort those who are suffering bitter persecution, pilgrims scattered and lonely in an evil world, first thrills them with the possession already assured them in the heavens, the inheritance of eternal life.

It Begins with Repentance. Is. 55: 6-9; Matt. 5: 3-16; Matt. 18: 1-4; John 3: 5-8; Acts 2: 37-39.

The Christian life as we are called to know it is rooted in an experience of the grace of God. That may come upon us in a sudden dramatic encounter such as Paul had on the Damascus Road: after long resisting of the patience of God and the playing of a "thrawn Janet" attitude towards all divine approaches, our human stubbornness may collapse without warning. Or it may be like the quiet opening of the bud which the sun and rain of the Spirit and the gracious influences of the Christian home have for long been maturing: there is a drawing of us with cords of love—the Christian love of a father or mother or friend—a daily teaching us to walk until of our own choice we make decision for the Christian way of life. However it come, there is a conviction that must be common to all who would essay the narrow road—the sense of a measureless gratitude towards the Christ "who loved *me* and gave Himself for *me*." One thing that war has done for us is to hallow and solemnize the privilege of living by awakening in us a sense of indebtedness beyond all calculation to those who have died for us: "Never was so much owed by so many to so few." A gripping reverence comes over any thoughtful person as he takes at the breakfast table foods that have come across the seas at peril of men's lives. Our freedom to pursue our ways of liberty and democracy has been purchased before our eyes at a great cost. If only in like measure we could awaken to what has been done for us in a sphere even more sublime, the work of Christ in revealing the gracious God in action and so making known to us the face of Him who holds all lives and liberties in His hands, before whom in the last resort we all must come for judgment and final destiny! Until that majestic truth has dawned upon us and stilled our hearts to awe and wonder we can hardly hope to experience the joy of the Christian life. The tree must first send its roots down before it can breast the storms that will inevitably bear down upon it: so must the Christian sink his roots in the depths of the riches of the love of God. And he will be most likely to learn of the truth and power of the Gospel who links his life to the fellowship of his Church.

The *Shorter Catechism* has a memorable definition of repentance: "Repentance unto life is a saving grace, whereby a sinner, out of a true sense of his sin, and apprehension of the mercy of God in Christ, doth, with grief and hatred of his sin, turn from it unto God, with full purpose of and endeavour after new obedience." These classic words sum up the truth of the matter—we must sense our sin and realize God's mercy—but the order is wrong. What breaks an obdurate heart is not the horror of sin, but, as we have stressed, the mercifulness of the God against whom we have sinned. As Dr. T. W. Manson has written: "Repentance is not striving to bring one's conduct into line with the Law or with the higher righteousness demanded by Jesus. Neither is it a painful scrutiny of one's motives with a view to substituting, let us say, unselfish for selfish motives. It is a return of the whole personality to God, a submission of the will to His will, the acceptance of His sovereignty. . . . The change itself is made possible by the new experience of God as Jesus reveals Him, that is, as the merciful loving Father who seeks and saves the lost."[1] We need to flood our minds with the light that Jesus casts on the character of God and of His Kingdom. Most illuminating are those characterizations in the parables and sayings of Jesus. Woe unto those who falsify the character of God—those who put the letter of His law above care for human beings He has created, who offer Him meticulousness in externals in place of charity, nicely proper tenths instead of mercy! He pillories the one-talent man who excuses his own craven timidity by slander against the divine nature, the envious one who questions the fairness of His generosity to the eleventh hour labourers, the unforgiving servant who abuses the grace of His pity, the Pharisee who in His Temple substitutes self-praise for the contrite heart before the throne.

But the old Catechism answer is wise in the fine phrase "repentance *unto life*." This is no vain wringing of hands over the irreparable past. Nothing is irreparable with God. It is a forward movement that is here begun into a new and richer existence. Hosea has set it down in this way according to the Septuagint: "Let us follow on to know the Lord, and we *shall find Him as a dawn prepared,*" as Dr. W. M. Macgregor comments, "a delightful phrase, which is a little gospel in itself. . . . Our day is nearly done, men say, and we now are bound to travel on in deepening gloom, to darkness and eclipse and defeat. It is not so,

[1] T. W. Manson, in *The Mission and Message of Jesus,* p. 328.

says Hosea; I tell you of One who can give you the dew of the morning again, and an outlook over the radiant possibilities of a whole new day. . . . His prevailing mercy admits of no delay, and is not checked even by the gathered power of years of evil living."[2] The divine appeal is always with us: "Son, give me thine heart" (Prov. 23: 26). But that Old Testament word is supplemented by the New Testament assurance that the Father has first given us His heart, as the prodigal experienced and the elder brother with all his churlishness could not forfeit: "Son, thou art ever with me, and all that I have is thine."

That life to which we are called is pictured before us in the words of Jesus. They draw us as the everlasting hills draw the fascinated traveller. So lofty these snow-capped peaks that kiss the clouds, so far away from us! But there is One who has climbed before us and He accompanies us all the way. And the air is tonic on the hills. We grow in strength as we breathe His grace. Out of such a facing of the heights comes the brave and humble spirit acceptable to Almighty God.

And Faith. Mark 5: 25-34; Mark 11: 20-25; Gal. 15-3: 7; Rom. 3: 21-26; Phil 3: 8-12; Heb. 11.

Faith is a word of manifold meaning. It has its place in the language of the common man and also in the systems of the theologian. We see it as a charming gift in the little child: it is that which for him holds open the door of the wonderland. That is a form of the gift we wish the years did not take away. It lingers in souls of rare spirituality, enabling them to look out upon the world with an undying expectancy: they never lose the child's eyes of wonder; so generous is their trust in the unplumbed mysteries of this engaging universe that they move through the dubieties and disillusion of the scientific and materialistic age with an undimmed ardour of outlook. There is moreover a measure of faith interpenetrating all our life's relationships, whether we are conscious of it or not. "Trust," wrote Dr. Robert Law, "is the key to life. In the end all our great certainties are rooted and grounded in trust. We take each other on trust. It is the bond by which human society subsists; our loves and friendships live by the mystic sense of trust. We take nature and its laws ultimately on

[2] *Repentance unto Life,* p. 17f.

trust."[3] In *The Winds of God* Dr. John A. Hutton sets out on one of his whimsical excursions of thought. Resolving not to believe, he plays with the dreadful idea that there is no God over us. "We set out upon our life tomorrow, as usual. But stop now. In the first place it is not as usual. . . . Indeed, I don't see why, if I take my own denial seriously, I should set out at all. Why should a man set out for anything, in a world which means nothing? To me it is clear that a man who thoroughly denies God, to be consistent should stay in bed. For, the moment he gets up, he accepts the whole idea of purpose in life: and if you are going to allow purpose at all you open the door once again to the Great Purpose —the Purpose which has for its end the Will of God."[4] Perhaps the plain man thinks chiefly of faith as "trusting God in the dark." Faith in the Christian sense passes out of the region of a vague and mystic hope and becomes the form of knowledge that is held with conviction. It is a fire of assurance and certainty, an actual "seeing Him who is invisible."

"Faith is the substance of things hoped for, the evidence of things not seen" (Heb. 11 : 1). Or, as Dr. Moffatt has finely rendered it, "Now faith means that we are confident of what we hope for, convinced of what we do not see." "Faith is a certitude without proof," says Amiel. "Being a certitude, it is an energetic principle of action."[5] In Hebrews that is displayed in a long roll of the men of action—Gideon, Barak, and the rest of them. But faith in the general theological acceptance of the term is derived rather from the Gospels and the letters of Paul.

Faith is a quality that Jesus required of those upon whom He sought to do any good work. It was said of certain cities that there He could do no mighty works because of their lack of faith. It was necessary to show an open-mindedness and confidence in Him before He could release upon any soul the power that lay within Him. The centurion had it, pagan though he was: accustomed by his profession to rely upon arms and force, he yet recognized there was a region where a power not material had sway; as a man moved by love for his servant he had touched the margin of that world, and in Jesus he recognized one who had authority within that realm. To people like the woman with the issue of

[3] *Optimism and other Sermons,* p. 32.
[4] P. 85.
[5] *Journal,* 7th Feb., 1872.

blood healing was possible because there was sensitivity to an overworld of the spiritual of which Jesus was the incarnation. Thus faith in the New Testament is not so much the intellect's acceptance of certain statements of truth as the personal self-committal of a man to the gracious unseen power that was revealed in Jesus. So also in Paul faith is that in man which answers to the grace of God: it is the soul's outreaching to receive and accept the love of God that approaches us in and through Jesus Christ. The prodigal son in coming home with the desire to be received back as a hired servant was casting himself on the love and goodness of the Father. So with us in our revulsion from sin and desire for amendment: we cast ourselves without reserve on that exceeding love of God made known to us in Jesus especially in His self-giving on the Cross. We recognize we have no merit of our own, no deserving, but we trust the Christ who, expressing God's mind alway, ever went out in pity and solicitude and healing to meet any soul in need or sorrow. In Christ alone God declared His will to redeem us, and to Him alone we look for salvation. As the *Shorter Catechism* finely expresses it: "Faith in Jesus Christ is a saving grace, whereby we receive and rest upon him alone for salvation, as he is offered to us in the gospel." Dr. Alexander Whyte in his commentary adds a word of John Ruskin: "I believe that the root of almost every schism and heresy from which the Christian Church has ever suffered, has been the effort of man to earn rather than to receive his salvation."

The Teaching and Example of Jesus. Matt. 5: 7, 13; Rom. 12; 1 Cor. 13.

Christians inevitably turn to the perfect life of their Master for inspiration and guidance. There surely was manhood at its highest excellence, human powers directed to holy purposes by a will disciplined and consecrated, the nature God had designed coming to flower at last in a flame of glory. To meditate on the Gospel story is to be awakened to the beauty and potency of grace and pity, purity and peace, love and sacrifice. The flavour of character portrayed in the Beatitudes, the integrity demanded of mind and motive, the appeal to sincerity in prayer and action—all these in the Sermon on the Mount strike home upon the sensitive soul. Where else is there such a ringing certitude that God in His mercy and majesty is fashioning His Kingdom among men, that the doors of man's prison house are open, that the gladness and liberty now available on the human plane are but a foretaste of the grandeur to come? In the light of that knowledge a man sets his face to the field of human endeavour, knowing that this earthly warfare is not fought at his own charges nor for his own petty interests. Recognizing that his chief end is to glorify God and enjoy Him for ever, he sets his course by the eternal principles of love and righteousness. Unequal in his own strength to the perils of the way, he yet remembers that, having risen with Christ and set his affection on things above, he is able through grace to mortify the fleshly members and to present himself as a living sacrifice in the service of his Father and brethren.

But how shall a man translate the ideal into the concrete? How far can a life and teaching belonging to the first century amid conditions of a simpler society and in a slave state supply the guidance needed for the complex texture of industrial and international civilization in the twentieth century? If every man is to sell all and give to the poor, to lend to anyone who asks him expecting nothing in return, to be a eunuch for the Kingdom of Heaven's sake, will not society pass through chaos to extinction? The individual can turn the other cheek; but what if the nation cannot be persuaded to that policy? If according to the parable God Himself does not forgive the unforgiving servant, but hands him over to the tormentors (Matt. 18: 34), how shall it be wise or possible to forgive seventy times seven an individual or a nation that brings ruin and desolation on the innocent, and how can there be punishment except by methods of force? The practice of lending without interest, in obedience to Luke 6: 35, may be the delight of a good man without nearer responsibilities, but can trade and commerce be organized without the principle of fair returns for capital involved? If "Go not into the way of the Samaritans" (Matt. 10: 5) had been erected into a dogma, how would the early Church have heard the call to make disciples of all nations?

We must remember in the first place that Jesus often spoke to concrete situations to meet the needs of particular individuals and in times of immediate crisis, and never intended such utterances to be treated as general laws. Secondly, His continual campaign was against the oral tradition of the Rabbis that was being erected into a hard and fast legalism; and surely then it is betraying Him to convert His utterances into a system of law. How often He makes clear by His handling of a situation that it is the letter which killeth and the spirit which giveth life. The very fact that He never wrote out any dictates, but met each case as the Spirit of God gave Him utterance, can only mean that the same illumination is at hand for us: it was expedient that He should go away, but the Spirit was to come to guide us into all truth. Is it not remarkable that the greatest of all His disciples, the Apostle Paul, makes but few quotations from the actual words of Jesus, but yet carried out His ideals and principles with unexampled loyalty? If human life were static and could be carried out by a set of rules, God would have made robots and not men. It is of the very essence of our nature as spiritual beings that conditions must be fluid and infinitely various. As our muscles without exercise become flaccid and useless, so our moral sense would atrophy did we not have continually to use our discernment and conceptions of value and choose everlastingly under the guiding of the Spirit between right and wrong.

The Indian trail that led by forest and marsh, lake and portage, is not the road that best fits the automobile or the aeroplane: routes change as conditions alter. As the centuries pass and the forest rushes back where settlements once throve, the treasure marked on the map by the old trail of long ago would be hard to find. But, given guiding by the unchanging stars and the sun, the directions would hold for all time. Jesus left men not an ordnance map, but a compass, not a path that could be charted only if life remained the same as in Syria of long ago, but a set of guiding principles that are changeless as the stars and the sun. First He set down the law of love towards God—and that meant putting foremost in our affections the Kingdom and its righteousness; then He set next the law of love towards our brethren. Thus centred immovably, believers must, in accord with His teaching and within the fellowship of the Church, follow the Spirit's guiding, so that Paul facing the Romans and their peculiar problems had one counsel to give, and writing to the Colossians in Asia had other warnings and exhortations—yet all according to the mind that was in Christ Jesus his Lord. The Spirit takes of the things of Christ and shows them unto us.

To Abide Within the Fellowship, Acts 2: 42-47; Eph. 4: 1-6; 1 Cor. 1: 9-13.

As God the Creator set men in families, so God the Spirit has gathered the redeemed into fellowship. The Christian is not intended to be a lone ranger. As his characteristic quality is love, the unit of the Christian organism is a company knit by the closest of spiritual ties. The first disciples had to break with their families and friends: ostracised by official religion, they had to seek a new association. The book of Acts describes this assembly most distinctively by the word *koinōnia,* which signifies a partnership or sharing. The sharing of the material goods of life was but symbolic of a sharing of their whole life, social and spiritual, and this sense of togetherness has ever marked the Christian Church. As Jesus confronted individuals and claimed men one by one for the Kingdom, so He also called brothers, pairs of them, into the first band, as if to carry family affection into a larger fraternity. But these first Twelve were singularly diverse in character and attainments, a doubting Thomas alongside a passionate Son of Thunder, an impetuous Peter beside a guileless Nathanael; for the test of love is to hold in fellowship the unlike and dissimilar. There is a richness in the society that can maintain unity in diversity: there is the continual interflow and exchange of qualities and properties that ripens and enlarges the individual and that in combination enhances the range of the whole.

The Christian society must ever retain that genius by introducing to each other and holding together in strengthening bonds of understanding the butcher, the baker, and the candlestickmaker. Often in a community the Church is the one meetingplace for the stolid builder and the clever watchmaker, the cultured librarian and the unlettered but Spirit-filled tailor, the shrewd banker and the working gardener. As a cross-section of trades and professions it is but carrying on the first tradition of Jew and Greek, barbarian and Scythian, bond and free. All join together in the common knowledge of their need and sin and their indebtedness to the one Lord and Saviour. As modern invention has abolished distance, and by radio, telephone and plane made one society throughout the earth, so in a deeper unity the ecumenical movement of the Christian Church binds all nations and continents. How much misunderstanding would pass out of the relationship of labour and capital and out of the bitter hates of race and race, East and West, if only the Christian fellowship drew still closer its professing membership throughout the continents and the islands of the sea! The fellowship of individual churches has made possible the missionary enterprise, and the missionary enterprise has built bridges across many yawning chasms of misunderstanding. Each Christian Church has enriched the civilization of its age and continent, infusing throughout its home and family life the spirit of love and promising eventually to displace the ruthless competition of commerce by goodwill and co-operation.

The individual, however great his gifts or graces, cannot make effective his contribution to the whole if he tries to work as a lone prophet. For a few such there may be a place, but for the many it is by sending their roots deep into the soil of the Church that they will yield a harvest for humankind. The Spirit can work through the individual, but the peculiar sphere of the Spirit is the Church. Recall the counsel of "a serious man" given to John Wesley in his early manhood, when he had been greatly affected by the *Imitatio Christi* and Law's *Serious Call:* "Sir, you wish to serve God and go to heaven. Remember, you cannot serve Him alone. You must therefore find companions or make them. The Bible knows nothing of solitary religion."[6] Within the fellowship of the Church have grown up the golden Scriptures, the glories of the hymnody, the soul-stirring music of Johann Sebastian Bach, the treasured liturgies, the books of devotion, the whole language and piety and testimony of the religious life. And how much the spread of education, the arts and sciences, owed in pioneer stages to the Church! The Church is the Jerusalem that is the mother of us all, and it is from membership in her that we can draw most fruitfully from the gathered traditions of the past, and share most lavishly in the comradeship and joy of the spiritual life of today. Within her fellowship we are kindled to devotion to whatsoever things are true and honest, just, pure, lovely, and of good report; we are moved to emulate every spiritual excellence, and, sharing in the necessities and anxieties of the saints, we come to know the height and breadth and depth of Christian faith and hope and love. Rubbing shoulders with all sorts and conditions of men, we

[6] Quoted by A. Birrell, in *Collected Essays,* p. 118.

broaden our sympathies and deepen our social aspirations, eschew division and class antagonism. We come to know ourselves and seek to promote in others the joy of peace and unity.

Give Heed to Prayer. Luke 11: 1-13; Luke 18: 1-14; Luke 22: 39-46; Luke 23: 34; Phil. 4: 6; Eph. 3: 14-20; James 5: 16.

Prayer is in one aspect the loneliest of human acts. A man removes himself like the Master, as it were, a stone's throw from his closest friends, and casts himself down in the presence of God alone. The unseen ladder where the ministering angels ascend and descend touches the pillow of the solitary. It is of the essence of religion that the individual soul communes in deepest intimacy with the God who calls each one by name. Our creatureliness demands that link with the Creator and Lord of our life. This is no mockery of mere self-persuasion, the bringing of the rebellious self into harmony with an inscrutable will that knows no change. It is a truly personal God who in the silence meets us, hears our plea, and ministers the grace the expectant soul requires. It is a real encounter with the Almighty who is also the All-Merciful, One whose ear is open and whose hand is ready to heal and to help as was the Lord Jesus in His earthly ministry. By this act strength is given from above and more things are wrought than this world dreams of. Did not Heraclitus say that you cannot find the boundaries of the soul by travelling in any direction? He who, in faith, asks, seeks, knocks, receives bread, power, entrance. Importunity is encouraged by the same Jesus who had sometimes, as in Gethsemane, to be content to say: "Thy will, not mine, be done." As flowers open receptive to the sun, so in prayer the spiritual awaken to the inflow of a divine energy. "We must not conceive of prayer as an overcoming of God's reluctance, but as a laying hold of His highest willingness."[7]

But solitary prayer is quickened and enlarged by the intercession of the many. The Lord's Prayer forms no chain out of "my" and "mine", but out of "our" and "us." If Jesus often prayed alone all night, He went as was His wont on the Sabbath day to the synagogue and shared there in the fellowship of common prayer. Jesus cleansed the Temple that the Father's house might be the house of prayer *for all nations.* He pictured His society as

[7] Archbishop Trench.

a Temple in which we are all living stones; and if He thought of the very stones of the earthly house as breaking into praise (Luke 19: 40), then surely we living stones must be vibrant with prayer and praise. We cannot read the letters of Paul without realizing with what intensity Paul had prayed with and for his converts.

Intercessory prayer is the life blood of the Church. It sweeps into our consciousness the needs of all men everywhere, and especially focuses our thought on those upon whom the burden of life has fallen most heavily, earth's countless sufferers and mourners. By its mere repetition we thus come to an awareness of and sensitivity to the wider human realities with the resultant deepening and enriching of our sympathy and sense of responsibility. Once we have set the world's heartbreak before God, we have been compelled to face the call of duty or obligation as it falls upon us. To lift up before the divine pity the warring world of our time is to sharpen our own conscience in relation to the rights of our cause and at the same time to challenge the Christlikeness of our attitude towards those who are our enemies. Rightly conceived, prayer is not the partisan appeal of two sides to the same God to give incompatible victory to each, but rather the purging of both contestants in the divine sight and the acceptance of that wisdom and righteousness that is higher and nobler than our limited conception.

Moreover intercession is never merely a chorus of human voices. "The Spirit Himself maketh intercession for us with groanings which cannot be uttered" (Rom. 8: 26). We have our Great High Priest: "Wherefore also he is able to save to the uttermost them that draw near unto God through him, seeing he ever liveth to make intercession for them" (Heb. 7: 25). "Nowhere is the Church so literally the Body of Christ as when she offers Intercession. No act more closely unites her with her Lord than when, vitalized by His life, instructed by His mind, and guided by His spirit, she pours forth her soul in entreating God's blessing for mankind. She is there indeed the representative of the seeking Saviour. She is there with all the company of the Saints before the Altar of God, offering her own life for the life of the world, that the world may be reconciled to God."[8]

Thus intercession is not to be valued merely by its reaction on ourselves: that is less than half its virtue. "The effectual fervent

[8] O. B. Milligan, *The Ministry of Worship*, p. 39.

prayer of a righteous man availeth much" (James 5: 16), and how much more the unified supplication of the many, laden with the anguish of bitter need! We believe that by prayer the windows of heaven may be opened and a blessing poured forth that outreaches the range of our thought and expectation. Shall not the Judge of all the earth do right? On Calvary it might have been argued that God could not by the same act bless persecutors and persecuted, and yet in the final disposal of that tragic event did He not both answer the cry of dereliction and transmute the desire of Caiaphas that one man should die for the nation?

To the Reading of Scripture.

"From a child thou hast known the holy scriptures, which are able to make thee wise unto salvation through faith which is in Christ Jesus.

All scripture is given by inspiration of God, and is profitable for doctrine, for reproof, for correction, for instruction in righteousness:

That the man of God may be perfect, thoroughly furnished unto all good works" (2 Tim. 3: 15-16).

Such is the classical definition of the value of Scripture. The records in the Old Testament of how God has spoken and still wills to speak to those who have ears to hear, the pages of the New Testament in which Christ becomes alive again to the believer, those writings in which the Spirit has harvested so discerningly of the faith and love and hope of the early Church—such is the treasure trove given into the hand of every Christian for his nourishment and growth in grace. Read in large tracts, the Bible fires the imagination with the splendour and awe of the righteous acts of God; read intensively, as psalm by psalm, or parable by parable, or pondered verse by verse, passage by passage, it confronts us with challenge, rebuke, consolation, as the Spirit ministers to our varying need. There are times when the words fall on deaf ears, times when we misconstrue and even pervert the teaching; for human unreason leads us astray: we must be in the spirit if we are to handle rightly the Word of God. To appreciate, *e.g.*, a prophetic passage or a letter of Paul, we need the patient study that fills in the background and lights up the historical situation, and to that must be added the Spirit's guiding that makes the episode of long ago contemporary to us. The anger of Jonah at the sparing of repentant Nineveh becomes at the touch of the Spirit our own resentment at the suggestion of forgiveness for the national enemies of today. Paul's counsel to those who are troubled about meats offered to idols becomes apt and modern as we are confronted with the problem of alcoholic beverages in the society around us. The pacifist teaching of the Suffering Servant of Isaiah shines out as strangely disturbing when we see it suggested for the India of today. The experiences of the Psalmists marvellously parallel our own oftentimes, and their greater faith rebukes us of the twentieth century who have the larger light of the New Testament and the example of Christian martyrs to strengthen us. There is no mood of the soul, hardly a problem of living in this complex age, that cannot be illuminated and resolved by an encounter with the Word that the Spirit makes alive. Inspiration, condemnation, light and power for daily living—all are there for the student who is willing to be taught of God. But, lest ignorance and partisan blindness betray us, let us use all the aids that modern scholarship can give us to explicate the text of Scripture, and let us turn to the open page only after we have sought the receptive heart and the guiding light of the Spirit.

Those who are not orthodox believers sometimes exhibit an appreciation of the grandeur of our Bible that might well put us to shame. In a preface to a series of Scripture "passages chosen for their literary beauty and interest" these words occur from the pen of Sir James Frazer, a scholar who had an unequalled knowledge of the world's religions: "The reading of it breaks into the dull round of common life like a shaft of sunlight on a cloudy day, or a strain of solemn music heard in a mean street. It seems to lift us for a while out of ourselves, our little cares and little sorrows, into communion with those higher powers, whatever they are, which existed before man began to be, and which will exist when the whole human race, as we are daily reminded by the cataclysms and convulsions of nature, shall be swept out of existence for ever. It strengthens in us the blind conviction, or the trembling hope, that somewhere, beyond these earthly shadows, there is a world of light eternal, where the obstinate questionings of the mind will be answered, and the heart find rest."[9]

[9] Quoted in J. H. Moulton, *The Christian Religion in the Study and the Street,* p. 226.

The reading of Scripture in church is sometimes taken as a convenient opportunity to look round and let the thoughts go woolgathering. That is an appalling irreverence. Read appropriately in all the dignity and beauty of the Authorized Version, what passage is there that cannot touch the mind or imagination? This is an appointed act in the worship of God. It is the soul seeking after God if haply he may find Him, as in a psalm like the forty-second, or it is God speaking His momentous truth for us men and our salvation—as in John 3. Let the reader fall out of view, the pulpit and every object that meets the eye, and conceive that out of a great silence, out of the heart of the sanctuary, a divine voice is breaking forth to declare, to plead, to protest, to console, to convict. Let us concentrate all our soul's power to listen and to wait with expectation, and it may be with us there in the holy place as it was with Isaiah in the year that King Uzziah died, or as it was with John of Patmos when he was in the spirit on the Lord's Day. There is a momentum behind the hallowed Word, a glory that springs forth from the sacred page, a mystery that enthralls the questing soul where divine grace reaches out to touch and transform our human need. That is a supreme moment in the sanctuary when in an atmosphere electric with expectation to the thousand listening souls the preacher, borne of the Spirit to a higher plane, speaks the healing and uplifting Word of God.

To Common Worship. Is. 6; Luke 4: 16; Mark 11: 17; Acts 16: 13; John 4: 24; Heb. 10: 25.

Worship is at once the unveiling of the Divine Presence and the response of the human soul. It is a movement from God to man and from man to God. The sanctuary is the place that *God* has appointed, the place where He comes in all the plenitude of His grace to meet face to face with those who are constrained to acknowledge Him as the Author and Redeemer of all life. The Creator has ever been minded to communicate Himself to His creatures. In the beauty of the garden, in the loneliness of Bethel, in the glory of the burning bush, in the heights of desolate Sinai, He chose to confront men and let them hear a whisper of His voice. From the golden sunrise and red lingering sunset, from the vastness of the flaming firmament, from the terror of the thunderbolt and the flash of the lightning, from the splendour that is spread as a garment on river and lake, meadow and forest, on the cloud-capped mountain and the restless stretching sea, God has spoken mystery and has constrained man to draw near and seek communion with the power behind the glory. Within the soul He has spoken in the still small voice, in the quickening of the moral conscience, in the need that must have speech with One higher and holier. In the joys and sorrows of individual lives, in national movements, even in the midst of war and tumult, out of the crises of history, the divine voice is ever calling demandingly. Thus comes that face to face of the Creator God and the created man that is worship. We must needs acknowledge the hand that has fashioned us, the wisdom that has guided us, the love that has redeemed us. Our nature cries out for that hallowing contact, and God in His mercy has drawn near and given us foretaste in worship of the final glory that is to come.

From the worship of the Hebrews we derive the rich legacy of the Psalms; in such a glimpse as Isaiah 6, we see the wonder and the glory of the throne on high, the mystery and the majesty of the God of the Old Testament. In the vision of the Apocalypse, chaps. 4, 5, we stand in awe before the praise and honour ascribed in the heavenly heights to the Author of our salvation and to the Lamb that was slain. The letters of Paul, the Magnificat in Luke, the prologue of the Fourth Gospel, radiate the spirit and language of worship in the early Church. With our coming together on the Lord's Day we enter into that heritage and join our voices to the cry of all creation in homage to the Lord God Almighty which was and is and is to come and to Him who has the keys of life and of death.

These are days when men have a new community conscience. Our lives are so interwoven that we stand or fall together: the war and its unnumbered perils brought home to us all this unity and interdependence. Must not that common life be lifted up to the God who is the Creator, Preserver, and sole Redeemer of its life? Are there not social sins, community plague spots, calls upon our common conscience and joint endeavour, which should be laid before the holy altar of the God of Righteousness? Does not the common weal depend on the integrity, devotion, self-giving, unselfishness, love, charity, and goodwill of all its members, and can that spiritual linkage be sustained in strength unless it is sanctified, dedicated, baptized into the spirit of Christ? Common worship is surely the consummation of the community life and spirit. Where there is no vision the people perish; and how shall a man see visions and dream dreams except he be found in the spirit on the Lord's Day?

There is always the odd person who claims that he can worship alone, and there are the many who prefer the sanctuary of the maples to any regular service of worship. Those who thus cut themselves off from the Christian communion would be surprised to be branded as graceless borrowers, and yet such they are in that they really carry into their solitary or their individualistic worship emotions and intimations of reality they have derived from the common Christian heritage. To ponder a Bible under the birches or to sing a hymn on sunset point is really to borrow from the ordered tradition of the Church. To let the soul outreach in prayer seeking Him who made the beauty of earth and air and sky is not *full* Christian worship unless it go on to sing the praise of Him who died. By all means let us seek God alone sometimes under the cathedral of the woods or in the music of the lake shore; but let us not forget that it was in the old country church or in the city congregation that we learned the imperishable truths of our religion, and that we thus have a debt to pay to our fellow-believers, and especially to those who come after us, that we share in and fully maintain the regular worship of the sanctuary. Would any one who loves his country wish to absent himself from those grand community assemblies of worship when dire peril threatens the state or when solemn national occasions like a coronation call all men to give thanks and supplication to Almighty God? Then why should any devout soul care to absent himself from the regular service when the redeeming acts of the Gracious Father are remembered and His cause the world over is borne up in prayer before Him? Then the community should best realize its oneness and rise to the height of its living experience when it makes solemn acknowledgment of the Over-ruling Majesty on high.

And the Sacraments. Luke 24: 30, 35; Acts 20: 7, 11.

The climax of common worship is found in the Sacraments. In baptism is declared that amazing grace of God that comes to meet us at the threshold of life and will sustain us to the end. Every baptism is an occasion when we must be stirred anew to give thanks for that grace and take our share of responsibility that that grace be mediated through the fellowship of the Church. The fitting place for that taking and renewing of pledges is the sanctuary of God. In the Lord's Supper the central act of God's redemption through the Cross of Christ is set forth in symbol and the Redeemer Himself is Host at His table. Surely every soul that acknowledges its own salvation and every one who realizes his own need must be there to give thanks and to receive anew. Opinion will differ as to how often the rite should be observed; but all who know the human heart with its truancy and its lapses into worldly ways will confess the need for seeking the Living Presence of the Saviour and renewing with thanksgiving our vows and prayers at His table. It is good to be recalled to the central reality of the faith—the Love that has condescended to tabernacle among us and redeem us from our sin—and there is no other way so effectual for bringing us back to the centre as this public celebration of the sacrament of the Lord's Supper. Do we not often notice that as the saints leave the act of worship there is a trail of glory on their faces?

As Those Who are of the Kingdom of God. Luke 4: 16-21; Luke 6: 20-37; Mark 12: 13-17; Rom. 13: 1-7; 1 Pet. 2: 13-17.

The Christian citizen has a very definite call to service in this world order. As a colony of heaven we are not removed from this present order, but rather have a responsibility heightened by our membership in a spiritual order. The poet with a song in his soul must needs sing it out through the imperfect medium of words. As the individual has set before him the imperative "Be ye perfect even as your Father in heaven is perfect," so the community is laid upon our conscience by the simple petition "Thy kingdom come, Thy will be done in *earth* as it is in heaven." It is not in human power to bring the Kingdom; but, having in our heart a picture of the heavenly realm, we cannot but strive to realize for men upon earth some foretaste of that perfect life to come. As sons of God we are called to live here and now in the spirit of love and righteousness that befits our final destiny.

Too often the Church has been betrayed into an otherworldly policy of indifference to this age and time. Many in the days of the early Church looked for the sudden coming from heaven of the Kingdom that marks the end of the age, and they felt in consequence divorced from earthly and temporal obligations. Moreover, the early Church was a feeble few in a great world of heathendom, and in the hands of a despotic Rome which allowed no democratic rights to her subjects. Yet even under that limitation Jesus did not despair of citizenship: He said "Render unto Cæsar the things that are Cæsar's." Paul made full use of his Roman citizenship to forward his missionary activity. He even set up the counsel of loyalty: "Let every soul be subject unto the higher powers. For there is no power but of God: the powers that be are ordained of God" (Rom. 13: 1). So also even in the midst of persecution the author of 1 Peter urges: "Submit yourselves to every ordinance of man for the Lord's sake: whether it be to the king, as supreme; or unto governors, as unto them that are sent by him . . . for so is the will of God" (1 Pet. 2: 13ff.).

In estimating social duty Jewish piety made much of works of pity and charity; and there is an obvious appeal to us Christians likewise in the care of the needy, the widow and the orphan, the unfortunates of every class. But Jesus did not merely stop holes in an old order. He rather set in motion forces creative of a new order. In modern states, furthermore, we are free citizens under the liberty of the Spirit of God. Constructive citizenship therefore is the Christian obligation. Man is a spiritual being: his interests must have precedence over profits or machines. Man is a person, not a mere "hand" or chattel to be hired at will and thrown on the discard without care for his welfare or the well-being of those dependent on him. Man is a brother for whom Christ died: therefore the state, the employing corporation, the individual trader, must give heed to the fact that immortal creatures are not mere market commodities to be bought and sold. Over little children Jesus cast a protecting shield; so must the Christian state. Education and child welfare are central, not peripheral, concerns. In the Christian view there is neither Jew nor Greek, barbarian, Scythian, male nor female, bond nor free. Those racial distinctions, class or cultural distinctions, sex differentiations, must go. On such principles as these the Christian citizen must ever be urging betterment of conditions in the society of which he is a voting member. The principles of Jesus cannot recognize man-made barriers at any frontier of human life. We are called on to "bring into captivity every thought to the obedience of Christ" (2 Cor. 10: 5.)

The reformer must remember the warning of Amiel that

"right apart from duty is a compass with one leg." Engrossed with thoughts of what society owes to him, he must not forget what he owes to society. And the Christian must not be the impractical saint in a hurry. He must admit that there are more ways than one of achieving social ends, and fellow-citizens equally sincere may stand for other ways of procedure. There are always genuine believers in the dictum: Improve the character of your citizens, and conditions will improve of themselves without legislation. The Church, it must be remembered, is a spiritual organism, and is not to be harnessed to the machinery of any party; it is a powerhouse which supplies light and heat, not the factory which turns the raw material into goods. There will always be differences of opinion as to how far the Church should be related to the political world. Some will point to the Lutheran Church in Germany and claim that there is a church which has kept strictly to a narrow spiritual function, eschewing political action, and see the result today—in a people that has needed leadership and has not found it in men of goodwill. Others will point to the political machinations of the Roman Church and show how that has depreciated her religious influence and led her into spheres of worldly intrigue. Really it is a matter where it will often be hard to draw the line between moral testimony and political activity. In our impatience it will be well to remember that our Lord Himself was more tolerant and large-minded than His disciples, and so be willing to grant the rightness of motive of those who do not go with us all the way (Luke 9: 49, 50). Already it seems evident that the post-war world will be minded for a more drastic reconstruction of the social order than has before been attempted; and, if we may judge from the Malvern report, the Scottish *God's Will in our Time,* and similar utterances, the Church is determined to set Christian principles in the vanguard. Yet there is the counter demand: Let the Church be the Church.

Our world rings from end to end today with the call to this new social order, and we hear loud and clear the watchwords of democracy and freedom: liberty, equality, fraternity. There is a willing and ardent responsiveness everywhere to this challenge from the disinherited and the sufferers of many lands. Blue prints of a fairer society are placarded before our eyes, and hopes spring freely from the disasters and frustrations of the yesterdays. War and competition abolished from the life of nations as peace and co-operation possess the stage under international agreement! Gardens to bloom profusely where now stand the "dark Satanic mills" where human labour has been cheap to hire and honest toil has been a soulless drudgery! New standards of food and health, and spacious homes in place of crowded, evil-smelling tenements! No youth denied its larger opportunity, no old age a prey to the terrors of want and loneliness!

But by what power can these mansions of promise be built and on what foundations? Victory alone cannot make a true peace nor equality a real brotherhood, nor will bricks and mortar and state subsidies create a New Jerusalem. A society that dissolves its Lord's Day into a weekly frolic can know no true rest. A society which loosens the marriage tie for frivolous oddities of temper cannot know the love that creates a home. Humanity that is made in the image of God cannot live its life off centre. Manhood cannot reach its full stature without the Christ, and womanhood has a passion of devotion that the Man of Nazareth alone can satisfy. Political organizations are empty frames until they own allegiance to eternal principles.

Where is there a social conscience that can rise above the national and racial except in the Church of Christ? Where is there a power by which to lift the mass of human clay except the power of God? Where is there a hope that will still live when the fashions of the passing hour die away except the Christian Gospel?

"We are to oppose the new paganism in the name of humanity, justice, liberty, brotherhood, and the indefeasible value of the individual human soul. That answer is well enough, so far as it goes, but I am sure that it must go further. These indeed are the ideals of the Christian ages, or some of them, or at least they sound very like them, but in the Christian ages they were all deeply rooted in something bigger and grander, in something that was no mere ideal but an eternal reality. They were rooted in the love of God as manifest in Jesus Christ our Lord. . . . It was Christ who taught us the indefeasible value of the individual soul. It was Christ who taught us the meaning of *fraternité* when He said, 'One is your Master, even Christ; and all ye are brethren' (Matt. 23: 8); and St. Paul when he said that 'we, being many, are one body in Christ, and every one members one of another' (Rom. 12: 5)."[10]

[10] John Baillie, *Invitation to Pilgrimage*, p. 125f.

That new democracy we envisage with peace and plenty, freedom and the liberal arts, must needs remember the way by which she has come into her inheritance. I have heard tell of a pushful spider that heard the call to live a larger life than a cold and leaky roof supplied, and so he spun out his fine filament one morning and slid down to a lower level, where there was good prospect of many winged passers-by. There he spread his net large and wide, and soon he grew plump and prosperous on the folly of poor flies. Overfed and sleepy to the point of forgetfulness, one day he was roving round his estate, when he lighted upon the gossamer thread on which it swung. "What's the use of that?" he asked and snapped the filament. So perished a good home and good hunting.

There is one sphere where Christian statesmanship is now overwhelmingly imperative—the international sphere. Guarantees must be devised which will secure peace among the nations, and that end so much desired will require standards of equity and freedom from vindictive passion that the Church can best proclaim. It is not too much to say that the sanity and righteousness and goodwill of the new order will depend on the realism with which Christian principles are asserted and applied.

A Foretaste of Final Redemption. Col. 1: 12-13, 27; Eph. 2: 4-10.

The Christian who thus disciplines himself in the fellowship of the Church and the service of the Kingdom becomes himself under the hand of God a transfigured personality. As Saul the proud Pharisee became Paul the slave of Christ, and the impetuous opinionated Peter became the martyr who turned back into the city of death, so the common self-seeker undergoes sanctification. Following Christ and entering into the spirit of His living, we may by grace grow towards the fulness of His stature. Not that we all keep on the way of progress or all attain to the heights. But there is the beginning of life on a higher scale with finer values and a richer content. We enter into that serenity that only they can know who have sought and found in God the Father who does not fail.

Is sanctification the end of the story? That old theological word does not mean "perfection." It describes rather a state or process. When Paul addressed the Corinthian Christians as saints he did not mean that they had attained: he knew only too well that they were at most "old strugglers" or halting beginners. As "saints" they were those whom the Spirit of God had chosen, separated from the thraldom of pagan gods, and set facing Christwards. Before them was a long and arduous process. The *Shorter Catechism* defined sanctification as a "work of God's free grace," as distinct from a single "act" like justification. It is not the triumph of a moment "to die unto sin and live unto righteousness." Sins are not easily mastered: they cannot be eliminated one by one by painful concentration of *human* effort. The method is rather indicated by the counsel: "When thoughts of sin press on thee, look over their shoulder seeking another thing, the which thing is God."[11] Victory comes by "the expulsive power of a new affection." He who keeps before him "the image of the crucified and victorious Christ" appropriates to himself a force that draws him onwards. He is marked for sanctification who keeps open the lines of communication with the eternal world, feeling the impact on his life of a great deed of redemption and the constraining grasp of the Holy Spirit. Love and prayer are the power lines. The true pattern of life is triangular: God, myself, and my neighbour. "Sanctification is essentially the return of man from the exile of . . . individualism and his incorporation in the triangle of relations to God and to his neighbour to which his life belongs."[12] Such a life never loses wholesome contact with the concrete, the tragic, and the real, and yet it has by reason of the inflow from above the foretaste of redemption.

[11] *The Cloud of Unknowing*, ch. 32.
[12] *Expository Times*, vol. li. p. 275b (1940).

XII. The Consummation.

We believe that the resurrection and exaltation of Christ, following on His crucifixion, gives assurance that the long struggle between sin and grace will have an end, the Kingdom be revealed in its fullness, and God's eternal purpose accomplished.

We believe that God will judge all men by Jesus Christ, the Son of Man.

We believe that, while salvation is offered to all, God does not take away or override the freedom with which He has endowed men. If they stubbornly refuse His mercy and prefer sinful ways, they shut themselves out from the light and joy of salvation and fall under the righteous judgment of God.

We believe that those who accept the offer of salvation and persevere in the Christian way do after death enter into the joy of their Lord, a blessedness beyond our power to conceive. They see God face to face, and in the communion of saints are partakers with the Church on earth of its labours and prayers.

So we acknowledge the righteous and merciful judgment of God and we wait for the coming of the Kingdom which shall have no end.

CHAPTER XII. THE CONSUMMATION

Hazard and Hope, two cruel gods are they
Who equally on all mankind do prey.

So writes the Greek poet Theognis, and so writing he reminds us that to the thought of his countrymen hope was a delusive thing. In the myth of Pandora, the first mortal woman of Greek legend, we are told that the supreme god, Zeus, wished to punish Prometheus for giving to men the gift of fire, and so he sent him a wife, Pandora, endowed with all the graces. To Pandora Zeus gave a beautiful box which when opened released upon the world all the evils except hope, which remained alone at the bottom of the box. Hope thus was generally regarded not as man's one remaining consolation, but as an evil: it is pictured as "blind," "airy," "easily led astray," that "on which exiles feed," just as it is to the poet Cowper, who describes it as the delusion that

Sets the stamp of vanity on all
That men have deemed substantial since the Fall.

It was only in later times that with the development of personal religion hope became almost a technical term for the assurance of a blessed immortality which was promised to the initiates in the mystery religions. Professor Burnet regarded it as the equivalent of faith to the Orphics.

The Bible, however, regards hope as an unquestionable good. To Paul the supreme misfortune of the Gentiles was that they were without hope and without God in the world (Eph. 2: 12). To him God was the author and giver of hope (Rom. 15: 13), and it would seem that in that word he saw summed up the uniqueness of the religion of his fathers, the promise that had been fulfilled in Jesus Christ: "for the hope of Israel I am bound with this chain" (Acts 28: 20; 26: 6). The long expectation of the people of Israel, the Messianic yearnings that had been cherished by prophet and Psalmist, that golden strand of promise that since the days of Abraham had been woven into the history of the faithful, had reached reality in the coming of Jesus Christ. Because a righteous God and faithful Creator had been the inspirer of that hope, it had been no delusion, but a glorious certainty. With Jesus the ages had reached their climax in the advent of the Kingdom, and to the individual in particular that brought the gift of eternal life. This was the grand theme of all the sacred writings: "For whatsoever things were written aforetime were written for our learning, that we through patience and comfort of the scriptures might have hope" (Rom. 15: 4). This then was the deepest note, the abiding message, of the Old Testament—that Hebrew history was not an endless up and down of frustration and tantalizing disappointment, but a mysterious movement towards a goal, the consummation of the Kingdom of God.

The Resurrection Gives Assurance. 1 Pet. 1: 3-12.

What that Christian hope really means comes to clear expression in the First Epistle of Peter (1: 3ff.), written to Christians suffering persecution. It is an inheritance beyond the reach of corruption, taint, or decay, reserved in heaven and thus under the sure protection of Almighty God. And most suggestively it is described as a hope that is *living*, and living *through the resurrection of Jesus Christ.* Peter may well call it a living hope; for he himself had been in dead despair until the presence of the Risen Christ was first made known to him (1 Cor. 15: 5). That is the element in the Christian situation of the first days that makes real this seemingly fantastic dream of some companies of humble folk, many of them mean slaves, scattered throughout a hostile and scornful world. Apparently defenceless and pitiable exiles in a society to which they do not belong, they are yet guarded by faith for a new life, the guarantee and sign manual of which a never-failing God has already provided by a unique demonstration of His power over this passing universe in the fact that He has raised from the clutches of death His son Jesus Christ. The implication is that He who has overcome man's last dread enemy of death can surely deliver to His waiting people the consummation on which they have set their hopes, the Kingdom of God with its gift of life on a new plane. It is the same radiant certainty that flashes out from Paul's great glimpse into the future in Romans 8. He sees men predestined to share the likeness of the Son of Man, called, justified, and glorified; and surely the God who did not spare His own son will unfailingly give us everything besides.

Nothing in earth or heaven, in the present or the future, can come between us and the splendour of God's love in Christ Jesus our Lord.

When Paul preached on Mars Hill to the people of Athens it was the Resurrection that was the stumbling-block. They laughed off the idea: they would wait and hear again of this matter. The Greeks, we must realize, did believe in the immortality of the *soul*. But to them it was unthinkable that a man in the totality of his personality—corruptible flesh as well as ethereal spirit—should rise again. Our notions of immortality are apt to be like the Greek conception; hence it is important to appreciate exactly what is involved here. Writing to Greeks and aware what hope meant in their thought, Paul exclaims to the Corinthians (1 Cor. 15: 12ff.): If in this life we merely had arrived at hope in Christ (and stayed there at mere hope, the verb implies), then of all men we are to be pitied most. But that is not our Christian position, he says. Christ actually has been, and remains, raised from the dead. That fact, he implies, makes hope into certainty. God to Hebrew thought was not, as to the Greeks, aloof from the course of human affairs. He came right into the stream of history and gave it direction and purpose. To the Greek, history was a constant alternation of ages, an endless cycle of recurrence, the idyllic era giving place to evil days, ever degenerating and running on into catastrophe, and then out of chaos a new golden age arising, and so on. Collisions of atoms brought the world together and in due time it would break up again. It was a whirligig of fate, the steersman now relaxing now resuming control. From such a materialistic swirl it was well that the divine in man, the soul, should escape.

The Struggle will have an End. Luke 12: 32-40; Rev. 20.

The Hebrew insisted that God's care was never removed from the world He had made. He was often hidden in mystery; but as a God of will and purpose He would break in upon the process of time and work His sovereign design. That holy intent of His was to establish His Kingdom, to make His will prevail in the course of human affairs. But men were often puzzled by the setbacks of history, and craved an assurance that He had not left His workshop of a world unattended. To the Christian believers, that proof was given in the coming of Jesus Christ; and, when dismay descended on them with the apparent desertion of the Crucifixion, irrefragable proof of the steadfast purpose of God was reasserted by the Resurrection. The God who had plucked Jesus from the jaws of death and balked the evil powers of their prey would surely go farther and establish His reign with sovereign power over all the forces of darkness. Jesus made men conscious in an unprecedented degree that the God above was a Father with goodwill towards men, with a love that would pass through any ordeal and persist over any human obduracy; and, when to that was added the testimony of the Resurrection that to fatherliness He had added almightiness with the mind to assert Himself here and now, there was nothing lacking to give complete and final assurance of victory to the Christian hope.

Jesus taught us to pray, "Thy kingdom come, Thy will be done in *earth,*" and He was ever active in the healing and the spiritual liberation of men and women in His day. Therefore it is incumbent on us also to labour and to strive to break every evil yoke that is laid here and now upon mankind. To make a pious gesture heavenwards and to leave it all to divine Providence is to sleep at the post of duty. It is your Father's good pleasure to give you the Kingdom, He said—but at the same time He sent out disciples to make haste on the King's business; and all through the centuries His spirit has been driving to service Pauls and Peters, Wilberforces and Shaftesburys, Lincolns and Schweitzers, with the great multitude of common devoted men and women. It may not be in man to build the Kingdom, but there are countless folk who can be reclaimed from evil and built into the living temple here on earth, and there are tyrannies and cruelties aplenty that must be broken to emancipate human personalities for the freer life and service our Master wills for His own.

In blazing words Professor John Line has laid this obligation to social action on the conscience of the Church. Describing the Incarnation as God's self-involvement in man's life, he sees a mandate thereby placed over us:

"For if God is self-involved with men, then where are we? We cannot call common what God has cleansed; we cannot be indifferent to what God has been at such pains to claim as His. Had God been indifferent to human need and despair, no

Incarnation would have occurred. It is God's concern for the world, in the opposite scale to indifference, that has given us the Christian Gospel; and His grace toward us constrains us to share this concern; to self-involvement with men in their uttermost need after the manner of God.

"Nor is this to be construed as just 'spiritual'; the spiritual is a false concept if emptied of the forces and tensions of man's actual life. It is pseudo-Christianity to be absorbed in the deification of our own souls, leaving the world and its ways to God. We ought to know by now that when we do this we don't leave the world to God; we leave it to the devil. Or we leave the human travail to others; for we may be sure that if Christians will not re-fashion human society, others will. The world won't stay as it is; and it will be our apostasy if the great things needed to re-stabilize human existence are done by Communists and Fascists, Christians being engrossed in trivialities. If others get deeper than Christians into humanity's struggle, it will be our betrayal of Christ. For He is at the heart of this struggle. This is the Incarnation again; therein God entered man's struggle with evil; or as before, the Incarnation is God's self-involvement, but not merely with man—with the very evil that would destroy man, that instead the evil itself might be destroyed."[1]

The Kingdom in its Fullness. Mark 12: 18-27; Rom. 8: 18-39; 1 Cor. 15: 3-57; 2 Cor. 4: 16—5: 10; 1 John 3: 1-3; Rev. 21-22.

Humanity, however, dare not ever settle on its lees and accept contentment within the limitations of this earthly home. With long periods of peace and social betterment it is fatally easy to resurrect the misleading doctrine of unending progress and set up as gods Parks, Plumbing, and Public Utilities. We need to remind ourselves that civilizations grow fat, corrupt, and sick with the seeds of death. We have all history against the notion that mankind can be organized and mechanized into a state of perfection. We have the fact of human nature to warn us that in the idyllic garden the serpent lurks: sin is not a negligible appendix to human life; Christ did not die to free us from an

[1] John Line, *Hope in God* (17th Annual Report of Board of Evangelism and Social Service), 1941, p. 47f.

evil that modern psycho-analysts can wheedle out by scientific practice. Nor have we any encouragement to believe that this solid earth can defy the sinister forces of the universe and continue its rotations without threat of death or change. What if some whirling comet strike this moving mass in shattering collision, or a dying sun leave us to perish in the freezing temperature of an ice age? Can science that knows so much provide another home, another scene for our passing habitation? It is well to hearken to the ancient admonition that here we have no continuing city: kingdoms on earth can not be everlasting kingdoms. Yet our Creator and Father has set eternity in our hearts.

Thus we are thrust back where later Jewish thought had come to rest—to the idea that earth cannot be the scene of the final consummation of God. Some indeed visualize an earth transfigured and glorified, while others transfer the scene to the heavenly sphere: the earth would pass away, and the righteous waking from their sleep would rise into the heavens as beings transfigured and radiant as the angels of God.

In the New Testament writers we find thought still taking shape within the inherited Jewish framework. The author of the Apocalypse pictures a climax for the earthly scene as well as a final consummation: he foresees a Millennium on earth before the curtain rises on the last scenes. As the patriotic Israelites had always yearned for a national kingdom eclipsing the grandeur even of Solomon's spreading domain, so the Apocalypse forecasts the binding of Satan and the reign of Christ on this earth, a first resurrection enjoyed only by the martyr saints, the rest of the dead remaining in the cheerless shadowland of Hades. But the perfected order of things cannot be contained within the limits of earth. Thus a further stage opens. At the close of the Millennium Satan is released and leads the forces of evil in a final assault on the Holy City and the saints, only to meet final defeat. Those evils that have always menaced human life, Death and Hades, are at last thrown to destruction in the lake of fire along with all those whose names are not written in the Book of Life. Only then comes the consummation in a blending of the earthly and the heavenly: the first heaven and the first earth and the fearsome sea have all passed away, and the New Jerusalem, the dream city that Jewish eyes have longed for but that human hand could never rear, comes down from God out of heaven (Rev. 20, 21). Finally there is realized the perfect bliss—God Himself dwelling amongst His people.

Thus the seer of Patmos is setting forth in picture form his great certainties. (1) The tangled history of earth, scene of defeat, disaster, and frustration, must have its culminating justification in the grand era of the Millennium. (2) The saints and martyrs have their reward in sharing that triumphant time with their Lord. The Jew had always valued this warm human earth and the body that God had given us to enjoy it. He could not conceive of a disembodied spirit, of an existence that was not clothed with an earthly tabernacle. "The body was no prison-house of clay which cribbed and confined man's spirit, it was the means through which the soul functioned. Body and soul were almost inseparable concomitants. What, then, the body made possible for the soul, the sweet intercourse of men, their mutual helpfulness, their kindly courtesies, all the relations which make courage and patience and gentleness and helpfulness realities instead of empty phrases, were assured for continuance in an earthly kingdom."[2] (3) But life in the full splendour in which God has conceived it transcends this common earth. He must dwell in the midst of His redeemed, and that calls for a new and more glorious firmament. The joy of living with Jesus had so caught the imagination of the Christian that nothing now could satisfy but the enjoyment of the Hallowed Presence.

Paul shares with his readers glimpses of expectation like those of John of Patmos. In his earlier letters he looks forward to conflict and crisis on the grand scale. The man of sin, incarnation of evil, now mysteriously restrained by the power of Rome, would yet break forth and bring an epic struggle to a crisis, and then would be the reign of the Christ in His Kingdom (2 Thess. 2: 1ff.). "For he must reign, till he hath put all enemies under his feet. The last enemy that shall be destroyed is death" (1 Cor. 15: 25-26; Rom. 5: 17; 1 Cor. 4: 8; 6: 3). But the significant note in even these earlier visions of the end is the passionate anxiety to share life with his Lord. When the dead rise, it is to be with the Lord for ever (1 Thess. 4: 17). In the later letters he has little to say of these cataclysmic events, but his longing is enhanced

[2] Adam C. Welch, *Visions of the End*, p. 242f.

to be with Christ, which is far better than life itself (Phil. 1: 23). In a sense that richer existence has begun already: our life "is hid with Christ in God" (Col. 3: 3); the Father through the work of Christ has already made us "partakers in the inheritance of the saints in light": He has already "delivered us from the power of darkness, and hath translated us into the kingdom of his beloved Son" (Col. 1: 12, 13). The work of Christ upon the Cross was a defeat of the evil powers and a foretaste of the final victory (Col. 2: 15). Even now beneath the suffering of the present time, another age is dawning with a glory beyond our conceiving. For this consummation with its unveiling of the sons of God all creation now stands on tiptoe. Flesh and blood cannot inherit the Kingdom of God: this mortal must put on immortality. We shall all be changed and share the likeness of His Son in a life of glorious freedom. No powers of the present or future, of the height or of the depth, will be able to cut us off from God's gift of love in Christ Jesus (Rom. 8: 18ff., 1 Cor. 15: 35ff.).

The Fourth Gospel carries into even richer expression these Pauline thoughts. In the death of Christ there has occurred a world crisis: the forces of evil have had their hour, but now judgment has come and the prince of this world is cast out (John 12: 31). Eternal life is a life of higher quality that begins here and now for every believer (3: 36; 5: 24; 17: 3; 1 John 3: 14), and yet there is a final consummation when the good shall rise to share in the resurrection of life and the evil to the resurrection of judgment (John 5: 26-29). The acceptance of the law of love is our passport to a new world: "we know that we have passed from death unto life because we love the brethren" (1 John 3: 14). Even now we are sons of God, but "it doth not yet appear what we shall be: but we know that, when he shall appear, we shall be like him; for we shall see him as he is" (3: 2).

When we ask what guidance Jesus has given us in the Synoptic records, we are surprised in the first place by His reticence about the detail of the last things. Asked whether few would be saved, He does not satisfy that curiosity, but bids men set their thoughts on striving (Luke 13: 23-24) to enter, for "strait is the gate, and narrow is the way" (Matt. 7: 14). As to the character of the after life He gives scant indication of His thought. Almost His last statement is that made at the Last

Supper to the effect that in the consummated Kingdom they would drink wine that was new, *i.e.* new in kind. We dare not press the symbolism of the Messianic Feast: it may be taken as but a picture of the abundant joyousness that will mark the life of communion in the higher sphere. More definite is the statement made in answer to the query of the Sadducees (as to whose wife a woman would be in the resurrection who had married seven brothers in succession according to the Levirate law): "Do ye not therefore err, because ye know not the scriptures, neither the power of God? For when they shall rise from the dead, they neither marry, nor are given in marriage; but are as the angels which are in heaven" (Mark 12: 24-25).

How are we to reconcile these two aspects of the Kingdom—a kingdom on earth to be the theme of our prayers and striving, and a kingdom under conditions of transfigured life beyond all our power to conceive? Jesus Himself was absorbed in the seeking of both without any suggestion of an inner contradiction. He set forth in the Beatitudes and His ethical teaching generally a way of life that was not only to be practised in the interval before the Kingdom dawns, but that defines the character of life within the consummated Kingdom. The law of love and sacrifice is our mandate if we seek the Kingdom here and now, but that must continue to be the standard of existence in the realm of a God who is love. In the fairer world beyond there must be depths of fellowship, riches of friendship, in those we know that will be explored only when we inherit a sensitivity and devotion beyond our present range of being. Sacrifice and vicarious suffering have an obvious function in our interdependent life here below; but they express so much our character and temper that we can hardly contemplate a perfect social whole of the unselfish where there can be no place for those qualities in us. There is a mystery here that the human mind cannot fathom. There must continue to be what theologians call a tension between the claims of the two kingdoms—that on earth here and that larger life we are to inherit. We know among us now those rare souls who soar far beyond us into the realm of higher reality and yet—indeed by reason of that vision of otherworldliness—they are immersed in every activity of citizenship and human welfare. The Kingdom beyond, so far from cancelling out our interest in the Kingdom here on earth, should set the imagination aflame and kindle to higher intensity our passion for nobler issues below.

> A man's reach should exceed his grasp,
> Or what's a heaven for?

Is this not the wisest provision of an over-ruling Providence, that we can be citizens of two worlds—that the foretaste of that which is above should stimulate and reinforce our devotion to the well-being of the other that is below? The visionaries, the dreamers, the music-makers—have they not throughout the Christian ages proved a living Jacob's ladder keeping open the paths that lead upwards from the sorrow-laden earth and mediating to the practical realm the light and glory of the higher regions? By divine grace it can be given to us to be

> True to the kindred points of Heaven and Home.

Let a modern convert to orthodoxy from socialism give his testimony. In the course of a moving chapter entitled "The Valley of Achor," D. R. Davies offers his confession that a man can work with zest for the transformation of the social order *"if History is a preparation for a sphere, for an order of being beyond itself."*

"History is the realm of the relative and the imperfect. It makes promises which it never fulfils and cannot fulfil. It promises to society perfect justice and peace and order. To the individual it promises perfect happiness and unalloyed joy. It promises tortured Humanity the ecstasy and bliss of perfect and permanent creation. None of these promises can it keep. But what if there is a super-History, in which the dreams and hopes and promises of History shall be fulfilled? What if the failures and evils of time are a testing, a training and a discipline for an order of existence beyond time and the world?

If that is true, then History acquires a new meaning, and it becomes abundantly possible to labour for the Kingdom of God, whose content and essence are too vast and profound to be expressed in time. . . .

If, finally, then, our dream of the perfect life shall be realized beyond time, it becomes possible to work with joy for a better social order."[3]

[3] D. R. Davies, *On to Orthodoxy,* p. 114-115.

May it not be the plan of an all-wise Providence that man should project his dream castles, strive for their realization, taste failure and defeat, and so learn to probe deeper into the fact of his own nature and the profounder needs of human kind? Chastened and humbled, he will begin to look up for aid, and then God comes with His gracious gift of life within the Kingdom. "History, then, is the providential preparation in time of what is only possible in eternity."[4]

God will judge all by Jesus Christ. Matt. 7: 21-27; 16: 27; 25: 31-46; Luke 13: 2-9; John 5: 22-29; 2 Cor. 5: 10.

Dominating all other aspects of the Kingdom to the mind of Jesus is the fact that it confronts each single soul with the issue of his personal destiny. The approach of the Kingdom sets all men in the Valley of Decision. In Christ God visits men with the offer of redemption, and the gravest of all choices is before us. Is it to be for us "Well done, thou good and faithful servant" or a sad "Woe unto thee because thou knewest not the time of thy visitation"?

This concern for the personal is manifest even in the name Jesus chose for Himself: "Son of Man." That name carries the mind back to the vision in Dan. 7, where we see portrayed the destruction of the world empires and the giving to the Son of Man of the everlasting kingdom. It is a kingdom of people—of the saints—a transfigured commonwealth—and this realm is to be signalized by the qualities of the humane as opposed to the bestiality of the dispossessed world powers. It is to this glorious hope of the Son of Man coming on the clouds of heaven that Jesus lifts His eyes from the threat of earthly power and the shadow of the approaching Cross (Mark 14: 62). The first thought that strikes us here is that Jesus sees Himself as the inaugurator and Lord of the coming Kingdom. He is to be the Judge: all power is given to Him on earth and in heaven. Judgment is not assigned to a law or a process, but to a Person —to one who is bone of our bone and flesh of our flesh, to one who has tasted the cup of human life, shared in our temptations and our sorrows. Judgment is at the hands of one who has made Himself known as Love and Mercy. This note appears in the

[4] *Ib.* p. 116.

great judgment scene of Matt. 25: "Inasmuch as ye have done it unto one of the least of these my brethren, ye have done it unto me." It is the kind of test in which all men and women can impartially share—the test of brotherliness, sisterliness, tenderness, pity, care, and love. The Judge on the bench identifies Himself with the hungry and the naked and the prisoner. It is a penetrating judgment; for the Judge has no need of alien witnesses: He has been there on the human scene as a spectator and participator who knows us and knows those whom we have helped or failed to help. The Judge incarnates in Himself a unique understanding of the weakness and the strength of the human personality He judges. Was there ever an earthly court so tender, considerate, and yet so searching, so probing?

Again we observe that predominantly the judgment is not in the mass, but person by person. In Jewish pictures of the last great Assize judgment is by nations and classes—especially of the enemies and tormentors of Israel, the despots and their mighty armies that had harried the sacred soil of Palestine: "there are no portraits of separate faces" (Leckie). But it is precisely this new note that marks the Apocalypse as Jesus has transformed it: the judgment comes upon men one by one. How often in the parables the figures are individual—just as in each day's journeying so much of the interest of the Master was given to a daughter of Jairus or a woman with an issue of blood. It is the way of love so to single men out whether to aid them or to try them.

God does not override Freedom. Mark 4: 9; John 8: 32; 12: 44-50; James 1: 13-15, 25; Gal. 5: 1, 13; Rev. 2: 7.

"Depart from me, ye cursed, into everlasting[5] fire, prepared for the devil and his angels" (Matt. 25: 41). These words coming from one who judges on the basis of humanity strike a chill and forbidding note, and many would ascribe them, not to Jesus, but to a later scribe's edition of the words of Jesus into which the unforgiving heart of man has poured some of its own bitterness. That may be; but we cannot neglect the cumulative testimony of other passages. "Cast ye the unprofitable servant into outer

[5] Literally "fire of the age," wrongly translated "everlasting." This conventional imagery is not to be taken literally. The idea is that all evil things of the material world unworthy to pass into the new age are to be destroyed or cleansed as by fire.

darkness: there shall be weeping and gnashing of teeth" (Matt. 25: 30). "Woe unto thee, Chorazin! woe unto thee, Bethsaida! . . . It shall be more tolerable for Tyre and Sidon at the day of judgment, than for you" (Matt. 11: 21-24). There is a similar word of doom on the city that rejects the messengers of the Kingdom (Matt. 10: 15). There is the grim rebuff that befalls the foolish virgins: "And the door was shut . . . Verily I say unto you, I know you not" (Matt. 25: 10-13). The curtain rings down on the interview with non-committal Nicodemus: "He that believeth not the Son shall not see life; but the wrath of God abideth on him" (John 3: 36). We cannot build dogma on picturesque phrases, especially where these are part of the scenery of the parables. Yet it is impossible to miss this insistent note that before man there is a choice and the choice counts momentously. "Inasmuch as ye did it not . . ." (Matt. 25: 45); "How often would I have gathered thy children together . . . and ye *would not*! . . ." (Matt. 23: 37); "Thou wicked and slothful servant, thou knewest that I reap where I sowed not, . . . Thou oughtest therefore . . ." (Matt. 25: 26-27); "If ye were blind, ye should have no sin: but now ye say, We see; therefore your sin remaineth" (John 9: 41). Men have their freedom: they have knowledge and insight. So they must accept responsibility. It is they who make these solemn decisions: in the face of their open folly doors must shut, and instead of the joy of the marriage feast there is weeping and gnashing of teeth. There is almost a relentless lack of pity for the unjust steward, for the neglectful Dives, for an Ananias or a Judas. There is no encouragement given to the idea that God will forgive because it is His business. The contrary is true: the reverse side of love is a face set implacably against all heedless and heartless inhumanity, against all callous and frivolous disregard of the divine direct appeal. There is here no mawkish nineteenth-century paternalism in the Judge that Scripture has portrayed. There is no spineless, slithering over evil, but rather a solemn affirmation of an irreparable past, an irretrievable future, where with open eyes and warnings all unheeded man has refused the better part. There is sin that is unforgivable. Where light has been given to walk by, where the ancient landmarks have been deliberately ignored, where our priceless liberty has been abused and the moral challenge has been flouted, there is a price to pay, and a burst of tears will not serve for redeeming. It is a terrible thing to have offended one of the little ones for whom Christ died.

When we examine the teaching of Paul and the Johannine writings, we are confronted with the same kind of evidence. Paul links death to sin. "The wages of sin is death" (Rom. 6: 23). Death here is not that lesser evil, the perishing of the natural body of a man, but rather that deeper death in which the individual loses the full richness of existence by falling out of touch with the life-giving Spirit of God. Biblical thought does not share the Greek idea that the soul is immortal by its own nature. Immortality in Scripture is the pure gift of God: "the gift of God is eternal life through Jesus Christ our Lord" (Rom. 6: 23). Beneath the attractive luring colours that sin often presents to the human eye is this fatal sting of death: it breaks our contact with the finer realities of the higher world; it destroys within the soul the higher capacity for truth, beauty, and goodness (1 Cor. 15: 55-56).

So John sees confronting us a universe of decisive contrasts, light or darkness, life or death. "Whosoever liveth, and believeth in me, shall never die" (11: 26). "He that heareth my word, and believeth on him that sent me, hath everlasting life, and shall not come into condemnation; but is passed from death unto life" (5: 24). "He that believeth not is condemned already . . . And this is the condemnation, that light is come into the world, and men loved darkness rather than light, because their deeds were evil" (3: 18-19). Evidently there can be in man an unresponsiveness, a hard-hearted callousness to the divine word of appeal, that must end in exclusion from the Kingdom of the saints.

There is little or no basis in Scripture for any lurid portrayal of everlasting punishment—a doctrine called by Lord Morley "perhaps the most frightful idea that has ever corroded human character." It cannot be denied that in days of persecution even Christian hearts were overwhelmed by a hot passion of hate and thirst for vengeance, and thus the gloating over the merited sufferings of the damned in some Jewish writings tended to reappear in Christian imagination. Tertullian is roused to exultation as he sees famous kings groaning in deepest darkness and persecuting governors set in flames more fierce than those with which they raged against the followers of Christ. Even Augustine taught in terms gross and materialistic. But the Biblical emphasis is on exclusion from the Divine Presence. Eternal life is a gift that God alone can give, and those on whom His favour does not fall cannot pass into life: thus they cease to be. In Matt. 25 the point of the parable is the placing, the sheep on the right, the place of honour, the goats on the left. "Come, ye blessed," the stress being on "Come," contrasts with "Depart from me" in the counter picture. To depart to æonian fire means simply to pass to extinction with the evil material world to which they chose to belong, or it may be pass to a purifying. Fire to the Hebrews was not a means of torment, but the agent of destruction or cleansing. The scenery of a single parable cannot be used to support a dogma. So also it is overstraining to build on the phrase "delivered him to the tormentors" (Matt. 18: 34), or on "many stripes" (Luke 12: 47).

"If we seriously believe in the fundamental Christian conception of God as being, before everything else, Love, can we suppose the 'many stripes' to mean unending and inexpressible tortures? Can a God of love have designed oubliettes for even the worst among His creatures?"[6] The severest possible punishment for a spiritual being is to find at the end of life that he has lost the power to continue in the Divine fellowship. Again, it is to be noted that the responsibility for ultimate tragedy rests with man who has loved freedom too well. "God does not cast into Hell as an Eastern sultan might cast a wretch, who had provoked his anger, to the lions; it is the persistently rebellious sinner who casts himself into the darkness by his very impenitence, just as it is I myself who dash myself in pieces if I insist in walking over a precipice. The 'second death' is a suicide's death."[7]

If they stubbornly refuse. Matt. 11: 20-30; 12: 31-37; John 3: 35-36; Rom. 1: 18—2: 11; John 14.

What then is the final issue of the striving of the Spirit of God with men? Does Love at last prevail over every evil and save all men, or can it be that many rebellious men ultimately stray beyond the reach of grace?

A. There are some who hold to *Conditional Immortality.* Man

[6] A. E. Taylor, *The Christian Hope of Immortality,* p. 114.
[7] A. E. Taylor, p. 123.

is free, they argue, and, as many persist in evil, they reach a stage where there can be no redemption. Like Esau, we sell our birthright, and there is no place for repentance though we seek it carefully with tears. That note sounds in the Epistle to the Hebrews. "For if we sin wilfully after that we have received the knowledge of the truth, there remaineth no more sacrifice for sins, but a certain fearful looking for of judgment . . ." "It is a fearful thing to fall into the hands of the living God" (Heb. 10: 26-31). "Strait is the gate, and narrow is the way, which leadeth unto life, and few there be that find it" (Matt. 7: 13-14; cf. Luke 13: 24ff.; Matt. 26: 28, Luke 10: 15).

Is this our verdict: as man had been created in Christ and redeemed by Him, he had no life save in Him, and it was not worthy either of the justice or mercy of God to tolerate to all eternity a dead universe, or a dead limb in a universe, which He had expressly redeemed from death?[3]

1. It is a view that is true to Scripture in that it takes sin seriously (Rom. 1: 18ff., etc.). Surely there must be retribution upon the soul that refuses the light and clings to deeds of darkness. Our experience can point to the deliberate flouting of the good with an open-eyed blasphemous gloating in naughtiness that corrupts the springs of thought and action. Is it only in the spiritual sphere that the unfit are to survive?

2. Is it not only the life that is hid with Christ in God that can have any permanent worth? If existence is persisted in on the bestial level, should it not perish as the cattle perish? If a soul has never developed any sensitiveness to the lovelier things of the universe, how can it ever be at home in the garden of God? Is it not better, even kinder, that the gross and sensual should cease to be with the wasting of the material body?

3. Is God's consummated Kingdom not the realm of the pure in heart? The end of history is the city of the New Jerusalem: "without are dogs, and sorcerers, and whoremongers, and murderers, and idolaters, and whosoever loveth and maketh a lie" (Rev. 22: 15). Does it not defeat the plan of redemption if evil can live on unrepentant? Is there not a point where the corrupt must cease to offend the presence of the living God?

Yet there are difficulties in this position.

[3] R. W. Dale, *Biography,* quoted by Leckie, *The World to come and Final Destiny,* p. 242.

1. It tends to suggest that it is by man's effort that immortality is won, whereas the whole testimony of the Bible is that eternal life is by God's free grace. If some perish by lack of virtue, then the saved are spared because they have listened to the voice of God, put their trust in Him, persevered in the way: they are spared through their own efforts in a measure. Is this not venturing to suggest that some deserve to be saved?

2. Is there not a self-righteous superiority in the idea that saints are so vastly better than sinners? We have all fallen short of the glory of God: we are involved in the social network of the world's sin, and who shall say that he has no responsibility for those who fall? Is our guilt measurable by sharply contrasting black and white or by shades of grey? Once we make allowance for all life's handicaps and inequalities, can we still confidently separate the sheep from the goats?

3. If God's image is in every man, can it be worn away from any? Is that not to say that evil is more powerful than good? If any single soul perish, has the great Father not fallen short of His perfect household since some are unreclaimed? Is not the All-righteous the All-loving too? Is His arm shortened that it cannot save?

B. There are those who put complete faith in the unlimited generosity of God and believe that somehow salvation will extend to all. "It is not the will of your Father which is in heaven, that one of these little ones should perish" (Matt. 18: 14). There was in the last generation in particular a widespread reliance on the divine love: there will be *universal restoration* for all sinners. Was that just a reflection of the indulgence of a luxurious and prosperous century—or is it a true appreciation of the great heart of the Eternal? "God hath shut up all unto disobedience, that he might have mercy upon all" (Rom. 11: 32). "For as in Adam all die, so also in Christ shall all be made alive" (1 Cor. 15: 22). "And I, if I be lifted up from the earth, will draw all men unto me" (John 12: 32). Are these words of Scripture large generalizations, a statement of the divine willingness to save all rather than a cold statement of doctrine?

1. This view takes account of the pitifulness and weakness of all men. It looks frankly at a cross-section of city life, and confesses that between the defiant woman in the dock and the

stern judge on the bench there may not be so much a difference of heart as a difference of temperament and opportunity. There are injustices in environment and in inheritance: life deals out to this one so much domestic bliss and to that one blow upon blow; and blood runs so hot in this woman's veins and so cold in that staid Portia; and the meshes of life are so tangled and intricate that to know all may be to forgive all. From the exalted viewpoint of the Almighty Mercy can there be any finely-drawn distinction? Is it not rather a case for pity for all: "Only the infinite pity is sufficient for the infinite pathos of life"?

2. Again this view takes the Gospel seriously. It believes that God is set upon a purpose of redemption and that no evil can finally defeat His will to redeem. He has permitted man to face life with a spacious freedom, recognizing that sin and suffering must corrode and chasten and defeat. But may not He will to make an end of the destroying forces and have pity on the work of His hands? Can He ultimately let sin claim its thousands? Must He not rather with a Father's heart reach out to rescue the last one of His children?

There are hesitations that rise in the mind as we contemplate this solution.

1. Does this view take sin seriously? Does it not undermine the whole moral struggle? What boots it to strive to keep the narrow way if in the end the broad way leads to the same heaven? Is there justice in the God who thus bundles together the serious seeker and the frivolous worldling? Is this not looking at an evil world through rose-coloured spectacles? Are Caiaphas and Judas to have the same discharge as the martyred Peter and Paul?

2. Does this view take man seriously? To what end were we all set down free in an evil world? Why give us the mockery of free choice when in the end we were all to be saved willy-nilly? If we were all to have the prize, why set the field for a contest? That travail of the spirit striving against the flesh, that struggle against tyranny and cruelty, that courage and sacrifice and unselfishness—was it all not a delusion if the frankly sensual and the pitiless despot and the cowardly self-seeker are objects in the end of the same generosity? Yet the parable of the Labourers in the Vineyard (Matt. 20) and Paul's grand conclusion in Rom. 8 give us pause.

After Death. Luke 16: 19-31; 1 Thess. 4: 13-18; 1 Pet. 3: 18-20; Rev. 6: 9-11.

To some minds the problem of the end is simplified by the conception of an interim period between this life and the next. Is there some cleansing experience that men unready at death can undergo before they pass to the eternal presence? Is there a purifying purgatory, as the Eastern and Roman Churches teach and as many Protestant thinkers have maintained?

In a parable like Dives and Lazarus we see the typical Hebrew belief in Sheol (or Hades, as the Greeks called it), a place of waiting where the dead had their abode in a cheerless, voiceless, shadowed underworld, and which later thought tended to conceive as a place of probation. In 1 Peter there is an allusion to an idea which must have circulated in the early Church that in the interval between His being laid in the grave and His rising again Jesus went into that realm of darkness and preached the good news to those who had not the chance to hear in their lifetime. The Fourth Gospel teaches us that we are being judged here and now according as we accept or reject Christ. But there is a sense in which no judgment can be complete until all those with whom we have been bound together in the bundle of life have also been judged. We must tarry till the final consummation. Scripture speaks of the dead as those that sleep. As we awake from a dreamless sleep all unconscious of the hours that have passed since we lost consciousness, so may not the blessed dead awake with no sense of long waiting to share the Resurrection morn? The believers of the early Church were concerned about the unbaptized infants and the spiritually immature and those who had passed away in pagan darkness. In Jewish thought there was faith in the efficacy of intercessory prayer, and such prayer might avail for the blessed dead, and some who passed into the Christian Church might bring this expectation with them. In the Christian society which has built up a firm and enduring family affection there must always be an eager concern for the souls of our beloved, and in spite of the discouragement of theologians many will continue to obey the instinct to pray for those who have passed beyond. Here too in this conception puzzled thinkers have seen compensation for the ragged edges of our human existence. Have the unheeding in this life a second chance in the waiting period before the end? Are the last moment penitents then brought under a rigorous discipline that breaks the stubbornness of the human heart and opens at last the windows of the soul?

Protestant opinion has often turned away from even the slightest consideration of this hope because of the tragic misuse that the Roman Church made of masses for the dead. Pious rites cannot buy a way into Paradise even when love drives. The eternal love, we say, needs no importuning from us. But neither does the gracious God need such urging in this life, and yet Jesus has taught us importunity (Luke 18: 1ff.).

Beyond our Power to Conceive. John 19: 24; 2 Cor. 3: 18; Phil. 3: 20-21; Rev. 7: 9-17; Rev. 21-22.

These are matters where our probing seems impertinent and dogmatism ill becomes us. Let us recall the reticence of the Master Himself, and be content to leave the issues in the Father's all-gracious hand. His love has thrown its mantle over those we love. What baffles our human minds is clear to His wisdom.

What lies behind the veil we cannot imagine or define. Heaven has been freely pictured as the place of reward and rest,

> the bliss of languorous hours,
> A glory of calm measured range.

But our modern industrial age has cherished rather a craving for activity, as in the words of Paul Hamilton Hayne:

> A heaven of action freed from strife
> With ampler ether for the scope
> Of an unmeasurable life
> And an unbaffled human hope.
>
> A heaven wherein all discords cease,
> Self-torment, doubt, distress, turmoil,
> The care of whose majestic peace
> Is *god-like power of endless toil.*

May it not be rather a larger magnitude of experience in which the virtues of activity and rest are inextricably intertwined? There is such a joy as the creative artist knows when after long questing and restless inner urgings there pours forth in a living glow of peace a masterpiece of the imagination in art or music.

There is that active yet restful interflow of mind and heart that comes to the sensitive soul when after long frustration and disenchantment he encounters love at last and opens out his nature in the atmosphere of understanding friendship. Professor John Baillie has set down this felicitous illustration:

> A night at an inn is one thing and the journey accomplished is quite another. In the inn we sleep, but when the journey is accomplished, we are in a sense more active than ever. We are now actively enjoying something that is worth having for its own sake, whereas the journey was undertaken only for the sake of this to which it has led. It may be we are only talking with the friend to whose house we have travelled, and that only for love's sake; yet it cannot be denied that our souls are now much more active than when we were jogging along in the saddle, or being jolted in the train or sitting behind the steering-wheel. *Fruition,* then, *is essentially an activity*—a higher activity than the activity of becoming or of unfulfilled quest.[9]

Here is a region where it is better that we should walk by faith and not by sight. To know what lies behind the veil would be to discourage all wondering and seeking and to miss the joy of finding. How many of the richest treasures of life are delightsome because there are ever new surprises? The sunrise morning by morning, sunset evening by evening, has the charm of unveiling its own particular freshness: it is always a discovery. Love is an adventure: to know all the lovelinesses of personality beforehand would be to tarnish it. And it is better that the bourne is that which eye hath not seen nor ear heard. It is enough to reach out in the dark and to touch a pierced hand and thus to know that a Friend who has proved His love has gathered us each one into His keeping.

> "We know Whom we have believed, and are persuaded that
> He is able to keep that which we have committed to Him."
> "To the only wise God our Saviour be glory and majesty, dominion and power, both now and ever."

[9] *And the Life Everlasting,* p. 278.